DELETED

Women's Antiwar
Diplomacy during
the Vietnam War Era

Women's Antiwar Diplomacy during the Vietnam War Era

Jessica M. Frazier

The University of North Carolina Press CHAPEL HILL

© 2017 The University of North Carolina Press
All rights reserved
Set in Espinosa Nova by Westchester Publishing Services
Manufactured in the United States of America

The University of North Carolina Press has been a member of the Green Press
Initiative since 2003.

Library of Congress Cataloging-in-Publication Data
Names: Frazier, Jessica M., author.
Title: Women's antiwar diplomacy during the Vietnam War era /
    Jessica M. Frazier.
Other titles: Gender & American culture.
Description: Chapel Hill : University of North Carolina Press, [2017] |
    Series: Gender and American culture | Includes bibliographical references
    and index.
Identifiers: LCCN 2016031010| ISBN 9781469631783 (cloth : alk. paper) |
    ISBN 9781469631790 (pbk : alk. paper) | ISBN 9781469631806 (ebook)
Subjects: LCSH: Vietnam War, 1961–1975—Women. | Vietnam War, 1961–1975—
    Protest movements. | Women—Political activity—United States—History—
    20th century. | Women—Political activity—Vietnam—History—20th century. |
    Feminism—United States—Foreign influences.
Classification: LCC DS559.8.W6 F73 2017 | DDC 959.704/31—dc23
    LC record available at https://lccn.loc.gov/2016031010

Cover illustration: Nguyen Trinh Thai, *Many Thanks to the People of the World
for Your Support* (pencil and tempera on paper, 1972). Courtesy of
Track 16 Gallery.

Portions of chapter 1 previously appeared in the author's work "Collaborative
Efforts to End the War in Viet Nam: The Interactions of Women Strike for Peace,
the Vietnamese Women's Union, and the Women's Union of Liberation, 1965–
1968," *Peace & Change* 37, no. 3 (July 2012): 339–65. Used here with permission.

For Todd,
Ava, and
Esme

Contents

Figures

Acknowledgments

Writing the acknowledgments section is a daunting yet gratifying task because so much support went into the completion of this book. First, I would like to thank the American Council of Learned Societies for its financial support through a fellowship that allowed me to dedicate a year to writing. I also received financial support from the Center for Historical Study of Women and Gender and the History Department at Binghamton University, as well as through a Faculty Development Grant and from the College of Environment and Life Sciences at the University of Rhode Island. Much of the research for this work was possible thanks to travel grants provided by the Sallie Bingham Center at Duke University, the Schlesinger Library at Harvard University, the Sophia Smith Collection at Smith College, and the Swarthmore College Peace Collection at Swarthmore College. I would also like to thank Don Nieman and Leigh Ann Wheeler for establishing the Wheeler/Nieman Grant through the History Department at Binghamton University. This grant supported research at the Center for Southwest Research at the University of New Mexico, the Charles E. Young Research Library at UCLA, and the Hoover Institution Archives at Stanford University. Jim and Ann Wolf and Kate and Günni Fuchs were kind enough to house me when I visited archives in Albuquerque and Los Angeles, respectively, and I thank them. I would also like to thank the archivists at these centers as well as those at the Chicago Historical Society, the Simon Fraser University Archives, and the Library of Congress for their assistance. For providing research support from afar, I would like to thank David Stiver at Graduate Theological Union Archives, independent researcher Virginia Martin, and archivist Lee Grady at the Wisconsin Historical Society.

Several people at higher education institutions have made life as an academic more fulfilling. At the University of Rhode Island, I have received warm welcomes from many members of the campus community, including Lynne Derbyshire, Cathy English, Tim George, John Kirby, Jody Lisberger, Erik Loomis, Rod Mather, Annie Russell, and Rob Thompson, among many others. I would like to give special thanks to Leslie Kealhofer-Kemp, who has provided both advice and entertainment. For providing comments, support, and guidance at various stages of this project, I would like to thank

Nancy Appelbaum, Mary Berkery, Elisa Camiscioli, Tom Dublin, Leslie Gates, Denise Ireton, Sarah King, Carol Linskey, Kelly Marino, Steve Ortiz, Giusi Russo, Sandra Sánchez López, Kitty Sklar, Eve Snyder, Diane Sommerville, Jen Tomas, and Leigh Ann Wheeler at Binghamton University. Leigh Ann deserves special recognition, as she has continually motivated me to produce my best work. Mary, Denise, and Kelly read several versions of several chapters; their suggestions made this work much clearer. Sandra has continued to support me both personally and professionally even though we now live on different continents.

Many others have contributed to my thinking about this research over the years, including Caitlin Casey, Ellen Chesler, Chelsea Del Rio, Andrea Estepa, Stephanie Gilmore, Justin Hart, Dan Horowitz, Suzzanne Kelley, Jessica Lancia, Kera Lovell, Edwin Martini, Matt Masur, Hang Nguyen, Grey Osterud, Shelley Rose, Benita Roth, Andrew Rotter, Amy Schneidhorst, Heather Stur, Michele Thompson, Kara Vuic, Judy Wu, Leandra Zarnow, and the anonymous reviewer at the University of North Carolina Press, as well as others I met at conferences and elsewhere who will unfortunately remain unnamed. A version of the first chapter of this book was previously published in the journal *Peace & Change*, and I would like to thank the anonymous reviewers of that article for their comments. I would also like to thank the editorial staff at the University of North Carolina Press for helping to guide this project through the publishing process.

The all-important research trip to Viet Nam in the summer of 2015 would not have been undertaken without an initial push from Hang Nguyen, one of the reviewers of the manuscript at the University of North Carolina Press. Judy Wu was kind enough to put me in touch with Mr. Bui Van Nghi at the Vietnam-USA Society. Ms. Hoang Tuyet Nga deserves special mention for coordinating my trip, for finding an English edition of Nguyen Thi Binh's memoir for me, and for tracking down the artist whose work adorns the front cover. Mr. Khong Dai Minh acted as translator and guide during my entire stay and took care of getting me where I needed to be when I needed to be there. I would also like to thank those who agreed to be interviewed by me, both in Viet Nam and in the United States.

Lastly, my family members have cheered me on throughout this project. My in-laws, Steve and Mary Guilfoos, were always interested to hear any updates on the project. My parents, Steve and Margie Frazier, and my sisters, Melissa Oliveri, Kate Fuchs, and Sarah Ernst, have expressed their enthusiasm for my academic pursuits in multiple ways. My daughter Ava actually wanted me to be working on my book manuscript when she got home from school so she could interrupt me with a "Boo!" and a snuggle. My daughter Esme was born during the final stages of editing; she has contributed the best way an infant can: by sleeping for long stretches of time. My husband, Todd Guilfoos, has made sure I have the time and space needed to complete this project. He is the best partner I could ask for. I dedicate this book to Todd, Ava, and Esme, and I look forward to our future together as a family.

Abbreviations

ARVN	South Vietnamese Army
COLIAFAM	Committee of Liaison with Families of Servicemen Detained in North Vietnam
CWS	Church World Service
DRV	North Viet Nam
IWC	Indochinese Women's Conference
MAI	Medical Aid for Indochina
MIA	Missing in Action
NLF	National Liberation Front of South Viet Nam
POW	Prisoner of War
PRG	Provisional Revolutionary Government of the NLF
RVN	South Viet Nam
SDS	Students for a Democratic Society
SNCC	Student Nonviolent Coordinating Committee
SRV	Socialist Republic of Viet Nam
VIET-MY	Committee for Solidarity with the American People
VOW	Voice of Women
VWU	North Vietnamese Women's Union
WIDF	Women's International Democratic Federation
WILPF	Women's International League for Peace and Freedom
WSP	Women Strike for Peace
WUL	Women's Union of Liberation of the NLF

Women's Antiwar
Diplomacy during
the Vietnam War Era

Introduction

A single photograph provides one of the few pieces of evidence that Lorraine Gordon and Mary Clarke, both white members of the U.S.-based organization Women Strike for Peace (WSP), were the first American peace activists to interview Vietnamese officials in North Viet Nam after U.S. bombing began.[1] On the back of the photograph, Mary Clarke wrote, "Hanoi, May 1965, Pres. Palace with Pham Van Dong (arranging Djakarta mtg), Lorraine Gordon, Mary Clarke" (see Figure 1).[2] Little other evidence of this visit exists, in part because Clarke and Gordon's trip to Hanoi was impromptu. They had introduced themselves to North Vietnamese diplomats in Moscow, where they were attending an international congress to commemorate the twentieth anniversary of the end of World War II. At the North Vietnamese embassy, Vietnamese officials invited Clarke and Gordon to travel on to Hanoi, where they would meet with members of the Vietnamese Women's Union (VWU) and Premier Pham Van Dong. The U.S. State Department forbade such travel, making it necessary for the two women to fly clandestinely to Hanoi and leave little trace of their transgression. Clarke and Gordon spent a few days in Hanoi before returning to the Soviet Union and then the United States.

Upon arriving in Hanoi, Clarke and Gordon would likely have been greeted at the airport by members of the VWU and been driven across the Red River to a hotel in the center of the city. Traveling through the city, Clarke and Gordon would have noticed the remnants of French colonialism in the wide boulevards and in the architecture of the Presidential Palace, built in the early twentieth century to house the French governor-general of Indochina. They likely would have also remarked on the number of parks and lakes in Hanoi, the prominence of bicyclists on city streets, and the magnificence of the ao dais that some of the women wore. Indeed, the beauty of Hanoi would have struck them as well as its situation as a nexus where East and West, tradition and modernity, a colonial past and decolonized present, met.

Monuments and museums across the city exhibited the 2,000-year history of colonial rule and revered Vietnamese uprisings against foreign invaders. Although many relics memorialized military achievements in particular,

FIGURE 1 Left to right: Le Chan Phuong, unidentified Vietnamese woman, Mary Clarke, Pham Van Dong, and Lorraine Gordon at Presidential Palace in Hanoi, 1965. Photograph Collection, Box "Dated Images/Billboards, etc.," Women Strike for Peace Records, Swarthmore College Peace Collection.

contemporary and present-day Vietnamese accounts identify three fronts in the struggle for independence: military, diplomatic, and political.[3] For Vietnamese, this study primarily tells the story of the political front— international antiwar activities and "people's diplomacy" during the American war. The establishment of people's diplomacy in the twentieth century began with Ho Chi Minh, who believed that fostering people-to-people relationships with individuals and citizen organizations was the first step to gaining independence for Viet Nam. In 1911, at the age of twenty-one, Ho Chi Minh (under the alias Van Ba) set sail aboard a French steamship and spent the next thirty years traveling the world. Mixing in anticolonial and communist circles, he "found a way to combine the national struggle with the dream of international revolution."[4] Seeking and receiving support from both state and nonstate actors, Ho Chi Minh returned to Viet Nam in 1941 to secure independence for the nation through military, diplomatic, and political means. Following Ho Chi Minh's example, people's diplomacy became a key aspect of Hanoi's three-pronged approach to ending the U.S. war in a desirable way. Pham Van Chuong, a press agent stationed in East Berlin, Prague, and Paris in the 1960s and 1970s, recalled that people-to-people diplomacy flourished because of Vietnamese and Americans' mutual "thirst for information," information unavailable through other means.[5] Although some would describe the activities of the Vietnamese and their American counterparts as spreading propaganda, others portrayed them as distributing educational material.

As North Viet Nam tried to shape its image in the international realm, women in the VWU, an organization closely tied to the North Vietnamese government, took on the task of cultivating relationships with American (and other) women. The VWU even had an international relations section dedicated to developing such connections. Staff of the VWU regularly attended international women's conferences and hosted delegations of women in North Viet Nam throughout the war years (and these activities continue today). Vietnamese women often acted in official capacities as representatives of the VWU, and U.S. women gained access to foreign relations debates as authorities on the war through their relationships with Vietnamese.

Investigating this alliance between American and Vietnamese women reveals an unusual story. Scholars studying women's international activism and transnational feminism have often identified cultural imperialism at work in such relationships.[6] For example, historian Helen Laville argues that during the early Cold War, U.S. women professed to promote international sisterhood but in reality, through international women's organizations, imposed the "American way of life" on women outside the United States.[7] Similarly, historian Jocelyn Olcott points to U.S. women's cultural imperialism at the UN's International Women's Year Conference in Mexico City in 1975 as they tried to set the feminist agenda for women around the world.[8] The present work complicates this body of literature by bringing to light an instance when U.S. women crossed geopolitical boundaries to criticize American Cold War culture, not promote it.[9]

As American women denounced the campaign to contain communism (and at the same time spread democracy), they solicited Vietnamese women's opinions on U.S. intervention. They even celebrated Vietnamese culture and gender roles, albeit in ways that at times proved problematic, but rarely assumed that American culture or feminisms were superior. Judy Wu's *Radicals on the Road* labels U.S. activists' admiration of Vietnamese society "radical orientalism," which she defines as "American activists idealiz[ing] and identif[ying] with revolutionary Asian nations and political figures."[10] While also noting this veneration of the Vietnamese, I ask what this means in terms of assumptions often made about U.S. women's transnational activism. I conclude that relationships between American and Vietnamese women were not clear-cut examples of U.S. women's cultural imperialism. Instead, they demonstrate the possibility of women from a decolonizing nation furthering their own agenda by collaborating with "Western" women. American women reacted in various ways to insights gained through such encounters, but rarely did these responses include implicitly or explicitly providing instructions to Vietnamese women.

Vietnamese women, as both subjects and objects, helped to mold American feminisms. In exploring the many facets of U.S. feminisms at the time, this work follows the lead of scholars such as Sherna Gluck and Benita Roth. Both have shown that an emphasis on the second-wave feminist movement as a monolith in the United States overlooks many burgeoning feminist ideas, actions, and individuals in the 1960s and 1970s.[11] Focusing on encounters between Vietnamese and American women brings some of this variety to light, as a wide array of U.S. women in social movement circles tended to place Vietnamese women on a pedestal as paragons of exemplary womanhood, but they did so in unique ways. Some WSP members developed a feminist consciousness through their exposure to Vietnamese women who both adhered to maternalist strategies and called for equal rights. For many women of color in rights-based movements, which criticized U.S. society as inherently imperialistic, Vietnamese women provided examples of how to be both revolutionary and feminine. White women's liberationists also looked to Vietnamese women as role models who had supposedly achieved many of the legal, economic, and social rights American feminists desired. American feminists and their VWU counterparts often portrayed women in the communist North as having made significant gains in terms of equality with men compared with U.S. women. By contrast, Americans and Vietnamese alike blamed discrimination, assault, and sexual objectification women faced in South Viet Nam on the "Americanization" of South Vietnamese society. American women's views of U.S. society as being in the wrong solidified their conviction that the United States should not intervene in Viet Nam. Foregrounding the international and transnational nature of U.S. women's activism in the 1960s and 1970s, this study shows that they developed unique feminisms as well as antiwar perspectives.[12]

A number of women in this study were never part of *the* antiwar movement per se, but they were part of the growing antiwar sentiment.[13] Historians Lorena Oropeza, Daryl Maeda, and Judy Wu have contributed to this recognition of the heterogeneity of antiwar activism, primarily through researching members of the "Third World Left."[14] A diverse range of arguments against the war existed, bringing to light the distinction between antiwar and peace activism. Peace activists were against war in principle, but many other activists were only against U.S. intervention in Viet Nam. Some even wanted the Vietnamese to win militarily and promoted revolutionary violence. Regardless, all looked to Vietnamese for inspiration, with U.S. women making particular contributions to depictions of North Vietnamese society as exemplary.

Portraying Vietnamese society as irreproachable only lasted through the war years, however. Following the U.S. troop withdrawal, this characterization began to fade when Vietnamese women's roles under the new regime did not meet the expectations of some U.S. feminists. Having held the Vietnamese in such high regard and having had the tendency to blame any shortcomings in women's societal roles on U.S. intervention, some U.S. activists felt let down by the inability of Vietnamese society to eliminate all vestiges of gender inequality. Some feminists even went so far as to denounce Vietnamese policies that reinforced gender roles. Thus, after the U.S. war in Viet Nam ended, some activists did impose American cultural values on Vietnamese society.

Change in Vietnamese perspectives over time is more difficult to determine because U.S. voices dominate most of the available sources, such as published works about U.S. women's trips to Hanoi. American women also wrote much of the informal documentation—diaries, notes, and correspondence—that provides emotional and personal reactions to meetings between American and Vietnamese women. Vietnamese women's voices are not absent from the historical record, however, as transcripts of speeches, personal letters to U.S. women, and recent interviews shed some light on their views. English-language Vietnamese periodicals, records from Vietnamese personal archives, and present-day Vietnamese-language documents complement these sources and provide additional insight into Vietnamese women's lives. The recently translated English edition of Nguyen Thi Binh's memoir also provides key information on female diplomats.

Any variation in Vietnamese perspectives is also difficult to discern because VWU members' contact with U.S. women was generally part of North Viet Nam's strategy to forge bonds with international activists to develop people's diplomacy.[15] Therefore, many of the Vietnamese sources available are by those who were closely connected to the North Vietnamese government and generally agreed with the official line on the war effort. Fairly consistently, it seems, members of the VWU and its sister organization under the National Liberation Front (NLF), the Women's Union of Liberation (WUL), used motherhood as evidence of women's continued femininity as they took on men's former responsibilities. North Viet Nam's Ministry of Culture, with the help of the VWU, clearly laid out Vietnamese women's role in the fight, identifying their "three responsibilities": to care for children, to produce food and goods, and to defend villages.[16] The Vietnamese version of motherhood often encouraged women's violent resistance to "U.S. imperialism" in the name of loyalty to family and nation. This commendation of women's participation in violence dated back to the Trung sisters of 40 A.D. According to legend, the two sisters led an army of Vietnamese against Chinese invaders after one of the sisters' husbands was threatened (and, in some versions, killed) by Chinese officials. Showing loyalty both to their country and to their family, the sisters had no choice but to fight the Chinese. Building on this ideal, in the 1960s, stories told by the VWU and WUL in periodicals and at conferences combined revolutionary militancy with motherhood.

In person, many VWU and WUL members also emphasized U.S. and Vietnamese women's shared identity as mothers, making a point of telling American women how the war had disrupted their roles as wives and mothers. Over the years, some Vietnamese and U.S. women developed personal relationships as they met numerous times in Hanoi as well as at conferences in Paris, Toronto, Djakarta, and elsewhere. They learned more about one another as individuals rather than as "mothers," allowing them to collaborate more closely to end U.S. involvement in Viet Nam. Although some U.S. and Vietnamese women used maternalism to justify their entrance into the international realm, their actions had less to do with "mothers' domestic duties" (both within the home and within the nation) than with strategizing with one another to gain influence over U.S. foreign policy decisions.[17] For that reason, this study moves past asking how U.S. or Vietnamese women entered the international realm to argue that they created a collaborative partnership to pressure the U.S. government to end its war in Viet Nam.

Evaluating the impact of such relationships on the U.S. domestic realm as well as on international circles shows the persistence with which North Viet Nam and the NLF used women's networks to influence international opinion. Histories written from the Vietnamese perspective on the war that are most closely related to this work generally fall into two categories: state-centered diplomatic histories or histories of Vietnamese women in the military.[18] Although both bodies of literature highlight the achievements of certain women, such as Nguyen Thi Binh and Nguyen Thi Dinh, neither provides much background on the political front of the Vietnamese war effort. Researching U.S. and Vietnamese women's international cooperation makes inroads into uncovering the significance of this aspect of the war effort against the United States.[19]

Because interpretations of the way in which the United States entered into the domestic affairs of South Viet Nam colored antiwar perspectives, before going further, it is pertinent to review that history and some of its controversies. America's involvement in Viet Nam dated back to the end of World War II, when the U.S. government lent material and tactical support to France as France struggled to maintain control over Viet Nam. After France lost in battle at Dien Bien Phu in 1954, it, China, the Soviet Union, Great Britain, the State of Viet Nam, and the Democratic Republic of Viet Nam signed the Geneva Agreement, granting Viet Nam its independence but temporarily splitting the country along the seventeenth parallel. Ho Chi Minh led the Democratic Republic of Viet Nam (DRV), and American-educated and U.S.-selected president Ngo Dinh Diem led the Republic of Viet Nam (RVN). The North and South were supposed to be reunited by an election in 1956, but the election never occurred because the RVN blocked it. The U.S. and RVN administrations feared a victory for Ho Chi Minh, ensuring a united Viet Nam under communism. Instead of allowing an election, the U.S. government chose to bolster Diem as leader of the RVN from 1954 until his assassination in 1963, and after his death, the U.S. government supported subsequent South Vietnamese administrations.

Following years of disappointment and struggle, in 1960, the NLF formed in opposition to the RVN administration. According to the U.S. and RVN governments, North Vietnamese wishing to reunite the country under communism established the NLF to subvert democracy in South Viet Nam. Officials from the NLF and DRV, however, claimed that South Vietnamese peasants founded the NLF after years of torture, imprisonment, and death at the hands of the RVN government. Both depictions contained some accuracy, as an indigenous anticolonial movement did indeed form in the South and Hanoi tried to direct it.[20]

Shortly after the establishment of the NLF, the U.S. government stationed the first American military advisors in South Viet Nam. Until 1964, U.S. military personnel in the RVN trained and equipped the Army of the Republic of Viet Nam (ARVN) but did not fight alongside its soldiers. That August, two U.S. destroyers stationed in the Gulf of Tonkin off North Viet Nam's coast reported an attack by DRV patrol boats. President Lyndon B. Johnson retaliated by ordering air strikes against North Viet Nam, and the U.S. Congress passed the Gulf of Tonkin Resolution, allowing Johnson "to take all necessary measures to repel any armed attack against the forces of the United States" in Southeast Asia.[21] Through this measure, an undeclared war in Viet Nam began.

Following Johnson's actions, U.S. peace activists quickly organized demonstrations and vigils to protest escalation of the U.S. involvement in Viet Nam, but, much to their dismay, within six months, Johnson announced Operation Rolling Thunder, a massive bombing campaign against North Viet Nam. American and Vietnamese women alike sought to bridge ideological differences at a time when the Cold War threatened to get out of hand. As one WSP member put it in 1965, while men in power "justify [U.S. intervention in Viet Nam] as a war against 'communism'—as if ideas could be destroyed by military force," women recognized the need to move forward through other means.[22] Therefore, U.S. and Vietnamese women fostered people's diplomacy, as exhibited by Clarke and Gordon's first trip to Hanoi.

CHAPTER ONE

Mothers as Experts, 1965–1967

Mary Clarke was no stranger to being on the "wrong" side of the Cold War divide. In fact, Clarke had first come to the attention of the Federal Bureau of Investigation (FBI) in the early 1950s because of her affiliation with the Communist Party. In the late 1950s, she had also traveled to the Eastern Bloc and to international peace conferences sympathetic to the Soviet view of the Cold War. In light of her past, her May 1965 trip to Moscow and on to North Viet Nam was not that extraordinary. Even so, the trip may have surprised some of Clarke's fellow WSP members, a fact that likely led Clarke and her travel companion, Lorraine Gordon, to conceal their brief stay in Hanoi.

Nevertheless, Clarke and Gordon knew that WSP members would support their efforts to contact North Vietnamese. At the third annual WSP conference, in 1964, WSP members identified the Viet Nam conflict as a potential seedbed for nuclear war and decided to seek an opportunity to speak with Vietnamese women and officials.[1] WSP leaders, like Clarke, distrusted the U.S. government's portrayal of the situation and wanted their own say in U.S. foreign policy. When Clarke and Gordon met with VWU members in Hanoi, they began to make arrangements for a conference between WSP, the VWU, and the WUL, to take place in Djakarta, Indonesia, later that summer. In Djakarta, WSP members asked Vietnamese women about the history of the conflict as well as the desired outcome for Vietnamese, and the Vietnamese wanted to know what the American public thought of the war.[2] Thus began an alliance based on exchanging information between women in the two nations.

Given the anticommunist climate of the United States in the 1960s, WSP members needed a strategy to avoid the likely red-baiting their entrance into foreign policy debates would engender. The group had dealt with such tactics before, when, in 1962, the House Committee on Un-American Activities subpoenaed some of its national leaders to testify to the possible infiltration of communists into the organization. During the hearing, WSP founder Dagmar Wilson successfully deflected Cold War criticisms, in part through maternalist rhetoric—a tool many women's organizations had used over the years.[3] At the turn of the twentieth century, female activists often expressed maternal concerns to argue against war and for women's involvement in international and municipal debates.[4] According to WSP historian Amy Swerdlow, none of the first WSP leaders in the early 1960s had any awareness of this history of women's peace activism and chose maternalist rhetoric because so many WSP members were in fact mothers.[5] Although the portrayal of WSP members as apolitical mothers succeeded in keeping the press from vilifying them generally, it did not convince everyone of the group's innocuousness. Indeed, even some WSP members questioned its actions. Some members and their husbands regularly informed the FBI of the possibly illegal and subversive activities of other WSP members.[6] One leader recalled being appalled when she received her FBI report years later and found that someone had told agents about intimate WSP gatherings at which she thought she could trust every woman in attendance.[7] Clearly, maternalism had not protected her from internal, not to mention government, scrutiny. Nevertheless, WSP leaders relied on maternalist rhetoric and depicted their Vietnamese counterparts in terms similar to those they used to describe themselves.

These portrayals mirrored those of VWU and WUL members, who also represented themselves as a body of mothers for the consumption of international audiences. They wrote open letters to American mothers, stressing their shared anguish over needless death and destruction. Quoting statistics on U.S. bombing and stating its consequences, particularly in terms of children's lives lost, VWU and WUL members provided both quantitative and qualitative evidence of the appalling effects of the war in North and South Viet Nam. In one letter, VWU member Bui Thi Cam identified numerous provinces where the U.S. military had "poured ... tons of bombs, napalm bombs included, and fired *phosphorous bullets*" (emphasis in original).[8] Going on to describe the physical effects of the chemicals, Cam stressed that U.S. bombing killed and injured children. Telling the reader "you are mothers and love children," she chose the emotions that American women were to feel as she also listed the number of GIs killed, wounded, or missing, further identifying her American audience as mothers of soldiers.[9] The portrayal of women on both sides of the war as first and foremost mothers was a mutual endeavor.

Even so, Vietnamese women challenged WSP's depictions of mothers as inherently peaceful and apolitical by promoting women's entrance into the military and politics. One narrative, titled "A Fighting Mother," chronicled the travails of a woman and her husband, both of whom valiantly fought for the revolution in the South. With references to the woman "carrying her baby in her arms" as she faced enemy soldiers, the story highlighted her roles as both a mother and a warrior as being central to her character.[10] This woman's motherhood enhanced her heroism, as the births of six children rarely kept her from fighting and strategizing for the NLF—her dedication to both family and country shone through. This kind of story of the people became popular in Vietnamese socialist propaganda in the 1960s. Making an example of an "average" person helped to build the illusion that the people, not the intelligentsia or diplomats, were behind the revolution.[11] Although WSP members tended to ignore stories of women's violence, through the repeated exposure to these alternative versions of motherhood, some WSP members developed new perspectives on women's roles.

WSP's characterization of Vietnamese women as sharing maternal sympathies began with Clarke and Gordon in the weeks preceding the July 1965 Djakarta conference. In an internal memo explaining the purpose of meeting VWU and WUL members, Clarke and Gordon described Vietnamese women as victims of American bombing "whose children [were] being killed."[12] According to Clarke and Gordon, Vietnamese women needed WSP members to publicize their plight in order to convince U.S. government officials to end the war. Through a face-to-face exchange with Vietnamese women, WSP could gain the leverage needed to "force a change in administration policy," Clarke and Gordon argued.[13] They also claimed that the fate of American women was "tied to that of Vietnamese women" because the conflict in Viet Nam "could erupt into nuclear war," a key concern for WSP members.[14] Taking this approach, Clarke and Gordon made U.S. intervention in Viet Nam a much larger issue that had the potential of directly affecting the lives of all American women, their families, and indeed the entire world. Women, however, could be in the vanguard to prevent such a catastrophe.

At the conference in Djakarta, ten American women met with six VWU members and three WUL members for four and a half days to show that women from warring nations could meet peaceably to discuss solutions. WSP decided who should attend the meeting based on who had the most potential to garner media attention after the event and who could afford to go. Of the ten American women, seven had participated in WSP actions in the past, and all could fundraise or pay the estimated $1,400 for the trip to Djakarta. Margaret Russell, a white founding member of WSP and chair

FIGURE 2 Left to right: Le Chan Phuong, Le Thi Cao, and Nguyen Thi Binh at Djakarta conference. Photograph Collection, Box "Dated Images/ Billboards, etc.," Women Strike for Peace Records, Swarthmore College Peace Collection.

of WSP's Committee on the Vietnam Problem in Washington, D.C., led the American delegation, which also included Mary Clarke.[15] Le Chan Phuong, secretary-general of the VWU, headed the VWU delegation and had met Clarke and Gordon in Hanoi in May.[16] Nguyen Thi Binh, vice chair of the WUL, led the WUL delegation (see Figure 2).[17] South Vietnamese women who supported the RVN administration could not attend the conference because the South Vietnamese government had made it a capital offense to confer with the enemy (members of the NLF or citizens of the DRV). Some WSP members questioned the significance of a meeting between American and Vietnamese women if RVN citizens were not present, but WSP leaders decided the conference would attract important attention regardless.[18]

Indeed, the Djakarta meeting did draw international interest and provided women the opportunity to get to know one another in a more intimate setting. The sessions generally ran from eight in the morning until noon and from three in the afternoon until seven in the evening. Between formal discussions, the American and Vietnamese women talked in smaller groups about their families, culture, and fashion. In the evenings, the delegates attended cultural events, prepared for the next day, and, on one occasion, had dinner with President Sukarno of Indonesia.

To begin the conference, the delegations decided to inform one another of their current and previous political work before moving on to discuss the war and its possible solutions. The American delegation began, taking one and a half hours to report on their domestic activism and on the political climate in the United States. Then, for the rest of the first day and into the next morning's session, the nine Vietnamese women introduced themselves, described the war's impact on their lives, and argued that if it were not for U.S. support of the RVN administration, they would now be living happily with their husbands and children in a united Viet Nam. VWU and WUL members provided information on their families in order to show that the war had had deleterious effects on every aspect of their lives, including their ability to mother.

At first, WSP members found the recounting of the war tedious, but they soon realized the importance of Vietnamese women's statements, which differed from the official U.S. version of the origin of the war and of the consequences of U.S. bombing on civilians. The American delegation also discerned the centrality of the war to Vietnamese women's lives because the VWU and WUL members could not introduce themselves without immediately referring to it. For instance, in her greeting, Le Chan Phuong spoke not of her role in the VWU but of the whereabouts of her children, whose village the U.S. military had bombed the night before. Uncertain of her children's fate, she evoked the sympathy of her American counterparts as she carried out her responsibilities as head of the VWU delegation. Like Phuong, each of the Vietnamese women at the Djakarta conference shared information about their families, including how many children they had and the locations of their children and husbands. They also listed family members wounded, jailed, or killed by the U.S. military or ARVN and described years of uncertainty as a result of the country's division.[19] These accounts exemplified the very real suffering of Vietnamese women while also serving as a tool for VWU and WUL members to secure U.S. women's assistance.

After hearing Vietnamese women's testimonies, WSP members appropriated these narratives to portray all Vietnamese women as mothers and victims. In a call to American women to join the antiwar effort, WSP stated, "We women shudder with the women of Vietnam, living under the constant horror of death from the skies, trying, often in vain, to protect their children."[20] With Johnson's bombing campaign over North Viet Nam under way, WSP members drew attention to civilian casualties, particularly children, to elicit sympathy and to justify their own stance against U.S. foreign policy.

Similarly, a joint communiqué written by the American delegation, approved by the Vietnamese attendees, and broadly addressed to American women highlighted the victimization of the Vietnamese.[21] The statement also stressed, however, the suffering of American mothers because of the war. That is, after describing the "break-up of tens of thousands of families" in Viet Nam and claiming that "nearly a million citizens have been jailed, maimed or tortured" in the South, the communiqué turned to the hardships of American women.[22] It stated that the war also "meant the death of several thousands of American men and the suffering of American wives and mothers."[23] "American mothers," it continued, "have not borne and brought up their sons to kill the innocent and to sacrifice themselves in an unjust cause."[24] Calling attention to the personal sacrifices Americans had to make to wage war, the WSP delegation asked American women to come out in opposition to U.S. intervention. As much as the statement was supposed to be about the afflictions of Vietnamese women, it was equally about the pain of American mothers. It implicitly suggested that American mothers would not sympathize with Vietnamese mothers unless their attention was drawn to the possibility of their own children's deaths, even as it explicitly asserted that American women understood the plight of the Vietnamese because they knew that living in "constant danger of death . . . is a life of terror."[25]

Although the VWU and WUL delegations approved this statement, it is likely that they wanted to include more information about women's roles in the resistance movement to better illustrate their determination to gain liberation, not just peace. WUL leader Nguyen Thi Binh, for instance, mentioned to WSP members that as a teenager she joined the anticolonial struggle against the French. Working undercover in Saigon, she was eventually caught, imprisoned, and tortured. Released three years later, she returned to her undercover duties in Saigon just before the final victory against the French at Dien Bien Phu. Following the signing of the Geneva Agreement ending French rule, she regrouped in the North in the fall of 1954, where she and her longtime sweetheart wed and started a family. Even so, she remained active in opposing the newly established RVN government in the South, eventually joining the foreign affairs section of the NLF. In the summer of 1962, she attended her first international conference as a representative of the NLF in an effort to further people-to-people diplomacy. It was in this capacity that she led the WUL delegation at Djakarta. Binh explained to the WSP members in Djakarta that her resistance to the French and to Diem's regime was consistent with her role as a woman defending her home and homeland.[26]

Although Binh's story would have shown her to be an exemplary woman in Vietnamese culture, it needed modification to appeal to an American audience. When Mary Clarke shared Binh's story in WSP's national newsletter *Memo*, she highlighted similarities between Vietnamese and American women and erased any hint of violence on the part of Binh. According to Clarke, Binh "had herself spent 4 years in jail, and also rarely sees her children or her husband who is in the Viet Cong army. She is very politically active, but said she would prefer 'to be just a plain woman.'"[27] Although Clarke mentioned in her article Binh's time in jail as well as the imprisonment of other South Vietnamese women, she neglected to explain all the possible reasons behind women's incarceration. She implied that the RVN government commonly jailed South Vietnamese women whose family members were thought to be part of the NLF, leaving the reader to assume that the RVN government had imprisoned Binh because of her husband's membership in the NLF. The RVN had arrested Binh, though, because of her own participation in the resistance movement. By acknowledging that Binh's husband was in the guerrilla forces, Clarke also made Binh seem similar to American GI wives worried about the fate of their own husbands in Viet Nam. Clarke's description of Binh as "very politically active," a term many WSP members used to describe themselves, also made Binh relatable to most American woman readers.[28] In short, Clarke's rendition of Binh's story resembled the lives of many WSP members: she was a wife and mother forced into activism in order to correct the injustices she and her family suffered.

Judging from discussions among American participants following the Djakarta conference, they deliberately portrayed their Vietnamese contacts in this way.[29] In the fall of 1965, Mary Clarke suggested that WSP publish a pamphlet based on what the VWU and WUL delegations had said, but debate ensued over whether such a publication would change anyone's mind. Whereas Clarke imagined the brochure as giving WSP members more credibility by squarely placing them in the field of international relations, Shirley Lens, a Djakarta conference attendee and WSP leader in Chicago, thought the pamphlet would be a waste of money. After reading a draft of the brochure, Lens scathingly wrote to Clarke that the representation of the VWU as nongovernmental and of the NLF as noncommunist would make WSP members "look like jackasses—just naïve women."[30] Lens further asserted that when she had cornered one or two of the WUL members in Djakarta, they had admitted to wanting a communist government; thus, Lens could not support any statement that depicted the VWU or WUL in a different manner. This refusal put Lens's fellow WSP members in a tough position as they sought a means to publicize the meeting without providing further ammunition for those arguing for U.S. involvement in Viet Nam from an anticommunist standpoint.

Authors of a WSP report sent to the Senate Foreign Relations Committee found a compromise between Clarke's and Lens's perspectives. Aline Berman, Margaret Russell, and Bernice Steele wrote an account of the Djakarta conference in which they obscured, but did not erase, communism as an issue. Instead, they challenged the official version of the war, arguing that the war began when former RVN president Ngo Dinh Diem violated the terms of the Geneva Agreement, with the support of the United States, by impeding the reunification of Viet Nam in 1956. When South Vietnamese peasants protested, Diem's regime killed them, leading to the indigenous formation of the NLF. In the early 1960s, Diem's administration continued to persecute South Vietnamese, sending the ARVN to spray the countryside with toxic chemicals supplied by the U.S. military. Even after Diem's assassination, Saigon continued its war on its own citizens with the aid of the U.S. government. The three WSP members also criticized the U.S. approach to peace talks, saying that the Johnson administration was "knocking on the wrong door" when it sought to negotiate with Hanoi, not the NLF.[31] They insisted that the NLF was led by southerners in response to Saigon's tyranny; therefore, the DRV had no authority to negotiate on its behalf. In an effort to deflate Cold War fears of communist expansion, the three WSP members also argued that communists did not control the NLF, although they did not deny that the NLF contained communist members.

To further obscure Cold War concerns, the three WSP members created a sympathetic image of Vietnamese women by highlighting their similarities to American women. "They are not different from us in their desire for a future for their children," the report explained. "It seems little enough for women to ask that their leaders find a way to talk and end this war."[32] However, Berman, Russell, and Steele did not appeal to the Senate Foreign Relations Committee as ordinary American women. In the cover letter to the report, they distinguished themselves as "the only group of American women who have had the opportunity to speak with the 'other side.'"[33] Dagmar Wilson similarly explained in an article in *Memo* that WSP members attended the conference in Djakarta to achieve "freedom from dependence on the judgments of the Viet Nam experts."[34] Creating a place for themselves in the international arena, the WSP members reinforced a bond between Vietnamese and American mothers, erased any hint that Vietnamese women violently resisted the U.S. or RVN militaries, and concealed the VWU's connection to the North Vietnamese government. Given their authority, Berman, Russell, and Steele then pressed senators to block U.S. collusion with Saigon.

Although the WSP members used maternalism to enter this debate, when they cited Vietnamese views on the war, some encountered backlash. Senator Milward Simpson of Wyoming quoted a male senior history major at Old Dominion College to attack WSP, even though this student had no credentials as an international relations expert. Simpson admitted that "No one [else] wants to tangle with a woman and no one wants to be against peace," but that would not convince him to change U.S. policy.[35] WSP members may have found a way to present themselves that was difficult to criticize, but they had not persuaded Congress to end the war. In fact, in June 1966, the United States increased bombings and began to target the DRV's fuel supplies.

VWU and WUL members informed WSP members of the ongoing situation in Viet Nam in a way that could contribute to WSP's domestic activism. In a 1966 letter commemorating American Independence Day, VWU members portrayed the war in Viet Nam as similar to the American Revolution against British colonialism. This time, however, the United States was at fault for ripping apart any shred of democracy in South Viet Nam, the VWU proclaimed, while the Vietnamese desired freedom and independence. Asking American mothers to stand up for the ideals on which the United States was founded, the VWU suggested that women should petition U.S. government officials on the Fourth of July as a way of showing their patriotism.[36] In a reversal of commonly held assumptions about transnational women's relationships, Vietnamese women actually instructed Americans on how to be good citizens.

Despite the growing alliance between WSP members and Vietnamese women, VWU and WUL members realized that the United States was the major, but not the sole, contributor to the war. Therefore, the VWU and WUL communicated their perspectives on the war to other audiences as well. Following the Djakarta conference with American women, the Vietnamese delegates stayed in Indonesia for a meeting with Australian women.[37] The outreach efforts of Vietnamese people's diplomats seem to have at least partially succeeded given that the Vietnam Courier, a weekly English- and

French-language periodical printed in Hanoi and distributed around the world, regularly published international statements of solidarity as evidence that "the whole world supports us [the DRV]."[38] Further promoting this unity, the North Vietnamese government hosted foreign delegations from at least seven different countries to visit Hanoi in 1966, one of which was a group of four American women.[39]

On December 22, 1966, the first delegation of American women invited by the VWU to tour the country arrived in Hanoi. Although none of the four women on the delegation identified themselves as WSP members, three of them used similar maternalist language to explain their reasons for going to Hanoi. One delegate, Diane Nash, an African American leader of the 1960 sit-ins in Nashville, confided at a 1967 press conference that she had decided to visit Hanoi after seeing a photograph of a "distraught [Vietnamese] mother holding a wounded or dead child."[40] Picturing herself in the Vietnamese woman's place, Nash visited war-torn North Viet Nam to find out the accuracy of the photo. What she discovered was worse than she had imagined. She saw evidence that the U.S. military bombed schools, hospitals, and churches, regularly injuring women and children. Shocked, she returned to the United States determined to end African American involvement in the war effort and identified herself as an African American mother when speaking to the press.

Weeks earlier, Nash had left New York for the month-long excursion, which few could afford or would be invited to undertake. Traveling with three other women—Grace Mora Newman, a Puerto Rican whose brother refused to serve in Viet Nam; Barbara Deming, a white peace activist who had visited Saigon in April 1966 with the Committee for Nonviolent Action; and Patricia Griffith, a white scholar—Nash flew through France, the Soviet Union, and China before finally landing in Hanoi almost a week later. The group toured North Viet Nam for eleven days before returning to the United States. In a magazine article, Nash made it clear that the four American women had little in common apart from their opposition to the war and that they represented no particular organization.[41]

However, the group did have more in common than their antiwar stances. First, they could all afford to take a month-long trip abroad. The women paid their own way to and from Hanoi, and the VWU covered their expenses while they were in North Viet Nam. Each of the women also had enough of a presence in social movements of the 1960s to be asked to visit Hanoi. The VWU had invited U.S. women to Hanoi through Dave Dellinger, an antiwar activist and the editor of *Liberation* magazine, who had recently returned from a trip to North Viet Nam. Members of the VWU often asked American visitors for suggestions about which U.S. activists they should invite to Hanoi in the future. For example, it was likely that a VWU member had requested that a female leader in the civil rights movement be included in the delegation to Hanoi so that the VWU could gain access to an African American audience. For this particular trip, a group of about twenty-five women active in antiwar organizations chose who would go based on their financial ability, their connection to particular communities in the United States, and their potential to solicit public attention.[42]

The greeting that the four American women received in Viet Nam illustrates the importance of these trips for the VWU. Upon deplaning, eight members of the VWU—Vo Thi The and Bui Thi Cam, both of whom had attended the meeting in Djakarta; Phan Thi An, who kept in contact with Deming for years after this first meeting; Ha Giang, a member of the Standing Committee of the VWU; Vuong Thi Trinh, who stayed at the hotel with the women; Le Thi Xuyen, a member of Parliament; and Tran Bich Thoa and Nguyen My Dung, both interpreters—welcomed them. The VWU organized daily trips for the women to visit parts of Hanoi and provinces fifty to sixty miles outside the city. A VWU representative, doctor, interpreter, photographer, and military personnel accompanied the group on its tours in and around Hanoi.[43] On most days, the group would leave early in the morning and return to the hotel to rest in the afternoon. In the evening, the VWU organized cultural events, arranged film screenings, and hosted dinners for the group. Such elaborate planning, especially during wartime, indicated the significance for VWU members of building relationships with American women.

The Vietnamese made it clear that they invited U.S. women as well as other Westerners to North Viet Nam to provide evidence that the U.S. military knowingly and indiscriminately killed civilians. One interpreter for American women's delegations, Pham Ngac, recalled that the itinerary for these trips was set up in such a way as to convince visitors that the United States was committing war crimes against Viet Nam.[44] Exposing U.S. bombing of the dike system as deliberate, for example, became a central objective of the Vietnamese, as it would illustrate the genocidal nature of the war—damage to the dikes had the potential to cause floods, famine, and death.[45] In regard to Diane Nash's trip, the VWU escorted her group to hospitals and introduced it to members of communities where air raids had recently occurred to provide evidence that the U.S. military regularly bombed nonmilitary targets. There, victims of bombings and chemical warfare told their stories in alarming detail.[46] For the Vietnamese, there was no better way for the American women to understand the North Vietnamese perspective on the war than to meet its recent victims.

The four women were also eager to learn about the day-to-day lives of Vietnamese during wartime. Even when left to their own devices, they sought to discover the consequences of the war for civilians. On a few afternoons, the American women roamed Hanoi without Vietnamese guides. During one of these walks, Patricia Griffith noticed how very few children she encountered in the city, even in a nearby park. For Griffith, a mother of four whose children ranged in age from three to thirteen, this absence struck her as the strangest aspect of Hanoi at war. In interviews about her trip, she mentioned it as epitomizing the effect U.S. bombing had had on the North Vietnamese—it tore apart families, the cornerstone of society.[47]

The four American women soon learned why so few children lived in the city: mothers feared for their children's safety. On a misty Christmas Eve, the group visited recently bombed districts of Hanoi, where it met with women living in the area. One of the women, a pregnant mother wearing a mulberry sweater and standing in the dirt road, told how she had evacuated her two children to the countryside to protect them from U.S. bombs. Close to the end of her pregnancy, with a month off from work, she finally sent for her son and daughter to join her again in Hanoi. After they had returned, she kept them home with her and only left them to go to routine prenatal checkups. During one such appointment, on December 13, 1966, she heard that the area of Hanoi where she lived had been bombed. She rushed home to find both of her children dead. Grieving for them, she declared revenge on the Americans who had taken her son and daughter from her.[48]

Nash captured the attention of her audience by describing the anguish of this pregnant mother in the civil rights periodical *Freedomways*. Stating that the woman had searched desperately for her children after the bombing but could only find "a piece of her [daughter's] head and hair," Nash described the mother as grieving woefully, rather than vengefully, over the destruction of her family.[49] "It is too much suffering for me," Nash quoted the Vietnamese mother.[50] In Nash's portrayal, this woman was a victim but not a fighter. She further spotlighted Vietnamese mothers' suffering when she relayed the graphic story of the death of a pregnant woman whose unborn baby had been "blown out of her body" and found "some distance" from the mother.[51] Through both of these accounts, Nash attested to the violent horror of the war as well as how it played out on women's bodies and in their private lives. Her narrative shared similarities with arguments against the war made by peace activists, and she also portrayed Vietnamese women in terms similar to those used by civil rights activists to describe African American women. For Nash, Vietnamese mothers exemplified the strength of those who carried on despite much personal sacrifice.

Like Nash, the VWU identified mothers and children as the frequent victims of U.S. bombing. On a few occasions, mothers testified to the deaths of children, and orphans told of the deaths of their parents to document the toll of the war on families. The North Vietnamese successfully made their case to Barbara Deming, who concluded that "above all [the war was] a war against children."[52]

But, for the American women's hosts, demonstrating the destruction of family life was not the sole purpose of the delegation's visit. They also wanted to show the determination of the Vietnamese, a determination that extended back to French and Japanese colonization. Le Thi Xuyen, president of the VWU from 1946 until 1956, lost her first husband during an attack by the French in 1939. That same year, her second husband lost his first wife and unborn child when his wife was arrested and beaten in a French prison. Despite these sorrows, Xuyen and her second husband found happiness together when they married in 1949. But they had to endure separation from each other and from their children and stepchildren because of U.S. military operations in Viet Nam. After decades of putting the needs of the revolution first, Xuyen, her husband, and others like them would not give in.[53]

VWU member Ha Giang insisted that Xuyen's story was not unusual. "Every wom[a]n in V[iet Nam is] a fighter," she proclaimed.[54] Why? Because since the defeat of the French in 1954, Vietnamese women in the North had gained equality. Giang listed women's accomplishments, including their high posts in the government, their better access to education, and their predominant role in particular fields such as women's and children's medicine. She contrasted this with women's lives under the French, when women had been paid less than men, if they could find work at all, had no chance at an education because it was expensive, and had no access to infant or maternity care. Most importantly for Giang, since independence, VWU executive members attended Ministry meetings in various sections of the government, meaning that women had representatives present in many major political discussions. With these new opportunities for women, the average Vietnamese woman would resist surrender to the U.S. military because she understood that American domination would mean suffering, illiteracy, hunger, and cold, according to Giang. Moreover, the VWU supported women as fighters by educating them about the war and by teaching them how to take over men's agricultural jobs, how to defend their villages, and how to maintain a home life for their children. The VWU argued that if women succeeded in all of these efforts, they would greatly contribute to the end of the war and foil Johnson's plan to sabotage the economic production of North Viet Nam.

Taken together, stories told by the Vietnamese pointed to the ideal of womanhood that included both maternal sacrifice and feminine strength. It quickly became clear to Barbara Deming that, for the Vietnamese, femininity did not exclude militancy, which troubled her because she recognized women's potential to act violently, but she nevertheless advocated nonviolent resistance. Deming came to see a contradiction in promoting women's equality through violence because it could so easily morph into an abuse of power.[55] At a Christmas Eve party held in honor of the American women, Deming unsuccessfully argued her case for nonviolence while also noting the qualities of Vietnamese women that the VWU intended her to see— grace and strength. For Ha Giang, Vietnamese women cherished peace, their families, and national independence; therefore, they fought to defend their homeland.[56]

Nash, who came from the nonviolent but increasingly more militant civil rights movement, could have but did not include stories of women defending their villages against American bombing raids. On a visit to a village outside Hanoi, the VWU introduced the group to a female vice commander of militia forces. The vice commander, Chi Thuan, told the American women that three weeks earlier she had led her troops in a defensive maneuver against U.S. bombers. Despite being wounded, she and those under her command continued to fight until the attack ended. A little over a week later, they again had to defend the town from an air raid and did so with gusto.[57] Patricia Griffith noted that such violent participation on the part of women occurred frequently, and she told reporters that women across the countryside carried rifles while working in the fields. This observation made her rethink the terms that she had used to describe the Vietnamese: "There are no innocent civilians in North Viet Nam," she declared at a press conference shortly after the trip.[58] The possibility of this kind of statement may have prevented Nash from similarly exposing Vietnamese women's military roles in that she may have foreseen that Vietnamese women's participation in organized violence could take away their status as civilians. Both Nash and Deming may have contemplated what Vietnamese women's militancy would mean in the United States, and both women hesitated to reveal Vietnamese women's roles in defending their villages. Instead, they focused on civilian casualties.

Foreseeing the pushback they would receive to stories that the U.S. military was causing widespread devastation to civilian areas, the American women asked the Vietnamese to provide more than statements made by alleged victims as evidence. Both Grace Mora Newman and Patricia Griffith requested that the Vietnamese provide documentation, including photos and films, to prove that the U.S. military bombed civilians and sprayed toxic chemicals. In response, Vietnamese villagers gave Newman part of a "Lazy Dog" cluster bomb as a gift on the fifth day of the trip. Cluster bombs contained three hundred smaller pellet bombs that exploded to release thousands of round pellets. Many victims had ten to twenty pellets enter their body, making extraction of all of them in a timely manner more difficult. Those victims who did not die from their injuries could be paralyzed or suffer from other long-term effects. In the early 1970s, Vietnamese doctors and others claimed that the U.S. military advanced the original design of the cluster bomb by making the pellets plastic and impossible to locate in x-rays. Deming, Griffith, and Newman presented one of the three hundred smaller bombs at a press conference in January 1967 as evidence that the U.S. military used antipersonnel weapons against civilians in North Viet Nam.[59]

Along with the pellet bomb and Vietnamese accounts of civilian injuries, the American women brought back their own stories of experiencing bombing raids in civilian areas. While they were touring a city about fifty miles southwest of Hanoi, an air raid siren sounded, and the Vietnamese rushed the American women to one-person bomb shelters along the street. These cylindrical shelters, spaced regularly along the side of the road, had a lid and sometimes contained two to three feet of rainwater as well as creatures attracted to such an environment. Uncomfortably standing in her shelter, Deming heard explosions and feared that a nearby building would fall on her. Sensing the anxiety of the American women, their Vietnamese hosts decided to move the group to a larger shelter where the women might feel less isolated and distressed. Newman hesitated, but, after some coaxing, agreed to go to the group shelter. Once in the shelter, she announced she was so scared she was "shitting green."[60] As Nash tried to calm her, Newman noticed a spider on the roof of the shelter. She was so unnerved by the spider that she left. After forty-five minutes, the all-clear siren sounded, and the group resumed its tour. Although this story could simply show the danger visitors to Hanoi might face during times of widespread American bombing, it also explains why these American women could not doubt that the Vietnamese told the truth about the bombing of civilian areas in North Viet Nam.[61]

Even with these different kinds of evidence, when the women recounted their experiences to American audiences, they often encountered skepticism. In a speech Barbara Deming gave at schools, churches, and town halls, she admitted that she did not want to believe that the U.S. government purposely bombed noncombatants. In light of what she had witnessed, however, she could not help but recognize that the U.S. military targeted civilian populations through chemical warfare, napalm, and pellet bombs. In the North, pellet bombs routinely injured or killed civilians and could not damage military infrastructure—which the U.S. government claimed was its sole target. Perhaps most convincing to Deming were the testimonies of children determined to tell the American women what had happened during air raids. One eleven-year-old boy, she recalled, "stood in front of us, the tears streaming from his eyes, sometimes shaking with sobs, but making himself tell us in detail" about seeing a group of his classmates killed by American bombs.[62] Still, many in Deming's audience asked whether the Vietnamese had staged all the death and destruction. After all, the American women had not "actually see[n] any American planes in the sky" or "any bombs falling."[63] Thus, some audience members seemed to suggest that "all that we had seen, all the wrecked schools and playgrounds and churches and houses, all the samples of the bombs themselves, all the grieving people with their stories of the day the planes came, all the wounded in the hospitals— all this was simply a very elaborate Hollywood production fabricated by these cunning orientals to dupe the four foolish American women."[64] Noting the possibly racialized and gendered undertones of audience members' disbelief, Deming asserted that it was not the Vietnamese who were trying to dupe her and other Americans; it was the U.S. government. The Johnson administration had first claimed it could accurately bomb military targets, but then, when evidence of widespread destruction in civilian districts came to light, it had to admit that sometimes American bombs hit other buildings by mistake. Deming pushed back against this story, too, asking "is it then by accident, too, that again and again and again, in place after place after place, the Lazy Dog [pellet] bomb is dropped—which is ineffectual against steel and concrete, but deadly effective against human flesh?"[65] With that, Deming challenged her audience to reconsider whose story of the war to trust.

Deming's questioning of the U.S. government's bombing tactics echoed that of Harrison Salisbury, a white Pulitzer Prize–winning reporter for the *New York Times*. Salisbury, who was the first reporter to tour North Viet Nam since U.S. bombing began, visited Hanoi in December 1966 and, in fact, met Deming, Nash, Griffith, and Newman in a bomb shelter. The American women saw him again in the hotel on the last day of their visit and asked him not to mention them in his reports. He assured them that he would not cover their story because he did not consider their trip newsworthy, as they had not done anything "spectacular."[66] In his coverage of the war, he reported on the bomb damage in Hanoi, where the U.S. government claimed no bombing had occurred, and cited North Vietnamese statistics on the number of casualties. Salisbury thus lent credibility to Hanoi, and Assistant Secretary of Defense Arthur Sylvester attacked him for doing so. Conversely, Vietnamese and antiwar periodicals praised him for exposing U.S. military lies.[67] In February 1967, he testified before the Senate Foreign Relations Committee (to which none of the four American women had access) at a hearing about the history and culture of the Vietnamese that was meant to help the Senate reevaluate American policies in Viet Nam. In his statement to the committee, Salisbury said that although "there has been much reaction in this country over my reports of the damage to civilians and the casualties among civilians, I myself was not surprised at the results from our bombings."[68] Implying that there was nothing extraordinary about the destruction of nonmilitary structures in Viet Nam, Salisbury instead questioned the U.S. military's tactics and choice of targets. He noted that the Vietnamese had successfully adapted to the U.S. bombing resources—they had dispersed their war materiel throughout the countryside along the highway and railroad leading to South Viet Nam to the extent that U.S. bombing could never cause enough damage to stop the supply line. The Vietnamese quickly repaired the railroad and highway and, when necessary, used bicycles loaded with six hundred pounds of supplies to bypass damage. There were no concentrations of resources anywhere to destroy. In this way, the DRV had rendered the U.S. strategy of bombing supply lines ineffective; therefore, Salisbury suggested a change in tactics as he intimated that the civilian damage was actually unremarkable.[69]

Even though Salisbury's statements undercut the accounts of the four American women, the women steadfastly argued that civilian casualties exposed inconsistencies between American ideals and the U.S. government's actions. Meeting with Ho Chi Minh on January 2, the group's last day in Hanoi, Diane Nash noted that he similarly observed the contradiction between American values and its deeds in North Viet Nam. Many antiwar activists and DRV officials made comparisons between the war in Viet Nam and the American Revolution by claiming that the Vietnamese wanted independence and freedom just as the American founding fathers had. As Deming later amusedly recalled, the Vietnamese often mentioned George Washington and Abraham Lincoln in speeches about how the United States' example encouraged Vietnamese revolutionaries.[70] Ho Chi Minh, however, spoke of his time in Harlem in the early twentieth century, where he "had observed and resented the exploitation of Negroes in the United States."[71] Instead of connecting the two nations by describing Americans as an inspiration for Vietnamese, Ho Chi Minh, and later Diane Nash, pointed out limits placed on access to American freedom both within and outside the United States. Comparing the treatment of the Vietnamese with that of African Americans, Nash asked African American youths to resist joining the military and face prison terms if necessary. For Nash, spending a few years in prison was better than dying in Viet Nam or murdering other people of color. Besides, the war only brought more pain and discrimination to the African American community, she argued, as a disproportionate number of African American GIs were killed in Viet Nam.[72] For Nash and Ho Chi Minh, the contradiction between what the United States stood for and how it treated African Americans and Vietnamese destabilized arguments in support of spreading democracy through force.

Couching her criticism of U.S. foreign policy in maternalist terms and challenging the treatment of African Americans within U.S. society, Nash received uncritical coverage of her trip from the African American press.[73] Likewise, when the three other women relied on maternalist rhetoric, their trip to North Viet Nam received much positive attention from such sources as the *Washington Post* and *New York Times*, which reported on the trip with little question of the women's veracity or patriotism. The press even collaborated in portraying the women's mission as maternal. For instance, one article described Nash as "a young, attractive Negro mother" concerned with the fates of Vietnamese and African American mothers and children, while another mistakenly called Deming "Mrs." and a housewife when she was in fact a writer in a relationship with two women.[74] Regardless, this portrayal of the four women as maternal and feminine protected them from vilification.

When Barbara Deming was not listed as part of this group primarily made up of married mothers, she received censure. On one occasion, Congressman Louis Wyman argued that Deming's account of the war was all but treason after he heard her speak at the University of New Hampshire. Deming's portrayal of the United States as the aggressor and her possession of an antipersonnel pellet bomb particularly irked Wyman. According to him, the only reason Deming's actions were not treason was that Congress had not declared war on Viet Nam. For Wyman and others, Deming's disagreement with the U.S. administration's portrayal of the war and her desire to expose what she saw as the immoral conduct of the U.S. military was nothing more than subversion and should be punished as such. Her entrance into international relations as a "so-called pacifist," as Wyman caustically called her, and not as a mother, permitted her less leeway in criticizing the U.S. government—only Deming was targeted in such an aggressive manner on the House floor.[75]

The State Department agreed with Wyman that such actions on the part of U.S. citizens should have repercussions, and in this instance motherhood would not shield anyone. Beginning in February 1966, it penalized those who traveled to North Viet Nam without special permission to do so by voiding their passports. At that time, the State Department revoked the passports of seven men who traveled to Hanoi in two separate groups in August and December 1965. Deming, Griffith, Newman, and Nash would have known that their trip might lead to such consequences, and indeed the State Department did take away their passports upon their return to the United States. By 1967, anyone who decided to travel to Hanoi anticipated this outcome. The courts soon curbed the State Department's ability to punish those who traveled to Hanoi, however. In January 1967, the Supreme Court ruled that the State Department could not criminally charge those who traveled to Hanoi because Congress had never enacted a statute that made travel to unauthorized nations a crime. Almost a year later, in December 1967, an Appeals Court ruled that the State Department could not refuse a passport to someone who might travel to an unauthorized location. Both of these rulings upheld Americans' freedom to travel, to monitor U.S. military actions, and to disseminate their own stories of the war.[76]

For members of the underground press, these rulings gave them an edge on reporting on the war, intensified by Hanoi's tendency to deny visas to many reporters. By January 1967, Hanoi officials had approved two of seventy applications for visas from American reporters in the mainstream press. American reporters in the RVN also faced many obstacles to obtaining complete information on the war. In the early 1960s, the U.S. administration set down a policy that U.S. advisors should defer to RVN officials' instructions regarding what to disclose to the press. Saigon severely limited information on the war because it feared that the NLF would use any admission of a military loss as propaganda to attract support and could use information on military matters more generally against the ARVN. The U.S. government agreed to limit coverage of the war because it did not want the extent of U.S. involvement known. Because it was in the interest of the RVN and the U.S. government to limit information on military matters, reporters found themselves shut out of news stories. Over the course of the war, the U.S. administration made guidelines more concrete as to what officials could and could not tell the press. The information tendered included the times of attacks and the names of Americans killed but did not include the use of unconventional weapons or the destruction of nonmilitary targets.[77] While this policy to limit information on the war caused tension between the U.S. government and mainstream media, it also created a need to gather news from alternative sources. Filling this void, U.S. woman peace activists continued to accept invitations proffered by the VWU to visit as they simultaneously strengthened the relationship between Vietnamese and American women.

Immediately drawing attention to their gender, race, and class status, WSP members Dagmar Wilson, Ruth Krause, and Mary Clarke traveled to Hanoi in September 1967 as middle-class, middle-aged, "respectable" white mothers and "housewives" who could lend credibility to reports that U.S. bombs frequently killed civilians. They also hoped to persuade American women in particular and the public more broadly to support antiwar political candidates, join antiwar organizations, and take part in antiwar demonstrations. In a speech after her trip, Wilson explained that she went to North Viet Nam because she believed "women [would] play an important roll [sic] in the international movement to challenge the right of powerful nations to inflict destruction on human beings."[78] The VWU seemed to agree, but it described U.S. actions as "war crimes," language that made the three WSP members shudder.[79] Even so, the WSP members did blame the U.S. government and depicted the war as an unnecessary endeavor that killed innocent civilians. They also found themselves questioning the very definition of femininity and motherhood on which WSP based its protests.

Photographs from the trip indicate what imagery WSP members and Vietnamese photographers thought would persuade the American public that the United States should cease its involvement in Viet Nam. The photos

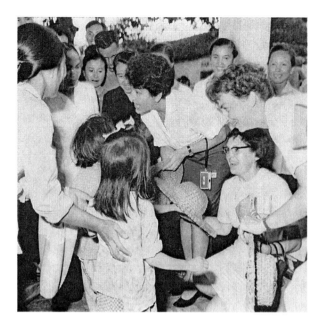

FIGURE 3 Left to right: Mary Clarke, Dagmar Wilson, Ruth Krause with children. Photograph Collection, Box "Demonstrations/ Protests; Billboards; Delegations," Women Strike for Peace Records, Swarthmore College Peace Collection.

documented life during war, and, more specifically, they presented both the symbols of resilience and the most sympathetic victims of war—children. In the October 1967 issue of *Memo*, the national newsletter of WSP, three out of twelve photos documenting the trip showed the WSP members talking to children, usually in a classroom setting (see Figure 3).[80]

Showing children at school highlighted Vietnamese efforts to maintain a semblance of normal life in the midst of war. All three women mentioned in later reports that children still attended class every day, but the Vietnamese had limited the school day to the early morning hours, when bombings were less likely.[81] In addition, these photos placed the WSP members in maternal roles, talking to and playing with children. Other photos portrayed the behind-the-scenes negotiating of WSP members with Vietnamese women and officials, including meetings Wilson, Clarke, and Krause held with the president of the VWU and the head of the permanent NLF mission in Hanoi. Two photos of the three women meeting with American prisoners of war (POWs) suggested that WSP members could negotiate effectively with North Vietnamese officials, unlike U.S. officials, who had not gained an accurate count of POWs in North Viet Nam let alone met with any of them.[82] Furthermore, the encounter between WSP members and POWs was not simply a brief exchange, but apparently a comfortable and catered interview. The photos showed them drinking tea, smoking, and chatting together, demonstrating the amicable relationship WSP members had with the North Vietnamese.

Two years later, one of the POWs with whom Clarke, Krause, and Wilson met drew a different picture of their meeting than the one displayed in *Memo*. After being released to a group of antiwar activists, among them WSP member Grace Paley, in August 1969, the former POW testified to the House Committee on Internal Security that the photo published in *Memo* misrepresented the meeting. According to the sailor, the photo made it look as if he had been sitting at an "L"-shaped table with the American women, but in reality he had been sitting at a table by himself facing Vietnamese officials, and the WSP members had sat off to his side. He did not explain the significance of the alteration to the photo; possibly the alteration itself seemed enough to condemn any WSP account of the meeting as false. Realistically, the editor of *Memo* likely spliced the photo so that it would better fit in the space allowed. The sailor also claimed that the WSP members showed little to no concern for his living conditions and that he had refused to send a message to his family through them because he thought they had made poor assumptions about how he felt about the war. Nevertheless, he did agree with the WSP portrayal of the meeting in one aspect—WSP members did have an amicable relationship with the Vietnamese. Arguably, this POW also had perhaps not an amicable but at least a tolerant relationship with prison officials, because he also met with antiwar activists Dave Dellinger in June 1967 and Tom Hayden in October 1967. Moreover, he was one of three POWs selected by Hanoi for early release in 1969. His testimony to the House Committee may speak to his desire to show his loyalty and patriotism to the United States, in contrast to the actions of antiwar activists he met in North Viet Nam.[83]

Just as significant as the photos WSP did publish in *Memo* are the photos it chose not to publish: photos of bombed-out school buildings or hospitals and a photo of Wilson with a helmet on in a bomb shelter during an air raid.[84] The editor of *Memo* wanted to show the Vietnamese people, not the devastation of the Vietnamese landscape or buildings, in order to put a human face on the suffering. Similar to WSP members' report to the Senate Foreign Relations Committee after the Djakarta meeting that Vietnamese women were no different from American women, the photos of Vietnamese people emphasized their shared humanity. Schoolchildren played and laughed; women met in living rooms and served food and beverages; Vietnamese women cared for children, the sick, and the community.

WSP meant to make Americans feel a connection to the Vietnamese and to sway American women to action through photos of schoolchildren, Vietnamese women, and cared-for POWs. The photos also showed the difficulty of life during the war, the perseverance of the Vietnamese people, and WSP efforts to end the war. Erasing Cold War boundaries of East and West and constructing similar versions of femininity for Vietnamese and American women, the WSP photos asked the viewer to sympathize with Vietnamese as people.

In a departure from WSP's conventional silence on Vietnamese women's participation in violence, Wilson, Clarke, and Krause also met with and photographed guerrilla women. Because WSP members usually stressed women's natural opposition to violence, Vietnamese women's militancy had to be explained in a way that preserved their image as sympathetic allies rather than as enemies and contributors to war. One photograph showed the WSP members making peaceful and friendly contact with a woman in the military.[85] It illustrated the ability of women to put aside their nations' animosity and hold a friendly conversation, presumably for negotiation purposes. Another photograph showed three women demonstrating the use of a lightweight machine gun.[86] Although these photos of guerrilla women might have compromised WSP efforts to depict Vietnamese women as peacemakers rather than fighters, they served another purpose by suggesting that U.S. soldiers fought women, and very young women at that, in North Viet Nam. American bombing raids not only injured Vietnamese women, but Vietnamese women also had to give up their conventional domestic duties as well as a peaceful home life to defend their nation against American aggression. Significantly, WSP published the former but not the latter photo in the October 1967 issue of *Memo*. Images that showed women's ability to set aside differences and to talk peacefully seemed more in line with WSP's purpose than images that showed Vietnamese women firing weapons.[87]

Although Clarke, Krause, and Wilson visited North Viet Nam to become "experts" on the war and the destruction it caused, the experience seems to have affected them more personally as well. Afterward, all three learned to sympathize with women who violently opposed U.S. intervention. Their Vietnamese interpreter recalled one of the WSP members commenting that the example of Vietnamese women made her rethink the inherent peacefulness of mothers, as circumstances might require women to react violently to protect their children from harm.[88] Wilson even stated that she "wanted to take up a gun and shoot back" when U.S. planes bombed nearby—an admission a congressman and the *Washington Post* censured.[89] Wilson seems to have recognized her misstep instantly and covered it "with a small self-conscious laugh."[90] Even so, the FBI took her words seriously and closely monitored her speeches at meetings across the country, on television, and on the radio. Even though she often began talks by declaring that she had visited North Viet Nam as a mother who simply wanted to end the war, FBI agents questioned Wilson's devotion to nonviolence and reported that she advocated civil disobedience and "militancy."[91] Some agents even suggested that Wilson supported the violent overthrow of the U.S. government. Clearly, maternalist rhetoric did not protect her from government suspicion once she had crossed the line and mentioned her willingness to defend herself through violence.

Wilson's comment also shows a departure from Nash's and Deming's silence about Vietnamese women's military roles. While Nash and Deming skirted the issue, Wilson, the figurehead of a women's peace organization, brought this violence to center stage and even sympathized with it. For her, going to Hanoi seems to have persuaded her to challenge American notions of femininity while she contradictorily clung to her status as a white middle-class mother as the basis on which she could protest against the government's actions. Not having the same social status as Wilson, neither Nash nor Deming placed herself in as precarious a position as Wilson did.

The two other WSP members said nothing so controversial, but their reports of the trip showed a similar sympathy for women who chose to fight. They no longer saw Vietnamese women as just victims who needed to be saved from U.S. attacks; instead, they admired their "indomitable character."[92] When Clarke spoke of a seventeen-year-old female guerrilla, she told her interviewer that the girl had entered the military after her parents were killed when she was eleven. Clearly a victim of the war, the young woman also inspired Clarke's admiration as a woman who had "truly [become] equal" to the men of her country by joining the resistance movement.[93] For Clarke, as well as for Wilson, their trip to Viet Nam provided a window on an alternative society—one in which men and women were equal. The fact that women gained equality through violence, a very alarming aspect of Vietnamese society for Deming, did not seem to register with these WSP members. Instead, they focused on the reason for women's violence—U.S. involvement in Viet Nam. The U.S. military needed to be stopped, and in the meantime, American women might learn about their ability to be equal through the examples of Vietnamese women.

Although experience in the war zone challenged Wilson's and Clarke's beliefs in women's inherent nonviolence, it did not transform the rhetoric of WSP. Despite Wilson's impolitic comment, she still described women's international mission as a "joint struggle against violence"[94] and reassured WSP members at the sixth annual conference that "we women have not changed—our goals are the same."[95] Krause most fully deployed the traditional rhetoric of WSP in her description of the visit when she quoted a Vietnamese woman who said, "I think that American mothers understand my sufferings. I hope that American mothers will help us to stop their children from coming to Vietnam and causing the suffering of Vietnamese children."[96] Through this Vietnamese mother, Krause reestablished American and Vietnamese women's common maternal bond and declared that they would work together to end the war.

Mary Clarke soon learned firsthand of the grief of Vietnamese mothers who had lost children. Shortly after her return to the United States, her twenty-eight-year-old son died of cancer. At a peace rally two days later, a fellow WSP member blamed the Johnson administration because, under its leadership, politicians spent more money on the war than on domestic needs like medical care. Clarke connected the war to her son's death by establishing a fund in his name for a children's hospital in North Viet Nam. Losing her son so quickly after witnessing the medical needs in Hanoi made her strive to do more than end the war—she wanted to alleviate the effects of the war on Vietnamese children, and she understood that peace meant more than ending a military conflict.[97]

For women such as Mary Clarke, maternalism was both a tool and a reality. As a tactic, maternalism helped to bridge differences between Vietnamese and American women. The VWU, WUL, and WSP all supported portraying women's concerns over the war as maternal and through that figurative bond gained each other's confidence. In some cases, American women made lifelong connections with Vietnamese women. Maternalist rhetoric also helped to protect U.S. women from harsh criticism, but it did not aid them in persuading supporters of the war of its unjustness. In reality, the majority of the women who traveled to Hanoi in these early years as well as those they met in Hanoi had children and so identified themselves as mothers in much of the press. This reality highlights the fact that middle-aged, middle-class, usually white heterosexual women could afford the month-long expedition, unlike their single, unestablished, or working-class counterparts. Although maternalism as a tool had its limits, women's actual status as mothers secured its place in their metaphorical toolbox.

Ostensibly, these first trips by American women to North Viet Nam established women's presence in the international realm, but their gender, race, and sexuality also shaped their experiences. Whereas WSP members could claim unbiased expertise as white middle-class mothers, women such as Diane Nash and Barbara Deming did not have the ability to portray themselves in the same manner. Regardless, even WSP members' social status had its limits, as Dagmar Wilson discovered. Women's nonviolence was central to their ability to claim a special place in foreign relations. American women's obscuring of Vietnamese women's participation in organized violence served both parties well as they looked to collaborate in the pursuit of persuading the American public and government to end U.S. involvement in Viet Nam. Standing in opposition to the U.S. government and questioning U.S. societal norms implicitly, if not explicitly, these women were unlikely ambassadors of U.S. culture. Instead, they allowed their experiences in Viet Nam to alter their own notions of femininity and motherhood. Some WSP members began a slow transformation from feminine to feminist consciousness when confronted with their limited roles in U.S. political circles. Even so, for the next two years, female peace activists established stable channels of communication with Vietnamese based on an even narrower definition of women's roles as mothers.

CHAPTER TWO

Strengthening Channels of Communication, 1968–1970

In May 1968, Susan Sontag, an author and American social critic, noted during her travels in and around Hanoi the centrality of familial language in Vietnamese culture. Although many visitors to Hanoi commented that the North Vietnamese referred to their leader as *Bac Ho*, Uncle Ho, Sontag pointed out that this title was not peculiar to Ho Chi Minh; in Viet Nam, people often addressed older unrelated persons as uncle or aunt. Sontag claimed that this language allowed the Vietnamese to see themselves as part of "one big family"—a forerunner to Benedict Anderson's "imagined community."[1] These familial lines literally as well as figuratively traversed the division of the country at the seventeenth parallel—in one case, a leader in the VWU even had brothers in the ARVN.[2] More generally, many Vietnamese in the North spoke of family members they had not seen or heard from in years because of the Saigon administration's barring of mail service between North and South Viet Nam.

Americans had their own stories of familial separation as the number of GIs deployed to Viet Nam increased. Tapping into this common experience, WSP members modified their maternalism. At a time when women were pushed to the sidelines of antiwar protests because of a focus on draft resisters, WSP promoted the slogan "Not My Son, Not Your Son, Not Their Sons," emphasizing women's maternal duties to resist war and conscription.[3] This motto had the additional benefit of providing women with an alternative to the solely sexual function of young women put forward by the common antiwar slogan "Girls say 'yes' to boys who say 'no,'" popularized through the distribution of a 1968 poster featuring folksinger Joan Baez and her two sisters.[4] Implicitly criticizing the sexual objectification of young women in antiwar circles, WSP members carved out a place for themselves as middle-aged mothers of draft-age sons as they sought to maintain a central position in antiwar demonstrations and sustain relationships with VWU and WUL members. Despite the recent revelations by Dagmar Wilson and Mary Clarke about the limits placed on women in U.S. society, the context of women's narrowed roles in antiwar protests suppressed the potential to center women's rights concerns in WSP's arguments against war.

Instead, WSP members continued to work collaboratively with Vietnamese women as allegedly apolitical and inherently nonviolent mothers, allowing the VWU and WUL to continue to disseminate information on the war through American women both to international women's groups and to American audiences.

American interest in the Vietnamese perspective on the war increased as accounts from antiwar activists who had traveled to Viet Nam and from reporters stationed with American troops in South Viet Nam forced the American public to recognize what kind of war the United States was waging. Hundreds of thousands of people had joined antiwar demonstrations across the country, young men burned their draft cards, and protestors participated in civil disobedience. By the fall of 1967, more Americans believed the war was a mistake than that it was not, and President Johnson sought to begin negotiations with the DRV.[5] Heavy bombing of Hanoi at the time of Johnson's offer likely kept the North Vietnamese from accepting. In February 1968, Hanoi and the NLF launched the Tet Offensive, which demonstrated the pervasiveness of insurgent forces in South Viet Nam. Following talks with top U.S. government officials about the United States' current military position, Johnson made known on March 31, 1968, that he would not run for reelection, an announcement that renewed the hopes of antiwar activists that the war would soon end.

But first the nations needed to agree to meet. Irking the Johnson administration, Hanoi chose to use informal channels of communication to state its willingness to negotiate and to suggest a location for the talks. Novelist Mary McCarthy and CBS foreign correspondent Charles Collingwood each met with North Viet Nam's prime minister Pham Van Dong in late March and early April 1968, respectively, and both brought back the message that the North Vietnamese "appear[ed] very confident" and had proposed Phnom Penh, Cambodia, as the site for negotiations.[6] The U.S. administration countered with Geneva, Switzerland, through official channels and waited for Hanoi's response.[7] While U.S. government officials negotiated with North Viet Nam to *begin* peace talks, women from the belligerent nations met in Paris to discuss the war and their efforts to end it.

In April 1968, the VWU, WUL, and WSP arranged a conference including women from seven additional countries to "establish reliable communication" between women (see Figure 4).[8] They invited two female representatives from peace groups in Australia, Canada, England, Japan, New Zealand, and West Germany, countries that, in some way, supported U.S. involvement in Viet Nam. In addition, seven members each from the

FIGURE 4 Left to right: Mary Clarke, Ha Giang, Nguyen Thi Binh, French Women's Union hosts, and various members of the WUL and VWU delegations, including Nguyen Ngoc Dung in the corner of the table at the Paris Conference of Concerned Women. Photograph Collection, Box "Dated Images/Billboards, etc.," Women Strike for Peace Records, Swarthmore College Peace Collection.

VWU and the WUL, and fourteen WSP members, attended the conference. The Paris Conference of Concerned Women to End the War took place two weeks before formal peace talks began, illustrating to its participants that women could agree to set aside their differences to talk peace more quickly than their political leaders.[9]

From the beginning of the conference, the positioning of women as concerned about the war because of their maternal status took center stage. In her welcoming address, Yvonne Dumont, the general secretary of the French Women's Union, the organization hosting the conference, described the common distress of mothers whose sons were fighting, killing, and dying in Viet Nam. Stating that "maternal love" crossed "social barriers and borders," Dumont erased any differences between women by reducing their identities to that of mothers, specifically mothers of soldiers and draft-age sons.[10]

The portrayals of conference attendees by Dumont and others belied the array of women present. The women's ages ranged from nineteen to sixty-five, and not all of the women were married or had children, although the majority were mothers. Not all of the women with children had sons, and not all of the sons were of draft age. In fact, of the fourteen U.S. women, only one mentioned having a son who had fought in Viet Nam, and her other son was a conscientious objector. On the one hand, VWU, WUL, and WSP organizers encouraged this diversity; they sought to include a woman active in the civil rights movement, a woman from a religious community, and a celebrity in the U.S. delegation in order to form a broad network of women working against the war. Their similar desire to include women active in antiwar organizations in other nations would likewise contribute to establishing international ties between women. On the other hand, they collaborated in projecting the conference as one between middle-aged married mothers of draft-age sons.[11]

Portraying all the women at the conference in this manner lent itself to having a workshop on conscription. The purpose of this session was to gather information on compulsory service in each of the nations as well as each nation's immigration policies, work possibilities, and living conditions for those emigrating to avoid the draft. Coming out of the workshop, American delegates set up a fund to help draft resisters avoid military service—highlighting one of the supportive roles women could play in the draft resistance movement. Although most of the delegations at the conference seemed to assume without question that draftees could only be men, the Vietnamese delegation clarified that males, but not females, faced conscription.[12] With Vietnamese women acting in central capacities to defend the DRV and infiltrate South Viet Nam, it made sense to mention the voluntary nature of their service.

In fact, one of the representatives of the WUL, nineteen-year-old Ngo Thi Tuyet, joined the resistance movement in the South at the age of twelve. An orphan by the age of fifteen, she secured information for the guerrilla forces. At eighteen, having been injured, she was sent to Hanoi, where she met Ho Chi Minh on a few occasions and was chosen to visit France, Cuba, Czechoslovakia, and China to tell her story.[13] At the Paris conference, she provided a moving account of life in the South during the war—so much so that during a break following her speech, more than a few of the women came up to her crying. One American woman, Marie Petersen, even declared Tuyet her adopted daughter. She gave Tuyet her address in the United States and pictures of her two sons. On the back of the photos, Petersen wrote that the young men were Tuyet's brothers. Although Tuyet never contacted Petersen, she kept her address and the photos as reminders of the sympathy women at the conference shared with one another.[14] This young woman's taking up of arms, however, undermined the overall portrayal of conference participants as concerned middle-aged mothers of sons and the depiction of women as inherently nonviolent, as did reports from other Vietnamese attendees.

FIGURE 5 New Year's Card from Bui Thi Cam. Box 3, Folder 44, Helen Boyden Lamb Papers, Schlesinger Library, Radcliffe Institute, Harvard University.

The head of the WUL delegation, Nguyen Thi Binh, likewise depicted Vietnamese women as fighters in her address to the conference. Although Binh first described the victimization of South Vietnamese women and children by U.S. and ARVN forces, she soon turned to the heroic efforts of Vietnamese women such as Ngo Thi Tuyet. She claimed that because of foreign invasion and the persecution of the Vietnamese, Vietnamese women had to defend their nation as combatants just as the Trung sisters had resisted Chinese invasion in 40 A.D. Reciting the Vietnamese proverb "when war strikes close to home, even the women must fight," Binh made clear that the Vietnamese version of womanhood included an obligation to take up arms in defense of their homeland (see Figure 5).[15] This participation in violence was natural for women because, as Binh explained, wives and mothers who longed for peace fought all the harder "to liberate their country from foreign invasion."[16] This violence, however, had no rhetorical place in the burgeoning transnational network of women; therefore, the other delegations obscured it in articles and statements about the conference while highlighting those aspects of Vietnamese femininity that corresponded to their own versions of motherhood. For WSP members, "faith, love, and compassion" best characterized both Vietnamese and American women's attributes.[17]

Conference attendees' sympathy arguably facilitated the creation of an international women's antiwar network. A second workshop focused on past and future cooperation among and between women in different nations.[18] Out of this discussion, conference attendees recognized a common problem: many of their fellow citizens lacked information on the war—information that could incite outrage. Although some delegates believed the dissemination of images of massacred Vietnamese children would stir enough indignation to end the war, others wanted to provide facts and figures to prove that women's knowledge of the situation extended beyond maternal emotions.[19] The Vietnamese came to the conference prepared with the history of and statistics on the war and even provided delegates with their interpretation of American ideals. In a statement to the Paris conference, VWU leader Phan Thi An described "true Americans" as those who promoted freedom and independence—what the North Vietnamese sought—as she distinguished between the acting U.S. administration and the American people.[20] Delegates generally adopted the Vietnamese perspective on the war and its solution, as evidenced by a joint communiqué written during the conference about its achievements. The communiqué similarly blamed the U.S. government, but not the American people, for the war. Combining facts on the war with mothers' supposedly inherent feelings, the joint communiqué stated that attendees had met with mothers who lived in North and South Viet Nam to learn what was really happening there; they had studied the legalities and illegalities of U.S. involvement in Viet Nam; and, as mothers, they had identified concerns about the war's effects on the children of Viet Nam as well as on their own sons who might fight in Viet Nam.[21] Accepting both a particular image of women and advancing a particular narrative of the war, delegates "unite[d] women in concern for the future of the world."[22]

Delegates left the conference looking forward to the end of the war, as Washington and Hanoi agreed to hold peace talks in Paris. Wishing the peace negotiators success, one American woman "hoped . . . the mood of give and take, the deep concern for the viewpoint of others, could somehow be carried from our conference to theirs through the air waves of Paris."[23] Indeed, the women who met in Paris got along so well that one WSP member even called the conference a "love-in."[24] WSP members had reason to hope, as Nguyen Thi Binh would soon lead the NLF delegation at the Paris Peace Talks.

Formal talks between the United States and DRV soon stalled, however, as the DRV demanded an end to U.S. bombing over North Viet Nam and the U.S. negotiator stipulated that the DRV simultaneously withdraw its troops from the RVN. Using a backdoor method to pressure the U.S. administration to continue the talks in a way favorable to the Vietnamese, VWU members reached out to the U.S. women they had met in Paris and provided them with statistics on the increased bombing in North Viet Nam as well as the number of GIs killed or wounded since the Paris Peace Talks began. They even went so far as to suggest to WSP members that they write letters to the families of GIs requesting that they ask their son or husband to desert. This tactic resembled one deployed by the NLF, in which older women in a village would reach out to ARVN soldiers, declare themselves to be like the soldiers' mothers, and try to persuade the soldiers to desert. Although it is unlikely that any WSP members acted on this suggestion, it illustrates the VWU's desire to guide WSP members as well as WUL members' domestic portrayal of themselves as mothers of soldiers.[25]

The VWU and WUL also appealed to women in the Eastern Bloc, specifically through the Women's International Democratic Federation (WIDF), an international women's organization (with no U.S. affiliate), to which both Vietnamese women's groups belonged. For its part, in 1964, the WIDF founded the International Committee of Women for Solidarity with the Women and People of South Vietnam for the purpose of tracking and reporting Vietnamese casualties at the hands of American and ARVN forces. Reporting these figures to an international audience, the WIDF was an important ally in efforts by the VWU and WUL to build a people's diplomacy.[26] Like the VWU, WUL, and WSP, WIDF members positioned themselves and other women as mothers concerned for the welfare of children. In October 1968, when the WIDF sent a delegation to meet with W. Averell Harriman, the chief U.S. negotiator at the Paris Peace Talks, it praised the "courageous actions of American women" who protested the war to save "the lives of their children."[27] The WIDF also held up VWU and WUL members as paragons of maternal and revolutionary ideals who simultaneously "advance[d] the cause of women's emancipation, the happiness of children all over the world, and . . . world peace."[28] For WIDF members, who primarily came from communist countries that promoted women's equality through their entrance into "masculine" realms, Vietnamese women's military roles could be celebrated alongside their maternal devotion.

Vietnamese participants at WIDF conferences expressed their gratitude toward the "vast international women's front" that had formed in support of the Vietnamese people while consistently characterizing Vietnamese women's roles in the resistance movement as stemming from maternal responsibilities.[29] At the WIDF's sixth international congress, in June 1969 in Helsinki, Finland, VWU delegation leader Phan Thi An commended Vietnamese women's heroism in the face of U.S. aggression when she told the story of a fifty-three-year-old mother who crossed a river under fire forty-five times in three days to supply North Vietnamese forces with ammunition. "Inspired by motherly love," Vietnamese women undertook unimaginable feats, An told her audience.[30] For An, Vietnamese mothers also had the task of carrying on after the loss of children; all three of An's daughters had died by 1966.[31] Nevertheless, her maternal responsibilities persisted, as all youths needed motherly attention to protect them and guide their actions. The VWU and WUL promoted this interpretation of women's duties both within Viet Nam and internationally as a way to end imperialistic aggression.

Declaring at its 1968 national conference that "for women, the war is not over until our men are home!," WSP made clear its own determination to continue its antiwar work.[32] For WSP, creating a transnational network of women against the war supplemented its efforts to drum up support for antiwar demonstrations. At the request of WSP, the VWU, and the WUL, WSP's sister organization in Canada, the Voice of Women (VOW), hosted a three-member delegation of Vietnamese women for two weeks in July 1969. This conference would allow more Americans to meet Vietnamese and would call attention to Canadian assistance to the military endeavors of the United States. The VOW set up gatherings all along the U.S.-Canada border from Montreal to Vancouver, introducing about one thousand Americans to the Vietnamese.[33]

Once again emphasizing that the common ground between American and Vietnamese women was based on maternal feelings, WSP member Cora Weiss described the conference as an opportunity for "fell[ow] mothers" to meet.[34] Similar to the description used at the 1968 Paris conference, those advertising the Canadian meetings portrayed the three Vietnamese women who toured the country as mothers whose sons were being killed in combat. In reality, none of the three women—Vo Thi The, a VWU member and professor of literature; Le Thi Cao, a WUL member and teacher; or Nguyen Ngoc Dung, an official representative of the newly formed Provisional Revolutionary Government (PRG) of the NLF—had sons fighting at the time.[35] But they were all mothers, and they could speak of the sacrifices Vietnamese mothers made for the resistance. For instance, Ngoc Dung did not see her daughter for the duration of the American war because she spent so much time out of the country on people's diplomatic missions.[36] All three women had also had relatives killed, imprisoned—Ngoc Dung's sister and nephew had both died as political prisoners in South Viet Nam, and her niece had been born in jail—or in other ways harmed because of the war.[37] All three Vietnamese women had attended the 1965 Djakarta conference and therefore were known to a few of the WSP members in attendance.[38] When WSP members glossed over some of these details in their reports of the conference, they deliberately did so to create a particular emotional response in their readers.[39] Although some observers, such as Susan Sontag, had complained about what they saw as the oversimplified and inauthentic way the Vietnamese spoke of the war, WSP members recognized this simplification as a means of gaining support for their antiwar cause.[40]

Nevertheless, tensions over what constituted inherent maternal responses continued to underlie the united women's front. VWU and WUL members took to telling parables to explain their own roles in the war as well as to imply that any mother placed in a similar situation would act in the same manner. Nguyen Ngoc Dung used the story of a woman who jumped into a lion's cage to rescue her child to show the extraordinary lengths to which mothers would go to protect their children. She argued that during wartime mothers acted in ways they would never imagine under ordinary circumstances, but, in the end, all mothers had the same inherent desire to defend their children and create a lasting peace.[41]

With ideas about motherhood pervading the conference, much of the favorable press on the Canadian meetings similarly focused on the common desires of American and Vietnamese mothers. In particular, many reports spotlighted a statement made by one American mother whose son had died in Viet Nam. "My only hope is that before my son was killed he never hurt anybody," she declared before the Vietnamese delegates, crying, embraced her.[42] Many newspaper articles covering the conference included a photo of this mother carrying a sign that said her son had died in vain.[43] Conference attendees also described moments when the Vietnamese, overcome with emotion, could not speak, and audience members similarly overwhelmed had "eyes full of tears."[44] These reports of shared maternal grief further cemented the bond between American and Vietnamese women in attendance in the minds of both the attendees and members of the press.

Just as in Paris, WSP and VOW organizers as well as the Vietnamese delegates told a particular war narrative—one that depicted the DRV and PRG as being on the side of freedom. Playing up the fact that the Canadian meetings took place over the Fourth of July, WSP members challenged conventional notions of patriotism as well as the official U.S. story of the war. Quoting one Vietnamese delegate as saying, "We have lived under foreign rulers for generations . . . all we want is to run our own lives . . . with leaders whom we have chosen," WSP member Cora Weiss depicted U.S. involvement in Viet Nam as hindering democracy and independence.[45] The Vietnamese women also contested U.S. portrayals of the war by sending women who could represent certain sectors of the Vietnamese population. For example, Le Thi Cao, a Catholic, as well as Nguyen Ngoc Dung, informed conference goers that religious followers in South Viet Nam did not support the Saigon administration as U.S. officials claimed but rather took part in the PRG. They implied that the PRG promised religious freedom and contradicted the Cold War assumption that communists would never allow religious practice. Highlighting this claim, Cora Weiss related in WSP's newsletter *Memo* that the PRG did not just represent the NLF but also included Catholics, Buddhists, peasants, and intellectuals in South Vietnamese society.[46] Collaborating in this way, WSP, VWU, and WUL members undercut Cold War portrayals of the war.

Cold War rhetoric, however, pervaded some news coverage of the events, and war supporters gained political fodder through the alliance of U.S. and Vietnamese women. For example, one reporter interpreted the gratitude of one of the Vietnamese women who thanked antiwar activists for trying to end U.S. intervention as "praise" by Vietnamese communists of antiwar organizations for their support of the communist cause.[47] Another reporter wanted the Vietnamese to admit that a "bloodbath" would ensue if the U.S. military withdrew its support of the South Vietnamese government, but the reporter refused to recognize that for many Vietnamese, particularly in rural South Viet Nam, neither Washington nor Hanoi proved effective at preventing civilian deaths.[48] Indeed, evidence suggests that soldiers on both sides of the war perpetrated untold atrocities.[49] Although no easy solution to the war existed, WSP members tended to see it as their patriotic duty to keep American GIs from killing any more civilians; therefore, they agreed with their VWU and WUL counterparts that the U.S. military needed to withdraw.

Promoting Hanoi's and the PRG's official stance on how to end the war helped stabilize the alliance between WSP, the VWU, and the WUL, which in turn allowed WSP members to broach controversial topics with the VWU and other North Vietnamese officials successfully. Encouraging the image of WSP as a body of mothers concerned for sons fighting in Viet Nam, in December 1969, three WSP members traveled to Hanoi and brought back with them 138 letters from 132 POWs, almost three times as many letters as any previous group of American visitors had succeeded in obtaining. Describing this act as "unprecedented," the three women launched themselves onto the national political stage as the POW issue captured the attention of the media, the American public, and the U.S. government.[50] All the while, the WSP members and much of the media maintained a maternalist view of their intervention, as the three American women claimed to understand the inherent desires of the mothers of POWs as well as those of Vietnamese mothers.

By 1969, the first American POWs captured had lived in captivity for five years, but Hanoi had not released a complete list of POWs, had not allowed a neutral international body such as the Red Cross to inspect POW camps, and had not provided POWs with consistent means to contact their families in the United States—all terms of the 1949 Geneva Agreement on the treatment of POWs. The DRV claimed it did not need to abide by the Geneva Agreement because the United States had not declared war in Viet Nam and because the U.S. military was acting criminally by targeting civilian populations. Nevertheless, the NLF and Hanoi had released a handful of POWs to U.S. antiwar activists on four occasions between 1966 and 1969. These releases demonstrated that they were willing to work with antiwar activists but not the U.S. government.[51]

Even so, interactions between Vietnamese officials and antiwar activists did not always run smoothly, as demonstrated by events surrounding the July 1968 release of three POWs. Three Americans—Stewart Meacham, a white member of the American Friends Service Committee; Anne Scheer (Weills), a white student organizer at Berkeley; and Vernon Grizzard, a white draft resister from Boston—escorted the POWs back to the United States, but not until after a two-week postponement of their departure from Hanoi left the six Americans wondering whether they would ever leave North Viet Nam.

Their Vietnamese hosts never fully explained why the Americans could not depart as scheduled, but Meacham and Weills guessed that the delay had to do with the U.S. government's announcement that it intended to intervene in the release when the six Americans landed in Laos by flying the three pilots from Vientiane to an airbase in Thailand. There, they would receive medical attention before returning to the United States aboard a military aircraft. While in Paris en route to Hanoi, Meacham, Weills, and Grizzard had tried to dissuade U.S. negotiator W. Averell Harriman from such a scheme because they feared this interference on the part of the U.S.

government would send a bad message to Hanoi and block future POW releases; after all, it would seem as if the pilots had immediately returned to the military to resume their duties. Ignoring the activists' concerns, Harriman, along with the U.S. ambassador in Laos, William Sullivan, set in motion a plan to intervene. Meacham and Weills could never be certain, however, that this threat had indeed caused the disruption to their itinerary because the Vietnamese remained silent on the issue.[52]

The Americans also could not coordinate with their Vietnamese hosts—as members of WSP, the VWU, and the WUL often had—to try to find an agreeable solution because of this reticence on the part of the Vietnamese. Instead, the six Americans simply waited until the Vietnamese informed them of their imminent departure—an announcement that came after the U.S. government released a statement that it would allow the three pilots to return to the United States via a commercial airline. Also demonstrating the reluctance of the Vietnamese to share information with the activists, Meacham, Weills, and Grizzard received no news on a list of MIAs (missing in action) they brought with them at the request of MIA relatives. Although the activists handed over forty-two letters for POWs and received fifty letters from POWs in return, the Vietnamese also refused to tell the activists how many POWs they held in North Viet Nam, claiming it was a "state secret."[53] Clearly, these activists were not marching in lockstep with their Vietnamese hosts.

Attempts to find out more about POWs and MIAs would not end with this episode, however, and in fact the issue became a rallying point for those who supported the war effort. After the election of Richard Nixon to the presidency, the U.S. government implemented new initiatives concerning POWs and MIAs, bringing more attention to the POW situation. As a gesture to show POW and MIA family members its concern, the military began to send a representative, not just a telegram, notifying next of kin of the status of their husband or son. The military also assigned a key contact person to each family to apprise them of any newly uncovered information over the weeks, months, and years to come. Recognizing the agony of families unsure of their husband's or son's fate, U.S. government officials also called for more scrutiny of North Vietnamese prisons and denounced the recalcitrance of Hanoi to abide by the 1949 Geneva Agreement. With the DRV refusing to allow inspections of POW prisons, debate in Congress as well as in the general public ensued over whether the Vietnamese tortured POWs.[54]

Amid this controversy, Hanoi announced on July 3, 1969, that it would free three more POWs in celebration of American Independence Day. This time, four antiwar activists—Grace Paley, a white WSP member; Linda Evans, a white Students for a Democratic Society (SDS) member; James Johnson, an African American veteran who refused to serve in Viet Nam; and Rennie Davis, a white member of the New Mobilization to End the War in Vietnam—escorted three POWs from Hanoi to New York City in early August. They planned to stay in North Viet Nam for three weeks, during which time they toured Hanoi, traveled down to the seventeenth parallel, and met the POWs during the final two days of their stay.[55]

If Hanoi had intended this next release to help garner antiwar support or at least counter allegations of torture, it selected the POWs poorly. Before the group left Hanoi, the antiwar activists observed that at least one of the prisoners seemed unlikely to contradict the official position of the United States. Grace Paley, horrified, recalled one pilot admitting he "liked bombing," even after visiting some of the ruins he had caused. He further insisted that a hospital with an antiaircraft gun mounted on top of it counted as a legitimate military target.[56] Unable and unwilling to understand such views, Paley argued that clearly he had not had a change of heart while a captive in Hanoi. Moreover, she and the other activists spent too little time with the POWs to build a rapport that could challenge such thinking. She brought her concerns to her Vietnamese hosts, telling them that the freed prisoners might say harmful things about their imprisonment. When Paley asked her hosts why they released POWs unlikely to help Hanoi's propaganda line, they replied that even if former POWs "say something on TV bad [sic] . . . at night they will go home and they will whisper the truth to their wife."[57] Writing this story for an American audience, Paley portrayed the Vietnamese as forgiving and willing to free POWs regardless of the political repercussions that might ensue as she simultaneously tried to undercut any allegations of abuse the three POWs might make.

The four antiwar activists also used the information they had learned about the war to redirect public attention back to the criminality of U.S. actions. After visiting areas just north of the seventeenth parallel, where Vietnamese lived in tunnels because of the constant threat of air raids, Paley described the war as typical American "overkill."[58] The indiscriminate large-scale bombing of bridges, whether made of stone, wood, or simple bamboo pontoons, illustrated to Paley and her companions the excesses of the war. Claiming that the U.S. military might spend as much as a million dollars to destroy a $120 bridge, Paley and her travel companions pointed out what they saw as the archetypical problem in U.S. thinking. This kind of unwarranted violence did not surprise Paley, however, because within the United States, Americans "overkilled flies, bugs, beetles, trees, fish, rivers, the flowers of their own American fields" through the use of toxics.[59] Comparing the way the U.S. military waged war in Viet Nam with the way Americans sprayed crops with chemicals, Paley found both tactical as well as moral problems with American actions at home and abroad as she presaged an aspect of ecofeminist thought connecting the oppression of people with the exploitation of nature.

Paley's observations largely fell on deaf ears, however, as rumors of torture continued to circulate. Even though Paley's group had received fifty letters from POWs to send to their families in the United States, this hardly seemed worth mentioning in the press. Because the Vietnamese had neglected to provide the activists with more substantial information on MIAs or POWs, the four activists had little means of entering the debate on the mistreatment of POWs. All the same, Paley insinuated that the three released prisoners themselves could hardly be trusted because they were "military men." Quoting one as saying, "I went into this a military man and that's how I'm coming out" as he requested a new uniform in Laos before returning to the United States, she implied that his perspective was tainted.[60] She also mentioned that this man had asked for a military debriefing before talking with the press, further suggesting that he was not speaking candidly, as she claimed the antiwar activists were. Paley's depictions of both the U.S. war and the POW situation point to her insistence on finding a way to collaborate with her Vietnamese hosts regardless of whether they directly or indirectly cooperated with her. Within a month of the POW release, what Paley feared would happen did, when two of the released POWs made public statements denouncing the North Vietnamese as inhumane torturers. In December 1969, before hearings conducted by the House Committee on Internal Security, the two POWs described their abuse at the hands of their captors as well as the suspected torture of fellow prisoners. Seeming to confirm the POWs' statements, Hanoi still refused to allow a thorough inspection of the prisons and withheld information on MIAs.[61] But, the DRV had implemented a policy calling for the humanitarian treatment of POWs. In November 1969, the Politburo resolved to "apply the points of the [1949] Geneva Convention [governing the treatment of prisoners of war] that are consistent with our humanitarian policies."[62] Stating that "Our humanitarian policy toward American pilots is aimed at further illuminating our just cause in order to win over the American people . . . and win the sympathy of world opinion," Hanoi made clear its objective to work with international antiwar activists.[63]

This timely decision worked in the favor of the December 1969 WSP mission, which held as one of its central objectives to convince Hanoi to release a complete list of POWs and to allow routine mail service between POWs and their families. With Nixon's initiatives prioritizing the concerns of POW and MIA families, some WSP members saw a need to address similar concerns, but in their own way. This new tactic would also establish WSP members as wanting reconciliation, not a DRV or PRG victory, as some supporters of the war had begun to claim.[64] At first, the Vietnamese hesitated to provide the three WSP members with more information and only reluctantly arranged a visit to a POW camp. Shortly before this trip, an Italian journalist had denounced the Vietnamese for not informing POWs of the moon landing, thereby reinforcing the Vietnamese disinclination to allow access to prisoners. Eventually, the WSP delegation succeeded in touring one POW camp, meeting with three POWs, and bringing back to the United States the names of and letters from about one-third of Americans held captive in North Viet Nam at the time—a major victory for the three WSP members. For some families, these letters confirmed, for the first time, that a husband or son was alive, and for even more families, these were the first letters they had received from their relative since his capture.[65]

While in North Viet Nam, the WSP delegation and North Vietnamese officials also established joint committees to oversee the exchange of mail between POWs and their families. The two committees—one based in Hanoi, the other in New York City—regulated the mail service, specifying that families could send one letter a month and one package every other month. Although families could send letters and packages through the post office, the WSP members and North Vietnamese suggested they send materials through the U.S.-based group (the Committee of Liaison with Families of Servicemen Detained in North Vietnam [COLIAFAM]), which sponsored monthly trips of three antiwar activists to Hanoi from its founding until the end of the war in 1973.[66] All the while, the WSP delegation claimed the authority to speak on behalf of POWs and their families by declaring a universal maternal feeling shared by American and Vietnamese women alike.

As mothers of teenage and preteen children, the three WSP members, Ethel Taylor, Madeline Duckles, and Cora Weiss, could easily have sympathy for mothers on both sides of the war. For her part, Taylor had become close with one couple whose son was a POW in North Viet Nam, and they had not heard from him since 1965. Learning of Taylor's forthcoming trip to Hanoi, the couple gave her a letter to deliver to their son and invited families of other POWs and MIAs to do the same. Consequently, Taylor took over one hundred letters with her to Hanoi, twice as many as previous delegations. Although none of the three women's children served—all five of Duckles's sons were too tall and Weiss's three children were too young, leaving only Taylor's one son eligible—the WSP members successfully presented themselves as U.S. mothers acting on behalf of their children as well as on behalf of mothers of POWs and MIAs, at least initially.[67]

VWU and WUL members continued to collaborate in this portrayal of American and Vietnamese mothers sharing a maternal bond. For instance, in December 1969 one Vietnamese woman wrote an open letter to American mothers asserting that no mother—Vietnamese or American—wanted to send her son to war and asking American mothers to act on their conscience by calling for an end to U.S. involvement in Viet Nam.[68] The Vietnamese women in Hanoi also reiterated to the three WSP visitors the three responsibilities of Vietnamese women, and they mentioned other slogans, all of which contained threes, such as the need for women to work hard, study hard, and fight hard. Weiss later commented that the Vietnamese seemed to have an inexplicable penchant for threes.[69] Even so, the three American women felt they understood the underlying desire of the Vietnamese. "Despite our entirely different culture, we spoke the same language," Taylor stated.[70]

Emphasizing women's maternal roles, the Vietnamese arranged meetings between the WSP members and Vietnamese children, including a survivor of the March 1968 My Lai massacre. News of the mass execution of about five hundred Vietnamese civilians by American GIs had only begun to surface in the United States in November 1969. The New York Times and other periodicals published a series of articles by Seymour Hersh based on his conversations with veteran Ron Ridenhour, who had tried to persuade members of Congress to investigate the decimation of an entire village. Whereas some in the United States refused to believe that such a massacre occurred or believed that, if it had, it was explicable, others argued that it illustrated the unjustness of the war and the need for the U.S. military to withdraw. The U.S. government countered with declarations of the anomalous nature of the massacre and with accusations that the NLF had acted similarly in Hue during the Tet Offensive in February 1968—thus, the U.S. military needed to remain in Viet Nam to prevent more bloodbaths on the part of the NLF.[71] With three WSP members deemed inherently sympathetic in Hanoi, the Vietnamese seized the opportunity to publicize their version of the story through survivors. To this end, a twelve-year-old girl, Vo Thi Lien, told the three WSP members what she had witnessed the morning of March 16, 1968, in her village.[72] "Cuddled up to" Ethel Taylor, Lien described indiscriminate killing as well as the rape and torture of her neighbors and relatives.[73] Her account left no doubt in the minds of Taylor, Weiss, and Duckles that the GIs had committed atrocities. Hearing these stories from the mouth of a young girl, the WSP members vouched to do what they could to spread awareness in the United States that current U.S. military strategy included such immoral violence. They found, however, that despite the international outrage that news of the My Lai massacre incited, the media cared more about what the American women knew about POWs and MIAs than what details they had learned about the massacre.[74]

Even the CIA seemed to be concerned solely with what information the WSP members had on POWs and MIAs. Approaching another American, Fox Butterfield, who happened to be visiting Hanoi at the same time as the three WSP members, CIA agents did not ask him about any other aspect of the WSP members' trip. On his way back to the United States, Butterfield told CIA agents in Laos that Weiss was trying to get a complete list of POWs from Hanoi and that Taylor had a package of letters to deliver to POW families. The concurrent visit of Butterfield, a *New York Times* stringer, his grandfather Cyrus Eaton, an industrialist from Cleveland, and his grandfather's wife, Anne, also highlights the distinct ability of these three WSP members specifically to gain more information on the POW issue. Although Cyrus Eaton reportedly broached the subject of POWs, the Vietnamese divulged nothing to him.[75]

At first, the WSP delegation's efforts to establish regular contact between POWs and their families received overwhelmingly positive press, which highlighted the joy of families hearing from husbands, fathers, and sons for the first time in years. One of the first articles assumed that only parents would receive word from their POW sons, perhaps illustrating the success of WSP members in portraying themselves as concerned mothers of draft-age sons. Subsequent articles focused on both mothers and wives of POWs receiving letters, but the POW wives mentioned almost always had children; thus, the articles still highlighted maternal emotions—mothers rejoiced with their children when they found out that "daddy" was still alive.[76] These first news stories substantiated WSP members' claims that they represented an apolitical group of mothers solely concerned for the welfare of children—either those left temporarily fatherless in the United States or the POWs themselves captured in North Viet Nam.

Soon, however, the POW issue regained its political undertones through some of the very same POW wives WSP members claimed to represent. By the end of January, about a month after the WSP delegation had returned to the United States, one POW wife stood up after listening to the testimony of Cora Weiss about the humane treatment of POWs and quietly contradicted Weiss. In a "quivering voice," the POW wife told Weiss, "'you're so very wrong on so many things.'"[77] In March 1970, the House Committee on Armed Services held a congressional hearing about the "Problems of Prisoners of War and Their Families" but did not invite a COLIAFAM representative to attend.[78] Instead, it relied on the testimony of four POW wives who felt blackmailed by COLIAFAM because it had the power to allow or withdraw contact with their husbands; consequently, the hearing took an unfavorable stance on the efforts by COLIAFAM and WSP to put POWs in contact with their families.[79]

On speaking tours, the three returning WSP members also noted an unwillingness on the part of some audiences to listen. Ethel Taylor recalled chants of "Hanoi Hannah" erupting as she spoke in one instance, and another in which the pastor seemed to have invited her to speak at his church just to show her that no one wanted to listen. As Taylor began her speech, row after row of the congregation filed out, as if on cue, until she spoke to empty pews. Despite this choreographed exit, one parishioner slipped Taylor a note with her name and address on it, asking for more information on WSP, as Taylor was leaving. This episode illustrated to Taylor the importance of speaking even to those audiences deemed unfriendly.[80]

Although WSP members had momentarily found a niche speaking as alleged mothers of draft-age sons, they soon had to rethink the terms they used to describe themselves. The backlash against WSP members following their entrance into the POW debate disrupted their previous reliance on essentialized notions of motherhood, creating new challenges and opportunities. Up to this point, WSP members had generally worked with women because of a belief in particular feminine qualities, but soon, with the rise of women's liberation, some members would begin to see women's roles in a different light. Even so, this initial reliance on maternalism would shape their future versions of feminism.

As the context of antiwar debates, foreign relations, and the war itself changed, WSP members continued to find ways to make their voices heard, especially through their contact with Vietnamese women. WSP maintained critical ties to the VWU and WUL, and some members used these relationships to boost antiwar activities in other organizations. The joint committees established to coordinate the exchange of mail strengthened people-to-people diplomatic efforts. This relationship could overwrite supposed Cold War distinctions between women of the East and those of the West and allow them to come together to negotiate as empathetic, mature, and responsible women. The similar language of the VWU, WUL, and WSP had created an authentic connection for some at the same time as it benefited the groups politically. In some ways, the versions of motherhood the three groups promoted contradicted each other, particularly in terms of mothers' use of violence, but the three groups' focus on the ways in which they were similar enabled them to form a transnational alliance that allowed the Vietnamese access to an American audience. While WSP members used this coalition to discuss the establishment of regular communication between POWs and their families in the United States, the VWU and WUL publicly admonished the U.S. government's disrespect for life and praised the efforts of American mothers to maintain American ideals.

The Vietnamese also wanted to establish contact with Americans outside mainstream pacifist and antiwar circles.[81] Using U.S. Cold War language of freedom and democracy, the VWU and WUL highlighted the injustice of U.S. actions in Viet Nam and complemented the rhetoric of activists of color in rights-based movements. These advocates often insisted that U.S. society needed a revolution to uphold the ideals of freedom, democracy, and independence. Working collaboratively, Vietnamese and Americans once again established people-to-people ties to further corresponding goals.

CHAPTER THREE

Developing "Third World" Feminist Networks, 1970

Following her April 1970 trip to Hanoi, Chicana Elizabeth "Betita" Sutherland Martínez concluded, "The white people of the West with their unnatural soul and their unnatural weapons are a death people."[1] Having seen bomb craters that disfigured the North Vietnamese landscape, witnessed people living in tunnels because of incessant air raids, and inspected an array of antipersonnel bombs dropped by the U.S. military, Martínez declared that only an uncivilized people could unleash such destruction. In contrast, the Vietnamese were a "life people"—they turned bomb craters into ponds, where they harvested fish, and they continued to sing and perform theatrical productions despite the devastation of their homeland.[2] As a "life people," Martínez asserted that Vietnamese mores were similar to those of Mexican Americans. Thus, she placed space between herself, a nonwhite Westerner, and white Americans perpetrating untold violence in Viet Nam. Describing the war as a clash between the civilized "Third World" and the uncivilized white West, Martínez impugned the U.S. government's mission to spread freedom and democracy to decolonizing nations.[3]

Martínez's criticism of the U.S. government may have rearranged the hierarchy of the Cold War, but it did little to undermine it. As historian Judy Wu has shown, many U.S. activists looked to Asian nations such as China and North Viet Nam as paragons of revolutionary society.[4] Having legally gained civil and political rights, some U.S. activists of color turned their attention to the economic and social ills that plagued their communities and curtailed "freedom."[5] Because these activists sought rights—economic and social—I refer to them as belonging to "rights-based" movements instead of to "civil rights movements." This language allows for continuity between the civil rights movement of the 1950s and early 1960s and the power movements of the late 1960s without obscuring the possibility of distinct purposes, methods, or activists. Many people of color in their respective rights-based movements connected what they saw as a pernicious "white society" to destructive U.S. foreign policy and sought to expose the cultural roots of U.S. imperialism.[6] In this way, some activists found a reason for people fighting for economic, social, and cultural rights in the United States to oppose the Viet Nam war—in Martínez's words, it was a battle between "life people" and "death people."

Illustrating ideological connections between domestic rights-based movements and socialist revolutions outside the United States is not new in scholarship on 1960s activism.[7] However, asking whether and how this connection shaped feminisms of women of color adds a new dimension to previous analyses. Scholars have noted the domestic challenges women of color faced when they tried to fight for both race and gender issues—they were often expected to choose and were labeled "sellouts" if they worked in white women's groups.[8] Vietnamese women, who fought for both their nation's sovereignty and women's rights, provided an important example to women of color that they could use as an inspiration and as evidence of the inseparability of race and gender. Through the example of Vietnamese women, women of color rejected the false dichotomy of fighting for their race or for women and insisted on struggling against all forms of oppression.

In April 1970, Elizabeth Martínez, cofounder of *El Grito del Norte*, a Chicano newspaper based in Española, New Mexico, went to Hanoi to inform her readers about "U.S. imperialism" in Viet Nam. Denouncing the "regular press" as biased against Mexican Americans, Martínez asked readers how likely it was that the press reported on the Viet Nam war accurately. Implying that the mainstream media would obscure the difficulties of people of color—whether they lived in New Mexico or North Viet Nam—particularly if the U.S. government was at fault, Martínez took it on herself to describe what she saw as "the truth" for members of "la Raza" (the people of the race).[9] She spent most of her article as well as her trip connecting what she learned about U.S. involvement in Viet Nam with the Chicano struggle in New Mexico and southern Colorado, where her readership primarily lived.[10]

Martínez herself had not grown up in a Southwestern Mexican American community, however, and had taken decades to form her identity as a Chicana. Even so, she had learned about racism, colonialism, and imperialism at an early age, growing up in segregated Washington, D.C., with a dark-skinned Mexican father who had witnessed the Mexican Revolution of the 1910s. Martínez's father regaled her with stories of Zapatista revolutionaries who wanted to redistribute land in Mexico to benefit peasants, as he cursed the U.S. military for aiding the Mexican government. As Martínez's father imparted his political beliefs to his daughter, both of them also experienced racism firsthand in segregated D.C. For instance, Martínez recalled bus drivers forcing her and her father to sit in the back of the bus despite empty seats in the front. Although Martínez's father tried to shield her from such racism and refused to tell her why they had to move to the back of the bus, living in biracial D.C., Martínez, who was neither black nor white, felt like a "freak."[11] Although she attended a white school and lived in a white neighborhood, she had few white friends. White parents would not allow their children to play with her because of her skin color. Instead, she made friends with African Americans who worked for her parents; and her white mother, aware of the troubles faced by her nonwhite daughter, arranged a few special parties every year to give Martínez a chance to play with children her own age. Still, Martínez saw herself as an outsider and sought community with others who did not fit into dominant U.S. society in some way.

During World War II, as one of the only nonwhite students attending Swarthmore College, Martínez remained on the margins. She absorbed herself in details of the war, stashing away each day's newspaper in her dorm room until she could hardly climb into bed. After the war, she pored over stories about concentration camps and wanted to help with the Jewish relocation to Israel. She even married a Jewish man so that she could participate in setting up a new colony in the Middle East, but ironically, her husband had no desire to move to Israel, and they soon divorced. Instead of moving to the Middle East, Martínez worked for the newly formed United Nations in New York City to "bring about world peace."[12] At the UN, she researched decolonization and discovered "a great big connection between colonialism and racism" during her investigation into medical care provided by colonial powers in Africa and the Pacific.[13] When Martínez found out that one doctor supposedly cared for 100,000 people in some places, she wanted to denounce such racist colonial policies, but her status as a UN employee limited her ability to do so. At the suggestion of her boss, Martínez supplied key information to the Philippine delegation before a meeting in Geneva to "expose the colonial powers."[14] Reveling in her triumph as the Philippine delegation did just as she hoped, she told a World Health Organization employee about her scheme while on a train en route to the Geneva meeting. Unfortunately, a nearby passenger appearing to be asleep turned out to be a member of the U.S. delegation. Upon arriving in Geneva, the U.S. delegate reported Martínez's misdeeds and insisted she be fired. Although Martínez's boss complied, he alleged that staff shortages forced him to rehire her the following day. Learning, at the age of twenty-one, the limits of working within the system, compounded a few short years later by Senator Joseph McCarthy's campaign against subversives in the U.S.

government, Martínez soon left her UN post. Nevertheless, she continued her campaign to unmask instances of racism and colonialism.

Martínez also sought a sense of belonging as she fought alongside other outsiders. Living in a world where people were either black or white, Martínez consistently chose to have relationships with white men, worked together with African Americans for civil rights in the New York office of the Student Nonviolent Coordinating Committee (SNCC), and eventually joined an all-white women's liberation group. Her personal and political relationships, however, always ended in frustration and disillusionment. The white men in her life turned out to have personal issues, such as drug addiction; her African American counterparts in SNCC wanted to remove all nonblack activists from their posts in the organization in the late 1960s; and the white women's liberation group all but ignored racism as demonstrated to Martínez on the night of Martin Luther King Jr.'s assassination. That night, the group held a meeting at which none of the white women talked about his death, a sign to Martínez that she needed to find a new group. With her personal and political relationships falling apart, Martínez was ripe for a new adventure.[15]

In 1968, Martínez found a new opportunity for her activism when she traveled with a SNCC delegation to Cuba, where she met scholar-activist John Gerassi, who invited her to move to New Mexico to start a publication (*El Grito del Norte*) about the Mexican American land grant struggle. Although Martínez planned to visit New Mexico for only two weeks, she stayed for eight years. She remembered years later, "I got off the plane, I looked at the mountains, I smelled the air: I fell in love."[16] More importantly for Martínez, New Mexico provided an environment where she as a Chicana could fight against sexism, imperialism, and racism alongside her fellow Mexican Americans, so she quickly "sent for my stuff to be shipped to me."[17]

Martínez supposedly saw her work on *El Grito del Norte* as "just another front in the battle against racism," but with her previous experiences in the UN and in Cuba, she brought an international perspective to the newspaper.[18] That is, Martínez envisioned *El Grito* as covering struggles all over the world, beyond just the United States. She thought it only natural for the Viet Nam war to receive attention in a newspaper dedicated to Mexican Americans' fight to regain control of land in New Mexico and Colorado. While Martínez brought a new perspective to the land grant struggle, her move to New Mexico also provided her with the opportunity to discover her own identity as a Chicana and explore discrimination perpetrated against her as well as others like her. Discussions of the lack of bilingual education for Spanish-speaking students, the denigration of Mexican American culture on the part of white society, and the oppression of women within the Mexican American community all found a home in *El Grito*. Although Martínez continued to see herself in some ways as an outsider in New Mexico, not having grown up there, she also found herself gaining a community by mentoring young Chicanas and contributing to a movement that related directly to her own life.[19]

Martínez, as well as other contributors to *El Grito del Norte*, made connections between the Chicano movement in New Mexico and the Viet Nam war by describing the Vietnamese as a poor people struggling to control their land. The Vietnamese effort supposedly mirrored that of Chicanos like Reies Tijerina, who, in the 1960s, led a movement to reclaim land in northern New Mexico that the Forest Service, industrialists, and the railroad had "stolen" from Mexican Americans.[20] On several occasions, Tijerina staged publicity-seeking stunts and more extreme actions, even going so far as to take hostages from a courtroom to gain the attention of the authorities and the Mexican American community.[21] While U.S. government officials denounced Tijerina and other notable Chicano activists such as Cesar Chavez by dismissing them as communists, *El Grito* writers challenged these characterizations in a way that undercut official reasoning for U.S. involvement in Viet Nam. Obscuring communism as an issue and instead portraying both Tijerina and the Vietnamese as battling the duplicitous U.S. government, *El Grito* writers described the war as just another example of the U.S. government trying to seize land from unsuspecting peasants.

With land being central to the Chicano movement in New Mexico and Colorado, Martínez began her account of her journey to North Viet Nam by portraying the beauty of the countryside. Indeed, she seems to have developed an affinity for Viet Nam in the same way as she had fallen in love with the landscape of New Mexico two years earlier, and she described Viet Nam in terms that would create nostalgic images of New Mexico in the minds of her readers. "There are mountains and valleys and caves and big skies and glowing sunsets [in North Viet Nam], as in New Mexico," Martínez wrote.[22] Not only did the landscapes resemble one another, but Martínez and her fellow *El Grito* contributor Valentina Valdez Martinez, who paraphrased the work of white male journalists in her articles, also told a story of the war that paralleled the history of Mexican Americans in the United States.[23] Just as Mexican Americans lost their land over a century ago because of the chicanery of the U.S. government and industrialists, rich Westerners more recently tricked Vietnamese into selling or otherwise giving up their land. In these accounts, Chicanos and Vietnamese shared not only a common enemy but also a common incentive—the reclamation of land.

For Martínez and Valdez, the story began with French colonization of Viet Nam. First, the French set up a system in which peasants had to pay exorbitant interest rates to work their own land. Then, French authorities illegally imprisoned some peasants in order to confiscate their land. The French treated Vietnamese ethnic minorities even worse, calling them "savages."[24] Isolated in the jungle, ethnic minorities had no political rights and little to no access to medical care or education. What education they had was all in French or Vietnamese, not their native languages. Fed up, the peasants rebelled against their French landlords, reclaiming their land and expelling the French. After the defeat of French colonists in 1954, South Viet Nam's new president, aided by the U.S. government, "schemed" to regain control of land taken from French landowners in the South and forced Vietnamese "*campesinos*" (peasants) to pay back rent and to sign over their land.[25] If the peasants refused, ARVN soldiers would "harass" them until they complied.[26] Having no one to turn to, Vietnamese peasants found themselves displaced within their own country, while Saigon and Washington profited from their land.

Telling readers that the U.S. government had employed similar tactics to "rob . . . our ancestors of their land," Valdez made it clear that what was happening to the Vietnamese was not just something taking place in a distant land to an unknown people but a reoccurrence of what her ancestors had experienced.[27] Reminding her readers that the U.S. government had tricked the native populations in New Mexico over a century ago into signing away their lands, Valdez concluded that the track record of the U.S. government spoke for itself. The U.S. government would use any means necessary to get what it wanted—land and money. In partnership with white industrialists, the government would sell raw materials from the land for a profit, leaving the *campesinos* with nothing, not even their way of life. Regardless of whether South Vietnamese peasants moved to Saigon or were herded into strategic hamlets—villages surrounded by barbed wire and guarded by ARVN soldiers—they had to give up their "customs" to survive in their new environment.[28] For *El Grito* contributors, because culture stemmed directly from one's relationship with land, without land, the Chicano and Vietnamese cultures would vanish.

According to *El Grito*'s writers, the newfound difficulties of Mexican American families living in cities—poverty, divorce, and isolation—arose from their separation from the land. They claimed that when Mexican Americans' ancestors had lived respectfully on the land, peaceful and civilized societies prospered. Conversely, "Anglo" society exploited land for profit, fostering hypocrisy and deceit. Obscuring any history of violence, poverty, or alienation within rural or precolonial communities, *El Grito* contributors placed full blame for the ills of Mexican Americans on white society. While men learned to take out their frustrations with not being economically successful on their families, women lost their status as important helpmates and leaders in their communities. If "Anglo" culture wreaked such havoc in the Mexican American community over the course of the last century, it followed that Mexican Americans should try to block its expansion overseas, particularly to South Viet Nam.[29]

Forms of discrimination also seeped into the school system, as attested to by thousands of Mexican American students across the Southwest. Valentina Valdez Martinez, who was about twenty in the late 1960s, had experienced overt racism in high school, when her white teachers taught her and her classmates that Mexican Americans were poor because they were "lazy, ignorant, [and] superstitious."[30] Brimming with anger, Valdez vowed to counter such stereotypes by teaching her Mexican American classmates their real history. She gave a speech in class that echoed the claims of Reies Tijerina about the theft of Mexican American ancestral lands following the Mexican American War in the 1840s. Blaming rich white "*rancheros*" for the poverty of Mexican Americans, Valdez glorified Mexican American antecedents who worked tirelessly to build, produce, and clean at the lowest wages.[31] Mexican American students across the Southwest similarly registered their anger at the overt discrimination within the school system by walking out of class, forming Chicano student organizations, and calling for bicultural education.[32]

Given this dissatisfaction with the education system in the Southwest, Elizabeth Martínez was fascinated to learn how the Vietnamese dealt with the similar situation of educating ethnic minorities in North Viet Nam. She found that in contrast to the experiences of Mexican American students in the Southwest, the Vietnamese provided a bilingual educational system that allowed minority children to speak their native language in school for the first four years while learning Vietnamese as a second language. In addition, government officials and soldiers had to learn about ethnic groups before working or fighting in a minority village, thus reducing prejudice among government workers. Applauding the cultural sensitivity of the

North Vietnamese, Martínez implicitly turned to them as a model on which to base demands to change the U.S. educational system.[33]

The Vietnamese, having spent centuries under colonial rule, also provided an example of how Mexican Americans could return to their roots by living off the land. Martínez's hosts took her to a cooperative that brought together about seven hundred households. Although at first North Vietnamese officials had faced difficulties in persuading some peasants to join, particularly in years after crops failed, through perseverance, Vietnamese formed self-sufficient villages that provided childcare, medical assistance, and protection from U.S. bombing through defensive artillery units.[34] Encouraged by the ability of the Vietnamese to return to the land and work in cooperatives sixteen years after the defeat of the French, Martínez echoed the desires of *El Grito* contributor Enriqueta Longeaux y Vásquez, who the year before had written an op-ed piece advocating that Mexican American women move out of public housing to form cooperatives in the countryside. Vásquez, a single mother of two, had lived on welfare in the 1950s after divorcing her abusive husband. Despite facing poor job prospects because of her ethnicity, class, and gender, Vásquez put herself through night school, joined a Chicano political organization, and began to write for *El Grito*. Recognizing her personal story as similar to those of other single mothers living in public housing and severed from their cultural roots, Vásquez sought a way for them to return to the land.[35]

Vásquez, who experienced abuse at the hands of both Mexican American men and whites, traced Mexican American history back to precolonial days to uncover the roots of sexism and racism. Taking aim at the colonization of indigenous peoples and the consequent abuse of women by men, Vásquez proclaimed that liberation for the Mexican American community must include liberation for women and a reclamation of "true" Mexican American culture. For Vásquez, Europeans had brought sexism as well as racism to the Americas. She declared, "Before Europeans came to the Americas, our highly cultured Indian woman usually held an honored position."[36] Blaming the influence of first Spanish and then U.S. culture for the woes of Mexican American women, she pointed to a noble past when "women held a degree of political influence never equaled in any *civilized* nation . . . then and now" (emphasis in original).[37] Other Chicanas joined Vásquez's quest to find stories of women's past leadership. The history of Mexican women fighting in the revolution against Spain in the nineteenth century as well as in the Mexican Revolution of the 1910s provided fertile ground for those looking for strong forebears. For example, one heroine acted as a spy during the Mexican Revolution, supplying key information to insurgents, while another printed a periodical publicizing the misdeeds of the Mexican government and rallying support for the rebels. Some of the women paid the ultimate price for their defiance of the authorities, and all were revered.[38]

Chicanas also looked to women outside the Americas as models of resistance. A special section of the June 1971 issue of *El Grito* on "La Chicana" somewhat inexplicably included photos of Laotian women with rifles and ammunition belts digging ditches and Japanese women linked arm-in-arm in protest against the government.[39] Valentina Valdez Martinez, in one of her stories on the Viet Nam war, romanticized the exploits of two militia-women, nineteen-year-old Blossom and twenty-two-year-old Lissom, who "helped five boys defend a village."[40] Having killed an ARVN soldier who was shooting at the village, "Blossom was the real heroine" of the story.[41] Although this woman took on the masculine role of protector, Chicanas were quick to point out that women's revolutionary roles did not erase their femininity. "After all, we have seen the Vietnamese women fight for survival with a gun in one hand and a child sucking on her breast on the other arm. She is certainly feminine," Enriqueta Vásquez reminded her readers.[42] For Chicanas, motherhood in and of itself established one's femininity and allowed women to take on men's duties without renouncing their womanhood or culture. Looking to other non-Anglo women for inspiration, Chicanas asserted their ability to "wag[e] battle for cultural survival" while remaining feminine and true to their heritage.[43]

Similarly, Martínez's report on her trip highlighted the femininity of Vietnamese women as mothers but did so in a way that more closely resembled WSP's version of Vietnamese mothers than Vásquez's depiction. Making only a passing remark about Vietnamese women's militia roles, Martínez ended her piece with a story of women's shared maternal grief. While visiting a village near the Gulf of Tonkin, a Buddhist nun pulled aside Martínez and her white female travel companion, Charlotte Bunch, to implore them, as women, to stop the suffering of Vietnamese children. Clutching Martínez's arm, the nun impressed on the two American women their maternal responsibility to end the war. Martínez took the nun's words to heart even though she believed she had many shortcomings when it came to mothering her own daughter. Somehow the nun's countenance defied Martínez's ability to object to portraying all women, let alone all mothers, as having the same inherent emotions.[44]

On the front page of the issue covering Martínez's trip, the editors of *El Grito* further emphasized women's dedication to the home regardless of their roles in the struggle against white U.S. society. Under the heading "Their People . . . Our People . . . ," three sets of photos—of children, *campesinos*, and women—brought attention to the similar situations of Vietnamese and Mexican Americans.[45] By far the most similar photos, pictures of a North Vietnamese woman and "la Chicana," showed both of them preparing food, wearing black short-sleeved blouses with hair pulled back by a white ribbon, and facing each other on the page. These mirror images projected the message that a woman from North Viet Nam and "la Chicana" had common experiences of womanhood. They had the same duties, dressed alike, and even wore their hair alike. Just as Vietnamese women maintained their femininity despite fighting in defense of their homeland, Chicanas could join the Chicano movement as equal partners in the revolution yet retain their roles as mothers, wives, and helpmates. Showing peaceful, domestic scenes, these images connected the Vietnamese with Mexican Americans through their common culture and love for the land.

The following issue of *El Grito* abruptly contrasted such bucolic images with news of the death of Ruben Salazar, a Mexican American reporter for the *Los Angeles Times*, who was killed by local police on August 29, 1970. During an antiwar demonstration at a park in East Los Angeles where thousands of Mexican Americans, including families, had gathered, police in riot gear began to line up at the back of the crowd. Many protestors, listening to the scheduled program, did not even realize that police had assembled behind them. Without warning, officers entered the crowd, swinging clubs and shooting canisters of tear gas. As people ran for shelter, the police beat and arrested dozens. Salazar, sitting in a nearby bar, received a fatal blow to the head from a tear gas canister blindly shot into the building. Police killed two other Chicanos in a similar fashion. *El Grito* pointed to this violence as evidence of Mexican Americans' inability to succeed in Anglo society—even a celebrated reporter at a major newspaper could die at the hands of the police.[46]

By this time, such violence on the part of U.S. authorities was unexceptional, however. Three months earlier, on the morning of her departure from Hanoi, Martínez and her companions had received a rude awakening when they learned of the killings of four students at Kent State University by the Ohio National Guard. The shooting occurred after days of student protests on the Kent State campus following President Richard Nixon's announcement of the expansion of the Viet Nam war into neighboring Cambodia. With a cease-fire having been put in place in northern North Viet Nam by former president Lyndon Johnson in the fall of 1968, Nixon turned elsewhere to demonstrate to Hanoi his intention to escalate the fighting, as he simultaneously implemented "Vietnamization" of the war, pulling out American troops and replacing them with ARVN soldiers. Abiding by his "madman theory," Nixon based his foreign policy decisions on the assumption that the threat of excessive force, including nuclear warfare, would compel Hanoi to negotiate.[47] But neither antiwar activists nor leaders in Hanoi would allow Nixon's strategy to hinder their attempts to end the war in a way that provided independence for the Vietnamese. While Nixon's veiled threat of nuclear war enabled antiwar activists to present the situation as similar to the biblical story of David defeating the giant Goliath,[48] the Vietnamese published accounts of social unrest in the United States to illustrate the American people's support for the DRV. Hanoi periodicals also covered stories of student protests and workers' strikes in Saigon, further demonstrating the dissatisfaction of both Vietnamese and Americans with U.S. policies.[49] As Martínez and her companions returned to the United States, they, like many other activists, sought a way to register their dissatisfaction with current American practices.

Across the nation, teach-ins, demonstrations, and student strikes proliferated following the shootings at Kent State. Looking for someone to blame for the unrest, Congressman William Scherle and others publicized a list of "subversives" who "preach[ed] riot and revolution—for money—on our college campuses."[50] On the list were Black Power advocates Elaine Brown and Stokely Carmichael, inspirational figures for many who wanted to transform U.S. society.[51]

Given the popularity of the Black Panther Party among "revolutionaries," it is not surprising that Hanoi would invite a delegation led by Black Panther Eldridge Cleaver to visit. In August 1970, the Vietnamese hosted the Anti-Imperialist Delegation, which traveled to North Korea, North Viet Nam, and China. The delegation itself contained an eclectic mix of people on the left, including Black Panther Elaine Brown, white journalists at underground and New Left periodicals, white women's liberationists, a member of a militant Asian American group, and a female Asian American member of a GI organization.[52] Focusing on the experiences and interpretations of delegation members Elaine Brown and Hideko "Patricia" Sumi reveals whether and how interactions between U.S. women of color and Vietnamese women shaped U.S. feminisms. Although Brown and Sumi

ostensibly had the same experiences, being on the same trip, their interpretations of Vietnamese women's roles were colored by their own previous exposure to distinct versions of racism and sexism.

For Elaine Brown, "it was easy to feel at home in Vietnam," but she never
felt quite at ease in the United States.[53] Growing up the only child of a single mother in the projects of Philadelphia, Brown was one of the only students of color at a school for gifted children. Although Brown had some
African American friends in her neighborhood, she lived between two
worlds and quite often felt like an outsider in both. After dropping out of
Temple University, Brown moved to Los Angeles, where she worked as a
waitress at a strip club and was introduced to civil rights thought through
her white lover, Jay Kennedy. After ending her relationship with Kennedy,
Brown edited a newspaper for the African American community and eventually joined the Los Angeles chapter of the Black Panther Party. Brown, a
singer-songwriter, also recorded songs to inspire African Americans to rise
up to gain "dignity, not just equality."[54]

Brown's lyrics reflected a shift in priorities for many rights-based activists in African American communities. After the passage of the Civil Rights
Act of 1964 and Voting Rights Act of 1965, which provided a basis on which
to claim political and civil rights, many turned their attention to economic
and social needs of African American communities.[55] Militant tactics, which
were present during the "non-violent" civil rights movement of the 1950s
and early 1960s, prevailed as new groups, including the Black Panther Party,
founded in 1966, emerged in the mid-to-late 1960s.[56] For inspiration, Black
Panthers turned to revolutionaries abroad—including Frantz Fanon, Ho Chi
Minh, and Che Guevara—even fund-raising by selling *Quotations from
Chairman Mao Tse-Tung* on street corners and college campuses.[57] Reciting
these works, the Black Panthers and other rights-based activists professed
that the United States needed revolutionary change, not simply reform.

In addition to the ideological connection Black Panthers championed,
they made actual inroads with Hanoi in 1969. That year, Eldridge Cleaver
and the DRV negotiated an exchange of prisoners—Hanoi would release
POWs if the U.S. government released Huey Newton and Bobby Seale,
cofounders of the Black Panthers.[58] Newton had been arrested for killing a
police officer, and Seale was one of eight political activists arrested for in-
citing a riot at the 1968 Democratic National Convention in Chicago. Although the U.S. government did not release Newton or Seale in exchange
for POWs, through this proposal, Hanoi and the Black Panthers publicly
established ties with one another.

During the Anti-Imperialist Delegation's visit, the North Vietnamese government celebrated this connection between African Americans and the Vietnamese through its commemoration of an International Day of Solidarity with the Afro-American People on August 18, 1970.[59] According to the North Vietnamese Organization of Solidarity with the People of Africa, Asia, and Latin America, the day was in observance of the 1965 Watts riot in Los Angeles. North Viet Nam's premier Pham Van Dong and General Vo Nguyen Giap attended the festivities, and General Giap even gave a speech calling for the release of Bobby Seale. In its coverage of the celebration, the *Vietnam Courier* praised the violent resistance of Black Panthers against the U.S. government. Declaring that "lucid leaders in the Black people's movement" knew the only way to achieve social and economic equality was through "solidarity with progressive White Americans and with the world revolutionary movement," it testified to Hanoi's desire to align itself with activists against "U.S. aggressive imperialism."[60] Similarly, the periodical *South Viet Nam in Struggle*, mouthpiece for the NLF and published in Hanoi, provided coverage of recent protests across the United States against the poor treatment of African American communities. It declared that "fighting a common enemy—US imperialism—the South Vietnamese people highly value the movement of the black people in the US."[61] To African American GIs, NLF propaganda leaflets stated that NLF forces would welcome deserters and that African Americans' fight was at home against the U.S. government, not in Viet Nam.[62] Capitalizing on the racial unrest in the United States, the DRV and NLF created a seemingly natural bond between African Americans and Vietnamese.

For Elaine Brown, the state-sanctioned violence perpetrated by the U.S. government at home and abroad united the fates of the two peoples. Linking African Americans, whose "own people are dying and suffering under racist, fascist terror right now, here in Babylon, here in the United States" with the Vietnamese who were "concerned right now with the survival of their people," Brown implied that U.S. authorities thought little of killing either African Americans or Vietnamese.[63] Echoing NLF propaganda, she and Eldridge Cleaver broadcast a statement over Voice of Viet Nam radio telling African American GIs in South Viet Nam that their enemy was the U.S. government, not the Vietnamese. "What we said in essence is to put down their guns. We told them to desert. We told them that in fact the best thing they could do, if they wanted to, if they had the guts to, would be to turn their guns against the people who are giving them orders to kill innocent Vietnamese people," she informed an interviewer in Berkeley.[64]

Although Brown advocated that African Americans and Vietnamese join forces to resist U.S. government aggression, she realized that ending U.S. imperialism only went so far. For Brown, the struggle for economic and social rights had to be accompanied by revolutionary gender roles. Upon joining the Black Panthers, Brown found camaraderie, but she also encountered overt sexism in some Panther chapters. During a meeting at a Black Panther member's house in Oakland in 1969, Brown observed the sexual objectification of a teenage African American girl. Prompted by a male leader to tell Brown what a "Sister's" duty was, the young girl recited, "A Sister has to learn to shoot as well as to cook . . . [she] has to give up the pussy when the Brother is on his job and hold it back when he's not."[65] As the male Panther members applauded this girl's understanding of women's duties, Brown felt disgusted. Shortly after this speech, a woman tapped Brown on the shoulder to inform her that all the "Sisters" needed to help out in the kitchen while the "Brothers" continued to talk about the future of the movement in the living room. Irritated, Brown bit her lip as she followed the woman into the kitchen. After spending the entire meeting cooking for, serving, and cleaning up after the men, Brown had had enough. As she dropped dirty dishes into a sink full of soapy water, she exclaimed, "At no time since I've been in the party have I seen such bullshit."[66] Overhearing her, one of the male members who knew her well stepped into the kitchen to calm her down. Seeing his mission was unlikely to succeed, he quickly retreated. The other "Sisters" in the kitchen said nothing, and without a participating audience, Brown ended her tirade. She soon left with a group of male Panthers from Los Angeles, and in the car they all agreed that the Oakland chapter had problems. Back in Los Angeles, Brown reached out to other female Panther members to form a clique of women who called out chauvinistic behavior.[67] Brown would not leave the party; nor would she allow such sexism to continue. Instead, she would "fight for the right to fight for freedom."[68] She and a few other women in the party became watchful of sexist attitudes and worked to "revolutionize" them.[69]

Brown and others insisted that African American women could gain equality with men without undermining the Black Power movement. Activist Myrna Hill argued that feminism and Black Nationalism supported each other because African Americans and women had the same enemies: imperialism and capitalism. Therefore, both movements needed to promote a socialist revolution.[70] Bobby Seale agreed. In a 1970 interview, he stated that sexist and racist oppressions were directly related because "the ruling class" had designed both to keep women and African Americans in their "place."[71] While Seale embraced and encouraged women's participation in the Black Panther Party, African American women debated how best to organize.

Part of the problem African American women faced in organizations such as the Black Panthers stemmed from Daniel Patrick Moynihan's 1965 report *The Negro Family: The Case for National Action*.[72] In it, he blamed the alleged matriarchal structure of African American families for the problems in African American communities, he assumed that the patriarchal family structure was best, and he ignored racism as a structural hindrance for African Americans. Historian Deborah Gray White argues that the report "legitimized the perception of black women as unnaturally strong and emasculating"; thus, African American women were put on the defensive and had to prove their femininity by being subservient.[73] The report also reinforced the idea that African American men, but not women, needed employment and educational opportunities. Making matters worse, no African American women's organization, only select individuals, protested the report. Dorothy Height, leader of the National Council of Negro Women in 1965, even agreed that African American women should support men as the dominant figure in the family.[74] White speculated that African American women's uncontested image as emasculators contributed to the emergence of masculine militancy in the late 1960s.[75]

In light of Elaine Brown's awareness of sexism in the Black Panther Party, her comment that "we were treated as human beings and as respected members of the human race" in North Viet Nam hinted at her oppression as both an African American and a woman.[76] Her identity as an African American excluded her from white society just as she experienced marginalization as a woman in an organization hesitant to allow women real sway. Indeed, the title of Brown's memoir *A Taste of Power* alludes to her continual lack of authority in the Black Panther Party, even when she became chair of the organization in the mid-1970s, during the exile of Huey Newton. When Brown took the reins of the party, she acted as a figurehead whom Newton could trust to do his bidding without trying to seize control of the organization. Although it is in hindsight that Brown recognized that she never would have real power in the Black Panthers, in 1970, she perceived the limits placed on her as a woman in a male-dominated organization.[77]

While "black women struggled with black men around issues of sexism, [they struggled] with white women around issues of racism."[78] Many African American women hesitated to join white women's liberation groups because the relationship between white women and white men was not the same as that between African American women and African American men.[79] As a representative of the U.S.-based Third World Women's Alliance (TWWA), which grew out of SNCC in 1969, explained at a women's liberation rally, "It is difficult for Third World women to address themselves to the petty problems of who is going to take out the garbage, when there isn't enough food in the house for anything to be thrown away."[80] Claiming that women of color faced larger problems than familial gender roles, many African American woman activists saw racism as undermining any organization that claimed to speak for *all* women because these (usually white) groups did not recognize the diversity of problems women faced based on race or class. But this did not mean that African American women renounced feminism. Instead, many sought camaraderie in organizations made up solely of African American women who had the goal of "develop[ing] black feminism as a dynamic theory and practice that promoted black liberation."[81] Within these organizations, African American women had the ability to collaborate on both "Third World" and women's issues without ignoring the unique problems that they faced.[82]

Central to countering the exclusion of African American women in social movement circles, many pointed to examples of African, Asian, and Caribbean women fighting for national independence as equals alongside men. Chairman Mao's writings also provided positive references to women's capabilities in battling sexism, racism, and imperialism simultaneously. After her second visit to China in 1971, Elaine Brown urged Black Panthers to "embrace China's correct recognition of the proper status of women as equal to that of men."[83] Similarly, Frances Beal, founder of the TWWA, told African American women, "We must begin to study . . . successful revolutions to discover the general truths which we can apply to our struggle here in the U.S. against imperialism, against racism and against male supremacy."[84] Patricia Haden, Donna Middleton, and Patricia Robinson also argued that African American women could learn from Vietnamese women, who had brought about "a new stage in history" by taking on the U.S. military.[85] According to Haden, Middleton, and Robinson, Vietnamese women had "prove[n] that no U.S. male, black or white, got what it takes to destroy a people who have decided in their guts to own themselves and their land. That is power U.S. males have forgotten, but not black women."[86] All of these women looked to revolutionary women abroad as examples of not only the ability to but also the need to fight against racism and sexism simultaneously.

Even so, Elaine Brown was not impressed by Vietnamese women's militia roles. In fact, she lamented the forced lifestyle of young guerrilla women, who kept a lookout for incoming bombers. "This shouldn't be part of a 16-year old girl's life—to have spent practically all of her life ... involved in watching the skies for planes," she stated.[87] Instead, they should have time to talk about boys, hairstyles, and makeup like girls in the United States. For Brown, girls should have the security of only having to worry about their looks and their potential heterosexual relationships. Vietnamese and African American girls, however, had no such privilege. Although for many people Brown's call for "revolutionary gender roles" could signify women's taking up of arms or renouncing men as sexual partners, for her it meant women and girls being free of violence perpetrated either by men in their communities or by the U.S. government.[88] She sought to end all violence against women of color.

Asian American women faced similar challenges of how and with whom to organize and had the additional task of making themselves visible within U.S. society. Asian Americans were noticeably absent from statements made by the Vietnamese, African Americans, and white activists alike during the 1970 Anti-Imperialist Delegation's trip, despite the fact that there were two Asian Americans in the delegation, Pat Sumi and Alex Hing. This omission reflected a larger concern of Asian Americans more broadly. In 1971, activist Evelyn Yoshimura identified the problem when she said, "To most non-Asians in the U.S., there is little if any difference between Asian Americans and Asians in America. We Asian Americans are either lumped with Asians, and therefore considered 'foreigners,' or we are invisible."[89] The small number of Asian Americans—less than 1 percent of the U.S. population in 1970—and the binary racial categories in the United States of either black or white hindered the acknowledgment of their existence. One activist recalled being told as a child in the 1960s by her black friend that she had to decide whether she was black or white.[90]

For many, the choice was to be white, black, or Asian, never Asian American. Pat Sumi realized in hindsight that she chose, for a time, to act white. She recalled, "Going to Japan [in 1963 to visit her ancestral home] was ... one of the things which kept me from falling all off into a white, middle class bag, marrying a white man, living in a white neighborhood, and telling everyone how assimilated I was."[91] Even so, Sumi did live with a white man for a time in the late 1960s, but having met her Japanese relatives, she constantly reminded herself that she was Japanese, not white. Even this declaration, however, distinguished her as Asian, not Asian American. Being

Japanese *and* American seemed impossible, as throughout her childhood she learned nothing about the history of Japanese living in the United States. Sumi, a Sansei, was born two months after her parents were released from an internment camp, and, like many Japanese Americans of her generation, heard little about her parents' life in the United States before or during World War II. She also learned nothing about Japanese Americans in school, where she was one of the only students of color. A perpetual outsider, Sumi aspired to seem white so she fit in.[92]

Another Japanese American woman took a different tack, declaring that she would marry a white man in order to be more Asian. She claimed her white fiancé wanted her to cook Japanese dishes for him and saw her "as a little Japanese doll in kimono," whereas the Asian American men she had dated wanted her to be as close to white as possible.[93] Although the author recognized that her fiancé placed her in a stereotypical role, she accepted it because "I am much more Oriental now, marrying him."[94] But even this celebration of this woman's heritage denied her identity as both Japanese *and* American.

Further complicating matters, up to this point, a panethnic Asian American identity did not exist. Many people of Asian descent living in the United States still separated themselves by ethnicity and felt strong ties to their ancestral lands. Since the nineteenth century, hostilities between Asian nations—China, Japan, and Korea, in particular—created barriers between people with ancestral ties to these countries who were living in the United States.[95] Not until the 1960s, when the first substantial generation of native-born Asian Americans left home to attend college, did Asian Americans begin to recognize "their common fate in American society."[96] While at college, students of Asian descent first became involved in antiwar demonstrations and, at those events, connected with other Asian Americans.[97] The nature of U.S. involvement in Viet Nam also helped to forge an Asian American identity as many activists came to label the war an act of "genocide."[98] They saw it as representing racism against all people of Asian descent and traced a historical campaign of aggression against Asian peoples that included the dropping of the atomic bombs on Japan.[99] They argued that if Asian Americans lived in Viet Nam, "we would be dead! *And the reason we would be dead is because we are Asian*!!!" (emphasis in original).[100] With this declaration, these youths formed a common racial identity while rejecting assimilation into white society.

Even as Asian American activists sought communion with Asians in Asia, in the context of the war, the conflation of Asian Americans and Asians on the part of white society could be alarming, especially within the U.S. military. Activists at UCLA claimed that even before setting foot in Viet Nam, "American soldiers in basic training are taught to repeatedly and viciously stab with a bayonet slant-eyed coolie-hatted dummies."[101] White veteran John Kerry, in his testimony to the Senate Foreign Relations Committee on behalf of the Vietnam Veterans Against the War about the Winter Soldier Investigation in 1971, described cadets confronting posters pasted to the walls of military barracks that depicted a "crucified Vietnamese, blood on him, and underneath it says 'kill the gook.' "[102] This was disconcerting for Asian American GIs, who testified that their fellow soldiers and commanding officers called them "gook," "charlie," or "Ho Chi Minh"—all derogatory terms representing the enemy.[103] Veteran Sam Choy stated that while stationed in Viet Nam his fellow GIs harassed him, saying that he "look[ed] like the Viet Cong."[104] Kerry affirmed that "racism [against Asians] is rampant in the military."[105] He argued that, "We fought using weapons against 'oriental human beings' . . . which I do not believe this country would dream of using were we fighting in the European theater."[106] While for Kerry the problem was a matter of military policy, for Asian Americans that policy could have dire consequences.

In the United States, many feared that GIs' violence toward Vietnamese would extend to Asian Americans.[107] Activist Peggy Saiki recalled a threatening encounter with a veteran at a miniature golf course in Sacramento in the late 1960s. "The owner's son, having been in Vietnam . . . c[ame] out and yell[ed], 'Get those gooks outta here,' " she recounted in a 2006 interview.[108] "That transference," she continued, "of his experience in Vietnam and not being able to distinguish between supposedly the people that he was fighting in Vietnam [and] Asian Americans in this country" taught her that "as Asian Americans . . . we are united with people who were being exploited and plundered in Vietnam."[109]

All women of Asian descent also shared a connection as sexist ideas about them proliferated in the military. Drill sergeants often told sexual jokes about women they had supposedly known while stationed in Asia. One officer insulted an Asian American GI by calling the GI's sister a prostitute and claiming he (the officer) had been one of her customers in Japan. This stereotype of Asian women dates back to the mid-nineteenth century, when a municipal committee in San Francisco reported that most of the women found in Chinatown were prostitutes. According to scholar Sucheng Chan, "This observation soon became a conviction, and it colored the public perception of, attitude toward and action against all Chinese women for almost a century."[110] At the same time, Asian women were assumed to be subservient. Put together, these stereotypes created an image of sensual, naïve, and obedient women incapable of refusing sexual advances.[111] As Viet Nam veterans at the Winter Soldier Investigation admitted "they had personally raped . . . and generally ravaged the countryside," Asian American women learned to be wary.[112]

Asian American women also faced sexism within their communities. They found that even their fellow male activists expected women to perform menial tasks such as answering the phones, keeping meeting minutes, making coffee, and, as one woman remembered, "cleaning the goddamn toilet."[113] Women often had "their ideas . . . usurped by the men," and taking on too much responsibility could earn them the label unfeminine.[114] Historian William Wei conjectures that men's treatment of women stemmed from decades of living as bachelors because of antimiscegenation and immigration exclusion laws. He suggests that men believed "that they had a 'right' to the sexual services of 'their' women, after years when Asian women were excluded from the country."[115] When women did obtain leadership positions, they found themselves perpetuating stereotypes by putting down other women or by emphasizing their alleged physical incapacities—such as claiming to be too weak to carry equipment.[116] For Sumi, it was in 1968, when she felt forced into acting like a "Japanese wife" while living in a pacifist commune where she cooked, cleaned, and did laundry for eight (likely white) men, that her consciousness as a woman and an Asian American surfaced.[117]

Although much of this sexism resembled that encountered in white mixed-gender groups, many Asian American women, like Chicanas and African American women, distanced themselves from white women's liberation because they viewed it as inattentive to the issue of racism. As Janice Mirikitani declared in her 1972 poem entitled "MS.," she wanted nothing to do with white women's groups until white women recognized racism and imperialism as critical issues. Her poem related an argument Mirikitani had with a white woman who wanted to be called "Ms." not "Miss." Although Mirikitani sympathized with the woman, she refused to "accommodate her" until white society "quit/killing us for democracy/and stop calling ME gook."[118] Thus, Mirikitani pointed out the centrality of racism to her lived experience while she also revealed her awareness of engrained sexism. Scholars studying the origins of Asian American feminism have provided similar evidence of women's feminist consciousness while explaining why Asian American women did not join white women's liberation groups.[119] The analysis should not end here, however. Mirikitani's poem also demonstrates Asian American women's tendency to refer to the Viet Nam war as they challenged the imposed dichotomy between racism and sexism. Therefore, asking how the international context shaped Asian American women's feminism shines a new light on this story.

Asian women's gender roles both inspired and limited Asian American women. Pat Sumi felt this tension during her 1963 visit to Japan. Although she knew she could not stay in Japan because she would never make a good "Japanese wife"—someone who would stay home and do her husband's bidding—she also felt in awe of the "arts of Japanese women."[120] She remembered her great uncle handing her "the weapon the Japanese women were expected to use to defend the castle when it was being stormed" and wished she had the physical and mental control to wield it properly.[121] Alas, her white American upbringing had kept her from learning these skills. This contrast in Japanese women's roles as both subservient and militant paralleled depictions of Asian women elsewhere. According to one underground Asian American periodical, despite the "low position of women in *traditional* Asian societies" (emphasis added), those living under revolutionary governments experienced newfound freedoms.[122] "In revolutionary societies such as China," it explained, "women have attained the highest positions in science, medicine, in the armed forces, as well as in the technical fields. In seeking change our women cast their eyes towards the example of these new societies."[123] Indeed, activist May Chen remembered looking to Asian women as "models" of women's new gender roles.[124] As a second-generation immigrant, Chen found what was happening in China particularly relevant, as her own mother had escaped an arranged marriage because of evolving cultural values. Although in many Asian societies there was a history of women's submission, Chen and others pointed to concrete examples of women's increased self-determination under new regimes.

Vietnamese guerrilla women provided prominent examples of women's ability to fight for their nation's independence while gaining equality for themselves. Sumi pointed out that Vietnamese women's militia roles demonstrated that women were not simply mothers of the next generation of revolutionaries but were loyal revolutionaries themselves. To illustrate this, she recounted the story of one South Vietnamese woman forced to give birth in prison. The woman, a member of the NLF, refused to give up important information on the NLF's whereabouts, even when her prison guards left her newborn just outside her cell, where she had to listen to it cry without being able to soothe it. Soon its cries turned to whimpers, and the baby died three days after its birth. For Sumi, this story exemplified women's ability to be equal participants in the revolution—not even maternal feelings kept them from performing their duties in the resistance movement.[125] Sumi's example, however, also seemed rather callous, as she upended assumptions about femininity and motherhood. This story reveals a problem with dismissing women's supposedly inherent maternal feelings in such a fashion. That is, portraying this Vietnamese woman as caring more about the revolution than about her newborn child either does her an injustice, obscuring the pain that she likely felt as she listened to her child die, or depicts her as inhumane and unfeeling, supporting racist notions of Asians as less human than their white American counterparts.

This conundrum may not have been lost on Elaine Brown, who, surprisingly, did not mention family or motherhood in her assessment of women's roles in North Viet Nam. This omission is noteworthy, especially because she had just given birth to her only child a few months before her trip. But perhaps given the history of African American women, who, under the system of slavery, often had their sexuality controlled by white men, motherhood in and of itself could not epitomize femininity, as it did for other women. Instead, Brown wanted freedom from violence, control over her own body, and the privilege to be "feminine."

In a later interview, Pat Sumi clarified that being revolutionary did not mean that women neglected their familial duties. When asked what Sumi had learned from women she met in Southeast Asia, she answered that women did not need to segregate themselves from men because "women could be beautiful, humane and have kids, take care of families and be revolutionaries at the same time."[126] Incorporating new roles into the family, women could remake society and fight against their "primary oppressor . . . capitalism and imperialism."[127] The North Vietnamese as well as the North Koreans and Chinese highlighted this coherence between women's revolutionary and familial duties. In these countries, officials asserted that every factory and collective farm had a nursery, allowing mothers to work, and kitchens, relieving women of cooking responsibilities. In North Korea and China, pregnant women received two months of paid leave, and mothers of three children received more pay for shorter hours. Women could also dress more comfortably in jackets and slacks, like men. Compared to Chinese, North Korean, and North Vietnamese women's lives just twenty-five years earlier, these rights were a great improvement, according to Sumi. Before revolutions in China, Korea, and Viet Nam, women had been triply oppressed by colonialism, capitalism, and sexism. According to Sumi, in Viet

Nam, married women took their husband's entire name and gave up their identity in doing so. In Korea, women had no education, and in China, women were physically incapacitated by their bound feet.[128] But, by 1970, Sumi stated, male revolutionaries recognized the importance of women's rights. Working side-by-side, men and women could end racism, sexism, and imperialism simultaneously.

Embracing these new societies, Pat Sumi as well as Elaine Brown and other Anti-Imperialist Delegation members upended U.S. Cold War portrayals of communism by describing North Koreans, North Vietnamese, and Chinese as "pursu[ing] a life which has a higher standard of living on the average than even the United States and a life which has infinitely more creativity and joy than that in the U.S."[129] Brown noted the artistic culture of the Vietnamese, who practically sang as they recited revolutionary poems and recounted the Vietnamese saying "let the sound of the song be higher than the sound of the bombs."[130] Sumi and fellow delegate Alex Hing, minister of information for the Red Guards, likewise celebrated the advanced state of civilization in Asia. Everyone had free medical care, education, and housing, as well as affordable food and clothing. Even though Hing and Brown admitted that in Viet Nam people lived in mud houses with thatched roofs and had little machinery to help with menial tasks, they argued that the economic and social benefits in Viet Nam outweighed the technological advances of the United States.[131]

Hanoi similarly proclaimed that the DRV created and reclaimed a Vietnamese socialist culture that provided benefits unavailable under capitalism, colonialism, or imperialism. Under French rule, the Vietnamese were "cultural[ly] enslave[d]" as prostitution, gambling, and drug addiction proliferated.[132] In South Viet Nam, these vices still flourished under capitalism, but in the North the revolutionary government had largely eradicated such debauchery. The Ministry of Culture of North Viet Nam worked to create a new society by disseminating poems, creating advertising slogans, and producing films aimed at influencing citizens to join the struggle against "U.S. imperialism" and for a reunified socialist Viet Nam.

Brown and Sumi believed they had "seen new people" in Asia—people who were socially responsible, politically conscious, self-critical, and "proud."[133] Unlike the "snake pit" that was New York City, Asians in socialist countries labored not for material incentives but rather for the good of all working people.[134] In fact, workers were willing to move to do harder labor for less pay if it was for the good of the people, according to Alex Hing. Instead of portraying socialist countries as "cold, stern, disciplined,"

Brown, Sumi, and Hing wanted to make it clear that Vietnamese had "warm, human concern for other people's feelings and well-being."[135] Brown told of the generosity of Vietnamese villagers, who, despite having very little, shared what they did have with the American delegation. For the Vietnamese, this generosity would have had its benefits, as it boosted local morale as well as impressed Americans who might help to end the war.

As Brown reflected on the trip during the eleven hour flight from Paris to New York, she considered her future in the Black Panther Party. With the slaying of many party members in 1969 and 1970—one young Panther having been killed while Brown was in Hanoi—she predicted the party would soon implode, even with cofounder Huey Newton's recent release from prison. As Brown deplaned, gathered her luggage, and faced the inquiries of U.S. customs agents, she continued to wonder whether the Black Panther Party provided a future for her. Waiting for customs to let her pass, she noticed a group of Panthers behind plated glass, watching as agents searched her luggage and removed items that she had collected in North Korea, China, and North Viet Nam. Finding her answers to questions of where she had acquired such items insufficient, two officers led her past the plated glass to an interrogation room. Before they reached the room, however, Huey Newton, a "beautiful man" whom she had never met, stepped out from behind the glass and embraced her, whispering in her ear that he had "listened to your voice and your songs over and over in my prison cell and dreamed of you."[136] Glowing from such a compliment, Brown endured a two hour interrogation, and upon her release readily joined a group of party members, who escorted her to a waiting car.

Even so, Brown felt "disoriented and strange" upon entering the "madness" of New York after having been in the "civilized world."[137] When Brown's group arrived at a hotel where actress Jane Fonda was hosting a celebration to commemorate Newton's signing of a book deal, she experienced "cultural shock" from the ostentatiousness of the guests and atmosphere.[138] She, like other women of color, more vehemently challenged the superiority of U.S. society following her travels in North Viet Nam. Elizabeth Martínez, Pat Sumi, and Elaine Brown all agreed that the Vietnamese had a more civilized society, and they looked to end U.S. imperialism's grasp on the Vietnamese as well as on their own communities. Identifying similarities in the mistreatment of Vietnamese and their own respective communities, Martínez, Sumi, and Brown sought to end U.S. society's cultural imperialism at home and abroad.

Even as Brown implicitly criticized supporters of the Black Panthers she encountered at the party in New York, she silently recommitted herself to the revolution and to the Black Panther Party. She also committed herself to Huey Newton, as they soon became lovers, entangling her deeper into the Black Panthers at a time when she could have forged a separate path for African American women. But Newton and Brown's relationship was no fairy tale. Brown soon discovered that Newton preached "revolutionary relationships," which meant that he could sleep with as many women as he wanted, whether she liked it or not. Because she wanted a monogamous relationship, Brown blamed herself for being too "bourgeois" and stayed with Newton and the Black Panthers despite her misery.[139] Brown's story demonstrates the inseparability of issues for women of color. Focusing on the needs and desires of black men did not release Brown from all of her tribulations any more than would working to end the type of sexism white women endured. Fighting against both sexism and racism as she experienced them as an African American woman was the only solution.

For many African American, Chicana, and Asian American women, Vietnamese women provided key examples of how they could challenge racism, imperialism, and sexism simultaneously. Although Martínez, Sumi, and Brown identified different aspects of Vietnamese women's roles as significant, for all three women, Vietnamese women represented the need and ability to fight alongside men for self-determination while simultaneously protesting sexism within their communities. While Martínez, Brown, and Sumi continued to work in mixed-gender organizations struggling against racism, imperialism, and sexism, over the next few years, some young white feminists found making connections between these interlocking forms of oppression a thankless task.

CHAPTER FOUR

Establishing Feminist Perspectives on War, 1969–1972

After attending an international women's antiwar conference held in Toronto in April 1971, reporter Renee Blakkan declared, "The [Viet Nam] war is a feminist issue."[1] Although feminist conference organizers would have applauded such a definitive statement, in the immediate aftermath of the Indochinese Women's Conference (IWC), Blakkan's declaration was lost. Indeed, in a recent interview, conference organizer and women's liberationist Vivian Rothstein lamented that there had been a "clash between women's movement goals and antiwar goals" at the IWC.[2] Rothstein and others expressed regret at the inability of U.S. women to bridge their differences to make the IWC a success.[3] She had hoped to form a feminist antiwar coalition, but instead women's liberationists seemed more divided than ever. Scholars studying the IWC have confirmed that North American women left the conference feeling confused, disappointed, and irritated with one another.[4]

In reality, some conflict should have been expected. For one thing, more than one thousand North American women from a wide array of organizations, including peace, women's liberation, civil rights, community, religious, and welfare rights, attended the IWC. Although some participating organizations regularly collaborated with one another, they still had different agendas. Scholars have often pointed to race, age, and class as factors that disrupted coalition-building between some of these groups. With this wide range of attendees also came many opinions on what was the most important topic to discuss with the Southeast Asian delegates, who totaled six—two from the DRV, two from the PRG, and two from Laos.[5] Given the disparity between the numbers of participants from North America and Southeast Asia, most North American women had very few opportunities to speak one-on-one with Southeast Asian women. Delegates often found themselves competing to ask about whichever aspect of the U.S. war in Viet Nam most compelled them. Even though the number of Southeast Asian women who could travel to Canada was out of the hands of the conference organizers, some women may have felt disappointed at not having the chance to have all of their questions answered and felt frustrated about time spent discussing topics they deemed inconsequential.

Historian Leila Rupp has shown other instances when conflict provided fertile ground for community-building, but in this case, division reigned.[6] Even within the seemingly homogeneous group of white women's liberationists, the central focus of this chapter, women held various views on the best way to organize, the underlying causes of women's oppression, and the overall solution to women's inequality. Although radical feminists generally agreed that women needed "liberation," as opposed to liberal feminists, who sought "equality," the term "liberation" itself had many interpretations.[7] With such disunity, organizers who were women's liberationists became sidetracked and felt impotent because they wanted to please everyone.

Yet, the conflict also forced those women's liberationists invested in hosting the IWC to contemplate why war was an important feminist issue. As central as the story of the discord itself has been to both contemporary and historical accounts of the IWC, it must not overshadow the accomplishments of white feminists.[8] Conflict before, during, and after the IWC within white women's liberation circles sparked debate about the relationship between sexism and imperialism and fostered a rethinking of war's relationship to women and society.[9] Much of the literature on second-wave feminism overlooks the international context, but I argue that the circumstances of the Viet Nam war generated feminist perspectives on military actions.

Before plans for the IWC even began, a few specific interactions between Vietnamese and young American women shaped emerging women's liberation thought. Vietnamese insistence on the inclusion of American women at peace conferences and on delegations to Hanoi created the opportunity for young female activists to gain attention, acquire leadership skills, and rethink their roles in mixed-gender organizations. For example, Vivian Rothstein attended an antiwar conference in Bratislava, Czechoslovakia, in September 1967 where female Vietnamese delegates suggested meeting separately with female American delegates. Rothstein, a twenty-one-year-old member of SDS, had convened separately with women only once before, at an SDS conference in 1965, and did not understand the purpose of segregating women from men at an international peace conference. The Vietnamese, however, contended that women had a special role to play in ending the war, and they believed that U.S. women could transmit an antiwar message more effectively than American men could. Nguyen Thi Binh, who attended the Bratislava conference as a representative of the NLF and WUL, later recalled that she thought American "women were inherently more open and tolerant than their male colleagues" and found work-ing with them particularly productive.[10]

Because of these convictions, when the Vietnamese invited a smaller U.S. delegation from the conference in Bratislava to continue on to visit Hanoi, they insisted on having women on the trip. Thus, Rothstein, along with SDS member Carol McEldowney, found herself in a seven-person delegation traveling from Bratislava to Hanoi despite her "terror" at entering a war zone—she could not even notify her family of her whereabouts, let alone say a proper "goodbye."[11] When Rothstein returned to the United States, she found the Vietnamese assumption that American women could be par-ticularly effective antiwar messengers true, as it was "disarming to people for women to speak out" about what they had seen in a war zone.[12] Through her contact with Vietnamese and because of her subsequent duty to report what she had witnessed, Rothstein developed leadership skills and a public persona.

Rothstein and McEldowney also brought back an idea of how women could organize themselves around multiple issues. While in Hanoi, VWU members told them about women's newfound leadership roles in all realms of society, including in the military. McEldowney later recounted to U.S. woman activists a story about how Vietnamese women successfully cam-paigned to join the ranks of antiaircraft operators. When male soldiers joked that they would have to carry both a woman and a gun if women were allowed to join their military unit, women decided to form their own units. After proving themselves capable and showing the advantages of female spies, whom ARVN soldiers did not see as a threat, Vietnamese women fur-ther argued that the struggle against all forms of oppression, including sexism, had to happen concurrently if the revolution were to succeed. Viet-namese men soon accepted women in the military and even allowed them to command defensive military operations. For women in the New Left, this account provided them with ammunition to combat sexism within movement organizations. Women's liberationist and SDS member Nancy Grey Osterud recalled reciting this story as proof that the Vietnamese en-couraged tackling all forms of oppression at once whenever men in SDS proclaimed "women's issues" as being outside the realm of current priori-ties. Male members of SDS had difficulty disputing such an argument because they, too, invoked the Vietnamese as the authority on revolution-ary struggle.[13] Nonetheless, upon her return to the United States, Vivian Rothstein decided to form an autonomous women's liberation group, the

Chicago Women's Liberation Union, which participated in a variety of activities to empower women in a similar manner as the VWU. Rothstein's experiences in Hanoi urged her to reevaluate her role in SDS—without leaving behind her conviction against the war, she became "an organizer of other women."[14]

Rothstein's decision to form a multi-issue autonomous women's liberation group anticipated questions facing women in the New Left throughout the United States. In the spring of 1968 in Seattle, white women active in SDS found a theatrical way to make the point that all forms of oppression were connected. A meeting set up for the October 1967 *Playboy* playmate of the month, Reagan Wilson, with women at the University of Washington was supposed to focus on how to attract men. Instead, a group of SDS women rushed the stage to perform a skit in which Wilson died from sexual objectification, just as so many Vietnamese had died from American bombs. The SDS women wanted to convey the message that white women and the Vietnamese both faced an integrated system of oppression. Within moments, members of the college football team, who were acting as stagehands, threw some of the women off the stage, injuring at least one of them. When news of the violence reached the public, it caused such an uproar that the university expelled the football players involved. Shortly after this incident, African American civil rights activist and feminist Florynce Kennedy arrived in Seattle for a prearranged talk during which she urged women in SDS to rethink their framing of the connections between the struggles of white women, African Americans, and the Vietnamese. It was not the similarity in oppressions that linked them but rather a shared struggle against their common enemy. For Osterud, who had participated in the guerrilla theater performance, seeing the struggle as the same, regardless of the form of oppression, defined her future activism, particularly in the Boston-based group Bread and Roses, which was one of the key organizations involved in planning the IWC.[15] But women's liberationists such as Osterud, who believed in struggling against all forms of oppression at once, constantly had to prove, explain, and justify their intention to work on multiple issues.

In the fall of 1969, some women's liberationists demonstrated their dedication to fighting all forms of oppression concurrently when they contemplated how to transform white and male supremacist thinking in the New Mobe (New Mobilization Committee to End the War in Vietnam), a coalition of antiwar organizations founded in July 1969. Following the New Mobe's first national demonstration, in November 1969, Charlotte Bunch, a women's liberationist and future IWC organizer living in Washington, D.C., criticized leaders of the demonstration for being "unresponsive" to the concerns of feminists, a point illustrated by the fact that they had not provided childcare.[16] However, Bunch did not suggest that women's liberationists leave the coalition; instead, she asked women in several cities on the East Coast and in the Midwest what they could do to make the New Mobe more sensitive to their concerns.[17] The answer was to form a Women's Caucus that would provide an anti-imperialist and feminist outlook on antiwar issues. Through the Caucus, Bunch and other women's liberationists advanced a more comprehensive, understanding, and inclusive antiwar position.[18]

Charlotte Bunch gained further insight into the importance of broadening antiwar perspectives when she traveled to North Viet Nam with Elizabeth Martínez and two other U.S. activists in April 1970. While Bunch admired the beauty that she saw in the Vietnamese landscape, culture, and people, she also noted challenges Vietnamese women still faced. She cited Vietnamese women's reluctance to speak with the American group unless the conversation was specifically about women as evidence that Vietnamese women held limited leadership positions. Discerning the shortcomings in women's roles cemented Bunch's conviction that a truly revolutionary movement needed a feminist perspective if women wanted to achieve liberation.[19] In a move similar to Vivian Rothstein's following her trip to Hanoi, in June 1970, Bunch founded the Women's Liberation Anti-Imperialist Collective (the Collective, for short) in Washington, D.C., a women's liberation group dedicated to finding connections between violence, imperialism, and sexism.[20]

Bunch's Collective soon undertook the major project of organizing the IWC in early fall 1970. Although the VWU first suggested to three WSP members in December 1969 that a conference be held in Canada, news of the meeting apparently took months to reach women's liberation groups. It is unclear why this would be, especially given that two WSP members were on the Steering Committee of the New Mobe with Charlotte Bunch. Neither WSP member, however, participated directly in planning the IWC, so perhaps that was the sole cause of the lack of communication.[21] It is also possible that WSP members did not see women's liberation as pertinent to the IWC—after all, female peace activists had different priorities than young feminists.

This sentiment notably changed, however, in the late summer and early fall of 1970, when WSP groups began to relate the war to feminist concerns as they simultaneously recruited young feminists to join their movement. WSP's participation in the Women's Strike for Equality demonstration on August 26, 1970, marked its evolving conceptualization of women's relationship to war. WSP added a fourth demand to the Women's Strike agenda, stating that the war needed to end in order to improve women's lives—the government spent money on military equipment that could instead provide social services for women and their children.[22] This development in WSP's characterization of the war did not replace its positioning of itself as an organization made up of concerned mothers but rather added a component to it. It was after the Women's Strike protest that WSP members invited women's liberationists to join their efforts in preparing for the April 1971 conference.[23]

Individual WSP members and women's liberationists did not always see eye to eye, however. At an international conference hosted by the WIDF held in Budapest in October 1970, three white women's liberationists, Ellin Hirst from Bread and Roses in Boston, Alice Wolfson from the Women's Liberation Anti-Imperialist Collective in D.C., and Peggy Morton from a women's liberation group in Toronto, met with two VWU, two WUL, and two WSP members to discuss preparations for the IWC. During these conversations, it became clear that the five North American women could not agree on an agenda for, or the purpose of, the IWC.[24]

Both WSP members and women's liberationists questioned the other's dedication either to ending the war or to promoting feminism. Historian Amy Swerdlow, who attended the WIDF meeting as a WSP representative, stated that disagreements centered on the proposed subject matter of the IWC. Whereas the two WSP members wanted to focus on "the Vietnamese predicament," the three women's liberationists "insisted that there be a thorough discussion of the relationship of patriarchy to militarism."[25] For Swerdlow, Hirst and Wolfson's additional demand that the IWC investigate "the role and status of women in Vietnam, including their attitude toward lesbianism," just seemed too much.[26] Conversely, for Hirst and Wolfson, the two white middle-aged WSP members lacked a feminist consciousness. They identified a "generation gap" between WSP members and themselves, diminishing the possibility of effective collaboration on the IWC.[27]

Wolfson pointed out that the Vietnamese women also embraced the "traditional" gender role of motherhood, demonstrated by their passing around of pictures of their children and grandchildren to the North American women in Budapest. But she simultaneously insisted that they embodied the ideal revolutionary womanhood, claiming that "these women have really progressed."[28] The Vietnamese, trying to foster people's diplomatic ties, succeeded in bridging gaps between themselves and the young white North American women because, as Wolfson recalled, "Instead of looking for those ways in which we are different, they [the Vietnamese] look for those ways in which we are the same."[29] Indeed, the head of the Vietnamese delegation, Phan Thi An, had practice building alliances despite differences as leader of the international relations section of the VWU. On several occasions, she had given presentations to, conferred with, and hosted women from around the world. Wolfson concluded that if only more American women could "touch and feel" Vietnamese women, "we would make the war stop."[30] The two WSP members agreed, and the five North American women decided to hold conferences in both Toronto and Vancouver in order to maximize the number of American women who could meet with the Vietnamese. But, the five women still could not agree on the purpose of the IWC and decided to host two consecutive conferences—one for peace activists and one for "liberationists," including women of color in "Third World" movements—in the two locations.

Upon returning to the United States, Hirst and Wolfson, along with a number of white "women's liberation organizers"—meaning those charged with the task of overseeing IWC preparations for the liberation portion of the program—decided to hold events that emphasized that the war was a feminist issue. Organizers, including members of Bread and Roses and the Women's Liberation Anti-Imperialist Collective, saw the upcoming tenth anniversary of the founding of the NLF on December 20, 1970, as the perfect opportunity to make their case. In Boston, New York City, Washington, D.C., and Chicago, women's liberation groups hosted rallies, demonstrations, and parties to celebrate the anniversary as well as "the birth of the U.S. women's anti-imperialist movement."[31]

To clarify what a "women's anti-imperialist movement" was, leading up to and following the December 20 celebrations, a group in Buffalo, New York, collected and distributed essays on the relationship between imperialism and sexism. These essays, written by members of the Chicago Women's Liberation Union, Bread and Roses, the Collective in D.C., and other groups,[32] generally began by echoing the Women's Strike for Equality statements made by WSP—namely, they alleged that the U.S. government spent public funds on ever more destructive and inhumane weapons instead of supporting social services. But then the authors often took the argument a step further. One essay pointed out that the shortage in government funding also charged women with the responsibility of cleaning up after the military—that women often provided care for injured veterans without remuneration.[33] It also fell to women to look after dependent children while their husbands were in Viet Nam on military duty or after they returned injured. Thus, the war and the military exerted a control over women's lives that exacerbated their inequality.

Women's exploitation by the U.S. government did not end at U.S. borders. Showing contempt for the lives and livelihoods of women in South Viet Nam, the U.S. military "use[d South Vietnamese] women as instruments for a particular kind of attack," one that would destroy the social fabric of the RVN.[34] Namely, GIs sexually assaulted Vietnamese women and razed villages, dehumanizing the Vietnamese. With nowhere to go, 400,000 South Vietnamese women turned to prostitution to survive (nearly one prostitute for every GI deployed in Viet Nam at the time).[35] Although historian Harriet Alonso points out that since the interwar period, U.S. woman peace activists "drew connections between the violence of war and violence against women," the violence against women was usually located within the United States—namely, war veterans who abused their wives and children.[36] Women's liberationists shifted this narrative by describing the "sexist torture" of Vietnamese women, thereby making the way war was waged a feminist issue.[37] American and Vietnamese women alike needed to fight "for power and control over our bodies, our minds, our destinies, [and] our environment."[38] Pointing to the actions of GIs, women's liberation organizers insisted that the accepted, and perhaps promoted, performance of U.S. masculinity made the war a feminist issue.

Through criticizing U.S. masculinity, feminists avoided characterizing women as inherently peaceful, another departure from WSP's rhetoric. Women's liberationists argued that in societies with strict gender roles, such as the United States, one gender had to be aggressive, thus causing conflict and war. By contrast, in an egalitarian society, this need for aggression arguably would diminish, and the entire society would be peaceful.[39] Through linking the conduct of the war to GIs' masculinity, the authors hoped to show that resisting the war made sense for feminist reasons—women's liberation groups would not only help women in other nations but also help themselves by forcing a rethinking of gender roles in the United States.

Problems with conference planning, however, overshadowed these intellectual contributions. As preparations continued following the December 20 celebrations, women's liberationists, female peace activists, and women of color in rights-based movements set up local and regional meetings throughout the United States from January to March 1971. Most of the regional meetings, however, involved women from only one of these categories, a fact often ignored by the attendees themselves.[40] Much of the indecision and conflict remembered about the IWC took place during and as a result of this intense planning period in the three months immediately preceding the conference.

Women's liberation organizers tried to involve as many women as possible in their planning process, but they had limited means of inviting women to meetings. The Vietnamese had requested that nothing about the IWC be published, not even in the underground press, for fear that the Canadian government would deny visas if it found out about the conference. Instead, word-of-mouth passed between friends and often went no further than a single contact in a city. Without an established network of women's liberation groups, not to mention one between white feminists and women of color, who were also supposed to attend the "liberation" portion of the conference, organizers had limited means of notifying all who might have been interested in the IWC, and thus they ended up making decisions for everyone. Just weeks before the conference began, the Canadian government finally approved the Southeast Asian women's visas.[41] By this time, it was too late, as some women who did not hear about the conference until February or March were already angry and frustrated at being left out. Unsurprisingly, some white feminists and many women of color did not appreciate having a conference planned for them.

The secrecy imposed on organizers also hampered the task of selecting a diverse set of delegates to attend the conference. In mid-January, the IWC conference hosts in Canada informed U.S. women that they could only find spaces that would hold five hundred women for the "liberation" conferences in Toronto and Vancouver, allowing two hundred U.S. women's liberationists on each coast to attend the IWC. For women's liberation organizers on the East Coast, allotting a certain number of delegates to each region seemed the best way to include a broad swath of feminists. Selecting delegates to attend the IWC did not seem like a problem at first but quickly grew into one, largely because no comprehensive national, or even regional, network of women's liberation groups existed. The organizers ended up defining the regions and distributing delegate slots rather arbitrarily, leading to a mishmash of representatives. Whereas each region for the Toronto conference, East, South, and Midwest, could send roughly the same number of delegates (67, 66, and 67, respectively), the Midwest encompassed areas as far east as upstate New York and western Pennsylvania and as far south as Arkansas.

With this broad definition of "Midwest," the region easily filled its allotted slots. By contrast, organizers in the South scrambled to find women to attend the IWC. Another problem was that many states were included in name only. Although one subregion purportedly consisted of Missouri, Kansas, Iowa, Nebraska, and Arkansas, all six subregional contacts lived in Missouri. In contrast, WSP leaders asked members to send nominations to a central committee, which then selected a cross-spectrum of participants. In the hopes of being more inclusive, women's liberation organizers actually created a more exclusionary and irregular process by leaving the selection of delegates up to unrepresentative contacts in each subregion and city.[42]

Women's liberation organizers also decided to involve more women in the conference planning process than could attend the conference itself—an unusual decision that caused more headaches than anything else. Because organizers wanted to make sure that all women had a chance to have their voices heard, they decided not to have particular individuals designated to attend subregional or regional meetings. Instead, women rotated on and off committees in an arbitrary fashion. Having felt their own exclusion in mixed-gender groups where women rarely held leadership positions, organizers feared impeding other women's participation and imperializing the conference planning process. But the result caused considerable disconnects from one meeting to the next. It also meant that when newcomers disagreed with decisions made previously, they could and would rehash and remake those decisions at subsequent meetings.[43]

Despite organizers' intention to be as inclusive as possible, the expressed indignation of women not fully included in the planning process came to their attention when a feminist group in Detroit began distributing a booklet called *Fourth World Manifesto*, attacking plans for the IWC. In the manifesto, the Detroit group made it clear that it felt patronized by the educational packet distributed by IWC organizers in December because it was "self-evident" that feminists should be concerned with imperialism—after all, women were the first group of people to be imperialized, it argued.[44] According to the manifesto, the reason conference organizers could not see the simplicity of the issue was because their interpretation of imperialism was one defined by men. The Detroit group urged other women's liberationists not to participate in conference planning but to crash the IWC instead. Women in D.C. and Boston decided that organizers in the Detroit area should speak with the women's liberation group without delay, but organizers in Detroit neglected to do so, and several weeks passed before the Collective in D.C. finally sent a letter to the Detroit women's liberation group correcting some of the misinformation.[45] By then, the damage was done.

All the while, women's liberation organizers ignored the fact that they were not actually co-organizing the IWC alongside women of color in rights-based movements as planned. Rather, women's liberationists and women of color met separately to discuss preparations for the conference. Notwithstanding the inclusion of a few women of color in planning meetings following the WIDF Budapest conference, women from the Third World Women's Caucus in Los Angeles felt that they had been "denied an equal participation *with* white groups" in the planning of the conference (emphasis in original).[46] Although women in the caucus believed that the conference, if organized properly, could build international solidarity among women, it could only do so if women of color took leadership positions and had direct contact with Southeast Asian women. Instead, they claimed women of color had little to no information about conference preparations, were treated as go-betweens for peace activists and women's liberationists who could not agree, and were used as tokens at meetings rather than treated as true participants. The Third World Women's Caucus rebuked white women who showed great interest in the struggles of Southeast Asian women but virtually ignored the struggles of people of color in the United States. Consequently, the Los Angeles group requested separate sessions with the Laotian and Vietnamese delegations in Vancouver because it did not believe women of color could participate equally in sessions that included white women. By February 1971, women's liberationists agreed to the caucus's request. Conference organizers on the West Coast decided to hold separate conferences for peace activists, women in "Third World" movements, and women's liberationists in Vancouver. Peace activists met with the Laotian and Vietnamese women on the first day; women of color met with them on the second and third days; and women's liberationists met with them on the fourth and fifth days.[47] In this case, conflict led to segregation.

On the East Coast, preparations for a single "liberation" conference continued with the assumption that women's liberationists and women in "Third World" movements would meet with the Southeast Asian women at the same time. While women's liberation organizers did not ask whether what they wanted to learn from the IWC was the same as what "Third World" women wanted to learn, women of color had decided that the IWC's current format did not fit their needs. As a result, the night before the "liberation" portion of the Toronto conference began, the plan to hold a joint conference started to unravel. Problems began when a few women of color, who had not previously collaborated with white feminists in organizing the IWC, appointed themselves to the Service Committee (a smaller committee in charge of last-minute decisions) and were permitted to do so because women's liberation organizers' desire for inclusivity allowed women to rotate on and off committees. The new women proceeded to overturn decisions previously made at meetings in the months and weeks leading up to the IWC. After four hours of negotiation, the Service Committee members compromised on a new format for the conference. The following day, however, an hour before registration for the IWC began, two additional women of color joined the Service Committee and told women's liberation organizers that they were canceling the cultural event planned for that evening and replacing it with discussions between women of color and Southeast Asian women. Further limiting the participation of women's liberationists at the IWC, these two women of color also suggested that women's liberation delegates should have only one session with which to meet the Southeast Asian women during the entire three-day conference. At that point, the conference effectively split, with women of color and women's liberationists meeting with the Southeast Asian women separately and with the cultural event greatly diminished.[48] Once more, disagreement over the setup of the IWC led to a segregation of attendees, a development not conducive to community building.

Women's liberation delegates, who did not know about the last-minute changes, felt greatly disappointed in the conference, and they blamed those in charge, the "elitist pigs."[49] With such accusations flying, women's liberation organizers chose to hide rather than explain the situation. While women of color came together to collect questions and to decide which topics they would discuss in which sessions, the women's liberation organizers floundered. Putting together a new conference schedule on such short notice created poorly run sessions with much unnecessary overlap. The frustration of women's liberation delegates did little to promote unity among them and fostered little productive discussion.[50]

Furthermore, the disagreements among women's liberationists anticipated by the Detroit group's *Fourth World Manifesto* tainted the IWC. Feminists quarreled with one another over whether one could be both anti-imperialist and feminist and over who defined what those terms meant. Although an Asian American delegation from the Bay Area brushed off the distinction between anti-imperialism and feminism as "a false dichotomy," the debate among women's liberationists permeated the conferences on both coasts.[51] While some feminist groups agreed with the Detroit women that they were in danger of being co-opted by women working in mixed-gender leftist organizations, others maintained that challenging imperialism and resisting the war was a way to combat sexism. Instead of discussing these differences of opinion, women's liberationists "showed a great lack of respect and humanity toward each other," observed Donna, a Chicana delegate in Vancouver.[52] Kathleen Gough, a Canadian feminist who also attended the Vancouver conference, believed women's liberation groups were "the most disparate and disorganized" because the delegates failed "to recognize the need for leadership, organization, and conventions of public as distinct from small-group behavior."[53] Instead, women's liberation organizers insisted that "freedom was individual autonomy" and sabotaged their own ability to orchestrate the conference.[54] Another feminist bemoaned the inability of white women to connect with African American women and the inability of white women to put aside their differences in order to build coalitions with one another. Unlike women of color at the conference, who "seemed to trust that [their] differences would work themselves out through struggle," white women honed in on areas of disagreement.[55]

The size of the "intimate" sessions between Southeast Asian and North American women may in part explain why women's liberation organizers did not fully achieve the unity they desired among American women. These discussions included two Southeast Asian women and fifty to sixty North American women. This imbalance differed greatly from what women experienced in Hanoi or at other international conferences, where the ratio of Southeast Asian to North American women was closer to one-to-one. Without Vietnamese women's ability to bridge differences, divisions based on class, lifestyle, and "level of consciousness" came to the forefront.[56]

Nevertheless, an article published in *off our backs*, a women's liberation journal, echoed Alice Wolfson's sentiment when it called the Southeast Asian women at the conference "sisters" to whom all North American women could relate.[57] This declaration vindicated the hopes of women's liberation organizers who had assumed women would have a particular emotional response to meeting Southeast Asian women—one that would unite U.S. women and show why women should work against the war as a way of combatting sexism. Many reports on the IWC portrayed American women as rallying around the Southeast Asian women whose stories of the war drove home the fact that the war was waged peculiarly against women (and children). For example, Nguyen Thi Xiem, a gynecologist and obstetrician from North Viet Nam, showed slides of babies malformed as a result of exposure to chemical defoliants, of wombs perforated with pellets from antipersonnel bombs, and of malnourished children living underground. While these photos brought conference attendees to tears, Xiem's delineation of U.S. bombing sequences, which seemed to target civilians, angered many. Xiem explained that first the U.S. military would bomb a village, then drop napalm to burn houses and cause villagers to leave bomb shelters. While villagers fought the fires, U.S. planes would drop antipersonnel pellet bombs, killing and injuring civilians—primarily women and children.[58] Thus, for Xiem, both the weapons and tactics of the U.S. war caused undue harm to women.

In South Viet Nam, women suffered from similar air attacks as in the North, as well as from wrongful arrest. South Vietnamese delegate Dinh Thi Huong recounted her years in the South Vietnamese prison system, during which time she underwent and witnessed torture. She spoke in detail about the abuses that she experienced and described the prison environment, in which up to thirty-two people, including children born in prison, lived in a ten foot by five foot cell with little food, no clothing, and no bathing facilities. Huong's persecution had not ended upon her release, as her daughter, who was nineteen in 1971, had been imprisoned four times since the age of thirteen. Huong had not heard from her daughter since her last imprisonment in 1970. Huong also insisted that she had had little involvement in the revolutionary struggle against the Saigon administration until she experienced firsthand the inhumanity of prison conditions. Her story not only highlighted the inhumane conditions in which South Vietnamese political prisoners were held but also pointed out that Saigon imprisoned innocent "housewives"—as she claimed to have been at the time of her arrest.[59] Following imprisonment, Huong and other women joined the resistance movement to prevent others from "suffer[ing] the same fate."[60] Nevertheless, under Nixon's Vietnamization program, the Saigon administration arrested even more Vietnamese as political prisoners, according to Huong and other Vietnamese delegates.[61] For those reporting on the IWC, Huong's story illustrated the unjustness of a war that promoted the imprisonment and torture of innocent women as well as their children.

In a continuing effort to reveal the violence of the U.S. military perpetrated against Southeast Asian women, after the IWC, women's liberation authors identified "special tortures against women."[62] For example, the insertion of foreign objects into vaginas, the removal of women's breasts, and the lack of sanitary care provided for imprisoned, menstruating women all highlighted "that the struggle against the Indochina war is intimately related to the struggle by women everywhere for dignity and equality."[63] The Southeast Asian delegates also spoke of rape, increased prostitution in South Viet Nam, the separation of parents from children and husbands from wives, and the torture of children as psychological warfare against mothers as ways in which war was waged not only against women but also against Vietnamese (and Laotian) society. "The totalizing effects of the war continue to make it impossible to distinguish the liberation of women from national liberation," stated white feminist Sheila Rowbotham.[64] In this way, the Southeast Asian women helped women's liberationists make connections between war and women's rights by taking war out of the male realm. For feminists, the war deprived Southeast Asian women living in combat zones of their rights—to control their bodies, to live and work in a safe environment, and to raise their children as they saw fit.[65]

Even with these intellectual connections of the war with feminist demands, women's liberation organizers wanted to declare a common enemy. They spoke of "imperialism" as the root cause of oppression of all peoples—people of color in the United States, white women, and Southeast Asians alike. In this way, fighting imperialism undermined racism, sexism, and the war, and resisting racism, sexism, or the war were forms of fighting imperialism. In exhortations such as "Sexism and Imperialism," "Women and Imperialism," and "Imperialism and the Oppression of Women," women's liberation organizers made sexism one pillar upholding imperialism and created a common ground on which to collaborate with women of color in the United States and Southeast Asian women fighting "U.S. aggressors."[66] This language also mirrored that of some rights-based activists of color, who stated that U.S. imperialism was the common enemy of all "Third World" peoples. When asked at the conference how to form unity between diverse groups of North Americans, the Southeast Asian delegates similarly urged their American counterparts to recognize that all of their problems stemmed from "U.S. imperialism" and declared the U.S. administration the common enemy of all those present. The Southeast Asian delegates also suggested that the first goal of U.S. activists should be to end U.S. involvement in Viet Nam because the war exacerbated domestic issues such as unemployment, racism, and poverty. Thus, the focus on resisting forms of "U.S. imperialism" stemmed in part from the Southeast Asian women's advice as well as from feminists' search for a common enemy.[67]

In line with the Cold War mindset pitting the capitalist West against the communist East, women's liberation writers tended to portray the contemporary version of imperialism as unique to capitalist societies. For example, one essay defined imperialism as "the external thrust which makes the continued growth of capitalism possible," and another called imperialism the "international face" of capitalism.[68] Describing multinational corporations' desire for profit as the driving force behind U.S. expansion into foreign markets as well as the reason for the U.S. government's involvement in other nations, women's liberation organizers saw the selling of American values and goods abroad as imperialism. The Southeast Asian delegates encouraged this perception of the U.S. government as imperialist and of capitalism as the impetus for repression inside and outside the United States. Although the Vietnamese reiterated that they did not blame the American public or individual GIs for the destruction of their nation, the U.S. administration and its imperialistic tendencies should be held accountable, according to the Vietnamese delegates. They went so far as to call for members of the Johnson and Nixon administrations to be charged with war crimes. In this way, Americans and the Vietnamese delegates distinguished the U.S. government from the American people and blamed capitalism for the destruction in Southeast Asia as well as the repression of women and people of color in the United States.[69]

Identifying imperialism as a common enemy, IWC delegates and organizers looked to Vietnamese women as the vanguard in women's struggle for liberation. Drawings of Vietnamese women carrying a baby and a gun proliferated on the front pages of women's liberation periodicals, in advertisements, and on fliers.[70] Going along with these images, articles about the IWC described Vietnamese women's revolutionary roles. In one such article, an Asian American woman at the Toronto conference credited WUL delegate Phan Minh Hien with alluding to the mass participation of women in military endeavors. "Coming from the battlefield," Hien addressed conference participants, "we bring you warmest greetings from the fighting women of South Vietnam."[71] She continued, "From the mountains to the plains, women, irrespective of age, are taking part in the revolution."[72] Likewise, a Vancouver conference participant wrote that the two Laotian delegates, who were primary school teachers, participated in the struggle by teaching children how to make wooden weapons. The Southeast Asian delegates also told stories of women who encountered Laotian or South Vietnamese soldiers, invited them to dine and drink, and once the soldiers were drunk, captured them.[73] Another participant at the Vancouver conference described Dinh Thi Huong, the woman imprisoned for years in South Viet Nam, as more than a victim of the Saigon administration—she was an "exemplary fighter."[74] Creating this image of Southeast Asian women as revolutionaries lent itself to looking to Vietnamese society for solutions to U.S. women's oppression.

If "U.S. imperialism" and capitalism were the problems, socialism was often the solution. Some women's liberationists, such as Osterud, had socialist parents, grandparents, and even great-grandparents, so the concept was not necessarily a new one. For Osterud, socialism provided a historical view of the movement for a more egalitarian society, a struggle that took generations. Therefore, she saw certain gendered expressions of discontent—vandalism often incited and carried out by men—as shortsighted and damaging to the overall goals of antiwar protests.[75] Censuring this destruction as a particular performance of masculinity prevalent within some antiwar circles, feminists looked to women in socialist societies for guidance.

To learn more about the process of building socialism as well as its benefits for women, women's liberation organizers asked the Southeast Asian delegates at the IWC to elaborate on women's newfound roles.[76] In response, the two VWU members described how women's lives had changed since the downfall of feudalism and colonialism and the rise of socialism in North Viet Nam, asserting that they had gained equality with men. Resembling reports VWU members often provided at international conferences as well as at meetings with U.S. visitors in Hanoi, the VWU delegates explained that, under feudalism, men could marry any number of wives, they controlled all property, and women had no right to an education. Under colonialism, women had no citizenship rights. With the combination of feudalism and colonialism, women had no ability to live independently. However, during the struggle for national liberation, women fought for their social, political, and economic rights simultaneously. "After our independence was achieved in the North, we began socialist construction. Then came the real equality of men and women," one of the VWU delegates declared.[77] According to VWU members, decolonization itself did not free women from male dominance, but the adoption of socialism did.[78]

VWU members went on to detail the benefits of a socialist society by listing gains North Vietnamese women had achieved. In the new revolutionary government, women held positions in the National Assembly and, closer to home, as village chairpersons, district-level committee members, and provincial committee members. Women also played important roles as guerrilla fighters, making up one-third of the defensive military commanders in villages. They transported ammunition, shot down planes, and protected their neighbors. Half of the students in high school were girls, and at the university level, a little less than half of the students were women. About 5,000 women were doctors or engineers, and approximately 50 percent of workers in factories, schools, and health clinics were women. With this kind of shift from women having little to no access to education to making up a fair number of politicians, educators, and guerrilla fighters, the VWU advertised the possibilities for women under socialism.[79] Thus, one conference attendee declared, "The [Vietnamese] Women's Union [has] laid the groundwork for the liberation of women."[80]

The VWU delegates promoted this interpretation by relating how socialism bettered their own lives. For example, Nguyen Thi Xiem, the obstetrician, spoke of the opportunities she received in North Viet Nam that would have been unavailable to her in the South. According to Xiem, because of the revolutionary gender roles in the North, she could become a doctor and carry out revolutionary work. She did so at the Hanoi Institute for the Preservation of Mothers and Newborns, where she searched for cures to diseases brought to North Viet Nam by American troops; she also treated war injuries. Conference attendees picked up on Xiem's newfound opportunities in a socialist society and quoted her as saying that she was "glad that I am not in South Vietnam like my mother and sister."[81] This statement implied that because of socialist policies in the North, Xiem had more freedom than did the women in the South living under capitalism.

In reality, North Vietnamese women's rights and desires would have disappointed many women's liberationists because the society still relied heavily on women's maternal roles. The two VWU delegates asserted that all women in the DRV wanted to have families and children, acknowledged that mothers still held primary responsibility for children, and verified that boys and girls were taught gender roles from a young age (one example was that boys would play ball, whereas girls would play with dolls). Although the North Vietnamese government provided day care, made abortion accessible, and created more equitable marriage and divorce laws, most Vietnamese still believed "a good woman is a good housewife."[82] Furthermore, despite Vietnamese women's clear assertions that sexism in Vietnamese society stemmed from feudalism and Confucianism established in Viet Nam during Chinese imperialism, some feminist analyses erased this history, making it seem as if sexism began as well as ended with capitalism and U.S. imperialism. This universalizing of the manifestation of sexism also made it seem natural that Vietnamese women wanted and had achieved the same rights that women's liberationists fought for in the United States. Immediately following the conference, several articles touted North Vietnamese women as having attained economic, social, and political equality, and only one mentioned any shortcomings.[83] Although in time this enthusiasm would fade, some feminists' inclination toward socialism led to simplifying the nature of and solution to sexism.

Even so, this exchange of ideas about the nature of war and its effect on women everywhere helped feminists establish a foundation on which to study women and gender during war.[84] By first recognizing women's oppression as well as the oppression of others based on race, class, and nationality, some women's liberationists could begin to see connections between struggles. Making these connections confirmed for some that U.S. imperialism and capitalism were the root causes of oppression, and socialism provided the solution to all manifestations of discrimination. Women's liberationists clearly desired to form a new society and looked to the Southeast Asian delegates to tell them how.[85] They held up North Vietnamese society, in particular, as a paragon of equality while criticizing U.S.-influenced South Viet Nam as an example of capitalism's adverse effects, including sexism. For these feminists, North Vietnamese women embodied the ideal revolutionary woman—a woman who not only had legal, economic, and educational equality but also could control her own body, express her opinions, and defend herself. The quintessential vision of a new society these women's liberationists promoted even stemmed from Vietnamese folklore. Citing a Vietnamese proverb, Bread and Roses members wrote that hell was sitting down to a banquet and finding chopsticks too long to use to reach one's mouth, whereas heaven was the same banquet but at which the people fed each other.[86] While this vision of a new society provided some women's liberationists with something to fight *for* instead of just against, their celebration of the North Vietnamese prevented them from recognizing some of the limits on women's rights in the DRV.

Nevertheless, women's crossing of social movement and national borders pushed them to see the war in different terms. While some women's liberationists sought to build and sustain coalitions with antiwar and other organizations, conflict with other women's liberationists, women of color, and peace activists alike momentarily impeded such efforts. Nonetheless, the IWC provided the opportunity to gather more evidence and to develop further ideas on the nature of war. Some feminists understood and theorized connections between many of the 1960s social movements as they sought to create a movement that spoke to the whole of their concerns and not just distinct parts. Although the IWC did not succeed in the way women's liberation organizers hoped—by building an antiwar, anti-imperialist, feminist coalition among conference participants—organizers created a space in which they could discuss the interconnectedness of struggles against racism, sexism, and imperialism.

As the war continued, activists persisted in contrasting the North and South Vietnamese societies in order to call into question which side of the war the United States should be on. While white women's liberationists had first made connections between power, violence, and American masculinity in the months leading up to the IWC, female peace activists traveling to Hanoi and Saigon followed suit as they considered how U.S. actions in South Viet Nam evidenced larger societal problems within the United States.

CHAPTER FIVE

Connecting U.S. Intervention with Social Injustice, 1970–1972

Returning to Paris six months after the April 1968 Conference of Concerned Women to End the War as a member of the first NLF delegation to the peace talks, Nguyen Thi Binh appreciated the warm welcome she received from Vietnamese expatriates, French citizens, and members of the international community living in France. She remembered that on the day formal talks between the DRV, RVN, NLF, and United States began in January 1969, crowds of people outside the Kleber International Conference Center waved NLF and DRV flags, demonstrating their support.[1] Even though Binh herself attended the official diplomatic sessions between foreign ministers, she and many of her colleagues in the DRV and NLF delegations believed in the potential of international antiwar activities to force an end to the U.S. war. When Binh was back in Hanoi for a brief visit in April 1969, Ho Chi Minh even "reminded [her] about the importance of taking part in the campaigns of people from different countries, since these ordinary people were the ones who truly valued justice and peace."[2] When Binh became foreign minister of the newly formed PRG in June 1969, she heeded Ho Chi Minh by maintaining old contacts and developing new ones with individuals and citizen organizations around the world.[3]

For Binh and other Vietnamese, having Paris as the setting for the peace talks contributed to establishing and maintaining antiwar networks because it was easily accessible to activists from Europe and North America as well as home to a significant and sympathetic Vietnamese community.[4] Phan Thi Minh and Nguyen Ngoc Dung spearheaded people's diplomatic efforts in Paris as members of Nguyen Thi Binh's delegation along with Binh's personal secretary, Nguyen Binh Thanh. In a recent interview, Minh recalled that her primary task was to collaborate with antiwar activists from around the world in order to determine what the international community thought of the present situation in Viet Nam and the current state of peace negotiations.[5] Through the information gathered for her by Minh, Ngoc Dung, and Thanh, Nguyen Thi Binh "mobiliz[ed] international support for our Resistance Movement."[6] The three women also worked with Maria Jolas, a French woman, to build international women's networks as part of the strategy to incite global antiwar protest.[7] Jolas helped to maintain contact with WSP members and women's liberation groups in the United States, setting up dinners and interviews between Vietnamese and American activists visiting Paris.[8]

At these meetings, Ngoc Dung, Thanh, and Minh contrasted women's roles under feudalism and colonialism with stories of Vietnamese society's acceptance of women's liberation under the influence of the DRV and PRG. They simultaneously asserted that "Vietnamese women have no higher desire than to . . . live . . . [with] our families, our husbands, and our children," and blamed the U.S. military for inflicting untold damage on Vietnamese society.[9] Upholding heterosexual family life as ideal, "liberation" for these Vietnamese women meant that women should receive an education and have job opportunities while men took on a share of the domestic chores.[10] Although this definition would have dissatisfied some feminists, Nguyen Thi Binh's poised, determined, and feminine presence on the world stage inspired countless women in different walks of life around the world. One women's group credited Binh with waking up British women to international relations when they organized a successful blood drive for Vietnamese in the North.[11] Women in the United States designed and wore t-shirts with the image of Binh printed on them and the caption "Live Like Her." For these women, Binh symbolized revolutionary gender roles that might or might not include having a family. The VWU contrasted images of women living in the North who had gained equality with those of "our dear sisters in the South [who] have still to face extremely barbarous repressions."[12] The task for Vietnamese women was to "liberate the South, defend the North."[13] Liberation itself was a two-step process, as the RVN first needed to be freed from foreign invasion; only then could women in the South gain the same rights as women in the North.

Complementing the PRG women's efforts, U.S. woman activists continued to travel to Viet Nam—both North and South. The context of American women's activism had shifted in two significant ways, however. First, the incarceration of Vietnamese political prisoners in South Viet Nam in "tiger cages" came to light when a congressional committee visited the RVN's infamous Con Son prison on an island about 140 miles southeast of Saigon on July 2, 1970.[14] Vietnamese and U.S. women used this discovery to portray the South Vietnamese as inhumane captors, in contrast to their counterparts in the North. Second, the context of growing feminist sentiment both domestically and internationally colored the views of female peace activists and realigned the goals of U.S. women's organizations such as WSP and the Women's International League for Peace and Freedom (WILPF). The U.S. military's complicity in the deplorable prison conditions in the South led WSP and WILPF members to perceive social inequalities in the United States as they also noted the distinguished positions of women in North Viet Nam. They came to describe Vietnamese women in the North as having gained "liberation," and they claimed that South Vietnamese society had actually deteriorated because of U.S. intervention. As women brought to light the ways in which U.S. involvement in Viet Nam worsened the situation for Vietnamese women, they also developed critiques of U.S. society, foreign policy, and gender roles.

This phenomenon contrasts with the more commonly told narrative of Western women's "rescue" of Eastern women. For decades, women's historians have highlighted instances when white Western women have supported imperialist endeavors by declaring that women in colonies needed to be saved from their traditional cultures. Scholars have shown that Western women asserted their own authority and claimed their own rights through these efforts.[15] More recently, scholarship on U.S. military pursuits in the late twentieth and early twenty-first centuries has noted that U.S. feminists and others have similarly called for U.S. military intervention in nation-states as a way of rescuing women who lacked rights.[16] Although in this case women's rights remained central to feminists' and other female activists' discussions on war and imperialism, U.S. women sought to collaborate with Vietnamese women, not save them from Vietnamese culture.

For the VWU, NLF, and American activists alike, U.S. intervention in South Viet Nam impeded women's rights from taking root and caused women's inequality. The NLF argued this point by enumerating the social ills in the South, including the increase in prostitution and pornography (loosening sexual mores was in no means seen as liberating for women) and blaming recent negative foreign influences for this degeneracy.[17] Sixty-seven-year-old white WSP and Church Women United member Anne McGrew Bennett put forward a similar explanation for distinctions she observed in northern and southern Vietnamese societies. Bennett visited South Viet Nam in May 1969 as part of a team of politicians, activists, and religious leaders investigating religious and political freedom; in December 1970, she participated in a COLIAFAM-sponsored mission to deliver letters to POWs held in North Viet Nam. Following her trips, she came to the conclusion that Saigon was "a corrupt slum dominated by Americans," and she contrasted this image with that of the people of Hanoi, who "moved with a certain posture of dignity and pride."[18]

As evidence of the negative influence Americans had in Viet Nam, Bennett cited the unsanitary prison conditions and the repression of religious leaders, all under the supervision of U.S. advisors in the South. The May 1969 team of American investigators in the RVN visited three prisons and spoke to numerous religious leaders and followers. During the tour of Chi Hoa prison, a civilian correctional facility in Saigon where 5,000 men and 100 boys lived, Bennett claimed she saw only one bed in the entire facility, and it was reserved for Truong Dinh Dzu, who had lost the 1967 presidential election. The rest of the prisoners had to sleep on the bare floor in cells scarcely big enough for all of them to lie down at once.[19] At Con Son prison, where the congressional committee would find tiger cages a year later, Bennett recalled that prison officials openly admitted that over 40 percent of the prisoners had never been tried, let alone sentenced, and guards even defended the imprisonment of religious and political leaders who advocated negotiation with Hanoi.[20] Such undisguised oppression alarmed Bennett as she tried to understand the role of the United States in upholding such draconian measures.

Officially, the team on which Bennett participated recommended changes to U.S. policy that could improve prison conditions in the South, but Bennett's inclination before and after her trip was to end U.S. intervention in Viet Nam, not mend it.[21] She had been active in WSP for years, attending the April 1968 Paris Conference of Concerned Women, where she found "compassion and understanding are not held within national boundaries."[22] She also attended international Christian conferences and encouraged churchwomen to take part in peace conversations. With an appreciation for transnational collaboration, Bennett decided to take it on herself to do more than suggest policy changes to end the injustices she witnessed in South Viet Nam.

Continuing her investigation into political and religious freedom in Viet Nam, a year and a half later Bennett traveled to Hanoi with a young white couple, Ron and Trudi Young (Schutz) of the Fellowship of Reconciliation and WSP, respectively. They were hosted by the Committee for Solidarity with the American People (Viet-My), the sister organization to COLIAFAM. Although Bennett had already witnessed deplorable prison conditions in South Viet Nam, the group requested a meeting with a former NLF POW in order to compare the treatment of POWs on both sides of the war. The Viet-My readily complied, introducing the Americans to an escaped NLF POW on Christmas Day 1970. Huynh Thi Kien, a twenty-two-year-old guerrilla woman, told Bennett that she had joined the NLF to avenge the deaths of family members in the mid-1960s (see Figure 6). Before long, however, she was captured, questioned, and tortured by ARVN soldiers. When ARVN interrogators asked her the location of the local NLF camp, she refused to answer. In response, her captors cut off her leg at the knee, allegedly in the presence of U.S. advisors. After she recovered from this incident, ARVN soldiers again took her to the interrogation room and tried to intimidate her by saying that her leg was still too long. Even so, Kien refused to talk and lost her leg at the thigh because of her silence, again allegedly under the supervision of U.S. advisors. Later, she escaped with the aid of a nurse in the prison hospital and, through the underground NLF network, made her way to Hanoi for treatment.[23] To finish this woman's story, Bennett wrote, "Huynh Thi Giong [sic], standing on one leg, swaying slightly, was like a bell tolling—calling for an end to atrocities."[24] Reducing Kien to an object with a singular purpose, Bennett reminded the world of the harm being done in South Viet Nam under the guidance of the U.S. military.

This simple message did not do justice to Kien's story for the VWU, however. In its published account, Kien continued to help the war effort after her medical treatment by becoming a nurse. Her own sacrifices had even been avenged by her fellow guerrilla fighters, who, during the Tet Offensive of 1968, killed those who had tortured her. Revenge, determination, and justified violence appeared throughout the VWU's rendition of Kien's story.[25] But Bennett only included Vietnamese determination to win in her account as she portrayed the North Vietnamese as humane, benevolent, and forgiving victims.

As for American POWs, Bennett seemed to have little doubt of their care. Nevertheless, Bennett and the Youngs wanted to speak with POWs to counter naysayers such as California congressman John Schmitz, who predicted that the DRV would hold POWs "hostage" and try them as war criminals once U.S. pressure—meaning a U.S. military presence in Viet Nam—to release them was lifted.[26] Compromising the ability of Bennett's group to meet POWs, however, was the recent unsuccessful Son Tay prison raid undertaken by the U.S. military in November 1970.[27] For a week, Bennett and her companions waited to hear whether they would be permitted to visit a POW detention center. In the end, Hanoi arranged an interview, allowing Bennett to respond to the kinds of arguments that Schmitz made by asserting her credentials as a people's diplomat and an expert on the war; unlike Schmitz, she had actually spoken with Vietnamese who looked after captured pilots.[28]

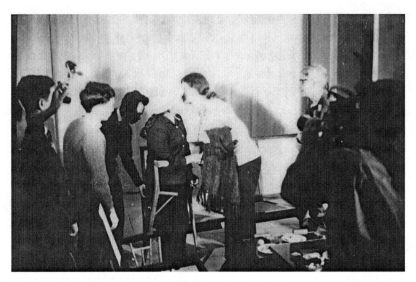

FIGURE 6 Huynh Thi Kien, Trudi [Schutz] Young, and Anne McGrew Bennett with Vietnamese hosts and photographers. Photo from Contact Sheets 15-16B, Negative Numbered 5A-6, Box 4, Folder 9, Anne McGrew Bennett Collection, GTU 89-5-017, Graduate Theological Union Archives, Berkeley, California.

Bennett's description of the POW camp in Hanoi provided evidence of the mercifulness of the Vietnamese. Pulling up to a detention center at 8 o'clock at night, Bennett immediately juxtaposed its appearance with prisons she had visited in the RVN as well as in the United States. From the outside, it looked like any other building: children played nearby, villagers left bicycles propped against the gate, and cabbage grew right up to the entrance. Even upon entering, the atmosphere continued to belie the purpose of the building. The guards had no visible weapons and did not search the group. At the center of the prison was a garden, which according to Bennett resembled a quadrangle found in many colleges and seminaries in the United States. To Bennett, the POW camp seemed warm and comfortable, unlike the "fortified, cold, harsh" prisons of South Viet Nam or the United States.[29]

Her conversation with the warden also impressed on her a feeling of openness and truthfulness she had not found in South Viet Nam a year earlier. The warden greeted the group amicably and invited questions, but ultimately wanted the Americans to judge for themselves whether the North Vietnamese treated POWs humanely. Telling his visitors "What you have heard a hundred times is not as good as what you have seen once," the warden gained their trust.[30] After this brief interview, he led Bennett and the Youngs to rooms where a few POWs lived. Pushing aside bamboo blinds, the group found five American servicemen in a twelve foot by eighteen foot room with three single beds. It had doors connecting to two more rooms with three and two beds, respectively, and at the end was a smaller room where the men could make tea or coffee whenever they wanted. The three American civilians sat on one bed while the five POWs sat across from them on the two other beds in the room. The warden, along with an interpreter and a few guards, stood near the entrance, and Vietnamese photographers moved around, taking pictures of the scene.

Bennett and the Youngs had half an hour to interview the POWs, during which time the Vietnamese remained silent. The interpreter spoke up only once, to tell the group when there were two minutes remaining. With the short time allotted for the meeting, Bennett and the Youngs had made a list of what they wanted to know, including the POWs' story of imprisonment, medical treatment, ability to speak with other captured pilots, and regularity of mail delivery. They also offered to answer questions and to deliver special messages to family members. The five men requested that Bennett and the Youngs assure their families that they were in good health and were treated well.[31] They spoke of their daily routine and showed the group Christmas packages they had recently received as evidence of their fair treatment.[32] The stories of the POWs' captures also indicated the dignity North Vietnamese civilians and the military afforded the men. Although all five had expected abuse, the villagers who had taken them captive greeted them with proud smiles rather than vengeful sneers. In some cases, the men stayed with villagers for weeks until the proper authorities could pick them up, and the villagers shared their food and shelter with them. Two of the men had been injured when they crashed, and doctors had treated their injuries in a timely and effective manner. Bennett asserted that neither had permanent handicaps or noticeable scars.[33] This last detail must have sharply contrasted in the minds of Bennett and the Youngs with the image of Kien, whom they had met just hours before. Although one cannot know whether the men spoke candidly or whether the camp Bennett visited was truly representative, this meeting influenced Bennett's portrayal of North and South Vietnamese society, confirmed her views on U.S. intervention, and shaped her future activism.

The disparity between prison conditions for POWs in the North and political prisoners in the South paralleled distinctions between the societies in Hanoi and Saigon, according to Bennett. In Saigon, the corruption of prison officials went hand-in-hand with that of the people on the street, who sold everything from stolen goods to their own bodies. The people themselves were not to blame, as they were refugees from the countryside who were forced into the city with little support from the Saigon government or the U.S. military. They had little recourse but to turn to crime to survive.[34] Bennett's condemnation of the role of the United States in creating the social ills she encountered in Saigon echoed that of her Vietnamese counterparts. Similarly emphasizing the centrality of U.S. interference in creating and supporting vice, the VWU pointed out to American activists on several occasions that the 300,000 to 400,000 prostitutes in Saigon primarily served the GI population. Under these circumstances, depravity reigned while religious values, healthy living, and loyalty to family and country were thrown to the wayside.[35]

After having found such moral decay in the South, Bennett was especially interested in meeting with Buddhists and Catholics in the North. The Viet-My readily agreed and combined these meetings with its own agenda, which, according to Le Mai, an official who worked with the Viet-My hosting American delegations, continued to be to show visitors war crimes committed by the U.S. military.[36] Therefore, it is not surprising that Bennett's first encounter with Catholics in the North highlighted this destruction. Traveling seventy-five miles south of Hanoi to Ninh Binh Province, before 1954 a center of Catholicism, Bennett and the Youngs spoke with the acting mother superior, Hoang Thi Ngo, at a convent. Sister Ngo stated that, beginning in 1954, after the Geneva Agreement had been signed, RVN propagandists tried to convince Catholics to move to South Viet Nam by saying that "Jesus Christ has gone south."[37] RVN officials could then use the relocation of Catholics to claim that religious repression existed in the DRV, according to Sister Ngo. The intervening years had been costly to the order, as evidenced by the ruins of the Catholic compound in which the group met with her. But neither the migration of Catholics to the South nor the nation's adoption of communism had caused the disrepair. Sister Ngo told the group that on March 11, 1968, U.S. bombers razed the cathedral, cemetery, monastery, and convent school, killing six nuns, including the mother superior. Thus, it was the U.S. military, not Hanoi, that obstructed the growth of Catholicism in North Viet Nam. Despite this destruction, Bennett found that Catholicism not only existed but thrived in the DRV, when she attended Christmas Eve midnight mass in Hanoi. She claimed she had never seen St. Patrick's Cathedral in New York City as packed as the cathedral in Hanoi that night; attendance was so great that many parishioners had to stand outside the church in the square.[38] This scene, as well as her observations of the prison systems in North and South Viet Nam, forced Bennett to ask why the North seemed to be so much more just, dignified, and moral than the South. She concluded that the United States had brought negative influences to the South, so she turned her attention back to U.S. society.

The apparent contrast in Vietnamese societies confirmed Bennett's opposition to U.S. intervention in Viet Nam as it also led her to challenge prescribed U.S. gender roles and current Christian practices. Within a year of her December 1970 trip, she began to speak out and connected problematic performances of masculinity with larger issues in the church and in the nation. As a Christian feminist, she asked at a commencement speech to the Union Theological Seminary in 1972, "Could it be that the drive for dominance, power [and] control by men is rooted in an identification of the male sex with the attributes of God?"[39] Referring to the Judeo-Christian origin story in which the first man is made in God's image, Bennett contemplated whether men felt the need to act in ways that proved their authority over other people and nations. She called for a redefinition of masculinity to prevent future military entanglements, as she connected her feminist, pacifist, and Christian beliefs in an evolving criticism of U.S. society.

Following Bennett's return to the United States from Hanoi, the treatment of political prisoners in the South took center stage for many female peace activists as an example of not just the deterioration of the society but also the tyranny that the United States supported. Groups, most notably the U.S. section of WILPF, solidified ties with those working in the "Third Force" in South Viet Nam—a movement dedicated to democracy but willing to negotiate with Hanoi and the PRG to end the war. Proponents of the Third Force faced imprisonment under President Thieu, making their stories of injustice distinctly palpable for WILPF members.

One advocate, Ngo Ba Thanh, received particular attention because she sought to bring women together to influence international relations. Her credentials as a middle-class educated Vietnamese mother and her previous connections to high-level government officials in Saigon also contributed to her being an attractive partner for U.S. women. Thanh was born in Hanoi in 1931 and received advanced degrees at universities in Europe and the United States in the 1950s, specializing in comparative law. A determined and energetic woman, she also had four children, whom she had to leave under the care of a relative living in France while she studied and taught. Thanh's husband was a marine scientist and moved to Saigon in the late 1950s to become director of the Fisheries Service under President Diem.

Thanh followed in the early 1960s when a colleague invited her to head a school of comparative law in Saigon. After relocating to South Viet Nam, Thanh organized the International Women's Association of Saigon,[40] bringing together ambassadors' wives from all over the world to further international cooperation.[41]

Thanh's position in the women's association also led to her visibility in diplomatic circles—a mixed blessing because she always spoke her mind, even when she attended government functions. Indeed, on one occasion, she told General William Westmoreland that he would lose the war if the United States chose to bomb North Viet Nam.[42] Her political beliefs mirrored those of her father, who was minister of labor and social affairs for the RVN. Despite her father's position in the Diem administration, he called for reconciliation between the two Viet Nams, causing his imprisonment on two occasions as well as his exile to North Viet Nam in 1965. From there, he moved to Cambodia in 1966 and finally to Paris in 1970, where he remained.[43] Following in her father's footsteps, Thanh became involved in antiwar activities and in 1966 was arrested for the first time. Released from prison in 1967, Thanh refused to be cowed. She more vehemently protested the war, denounced the Thieu administration, and called for negotiations with Hanoi and the NLF.[44] These activities led to a second arrest but did not impede Thanh's activism. At Thu Duc, a women's rehabilitation center primarily dedicated to teaching prostitutes new trades, Thanh undermined the authorities by knitting the words "peace" and "freedom" into sweaters and by educating her fellow inmates on the war.[45] It seems that any efforts to repress Thanh's activities made her even more determined to voice her objections to the Thieu administration.

Thanh's antiwar work also caused repercussions for her family. In the late 1960s, her husband lost his job as director of the Fisheries Service, and with his dismissal, the family lost their government housing. Thanh, never one to back down, threatened to move her family to the lawn of the Presidential Palace to show the world the treatment of a former government official because of his wife's peace activities.[46] Shortly after making this remark, Thanh's husband received an appointment as a professor at the Institute of Oceanography, a position that included housing. The new accommodations, however, came with police surveillance. Even so, Thanh continued her activism, writing antiwar newsletters and sending them out with her children to distribute. On one occasion, her youngest daughter, who was in her teens, was stopped by police as she left the house. They checked her bag for antiwar material, which, if it were found, would cause her arrest. Luckily, she had put candy in her bag and had stuffed the news-letters her mother wrote into her dress to conceal them. Evading police scrutiny became a way of life for Thanh and her family.[47]

Both politically savvy and genuinely interested in international cooperation, Thanh sought opportunities to bring this kind of persecution to light in international women's peace circles. In 1970, Thanh founded the Vietnamese Women's Movement for the Right to Live (Right to Live, for short),[48] giving her the chance to reach out to women's international organizations to share her story as well as the stories of other political prisoners in South Viet Nam.[49] One of the first acts of the Right to Live movement attracted the attention she desired. When Vice President Spiro Agnew visited Saigon in August 1970, Thanh's group decided to write him an open letter exposing the harsh treatment of political prisoners. Agnew, however, refused the letter. Nevertheless, WSP members obtained a copy of it and hand-delivered it to Agnew's office in Washington, D.C.[50] Although Agnew still would not read the letter, Thanh had successfully tapped into an international women's network that could push the agenda of her organization in the United States.

WILPF members took particular notice of Thanh's new organization because of its commitment to nonviolent means of ending the war and because it was tied to neither Saigon nor Hanoi. Speaking of the need for reconciliation, not war, Thanh's group easily meshed with WILPF's platform; thus, WILPF granted it affiliation.[51] For WILPF, Thanh's story came to symbolize everything that was wrong with U.S. policy in South Viet Nam, particularly the United States' support of what WILPF members considered an inhumane regime that denied political freedom to anyone who opposed it, whether they were communists or not. Within a few short months, the Right to Live movement hosted a WILPF delegation to better acquaint its members with the current situation in South Viet Nam.

Katherine "Kay" Camp, president of the U.S. section of WILPF, led the international delegation and observed what she considered to be stifling features of RVN society. As soon as she landed in Saigon, she found the atmosphere in South Viet Nam oppressive. She recalled standing in line at Immigration Control at Tan Son Nhut Air Base, sweating in her knit turtleneck and camel-hair slacks; she had not dressed appropriately for the hot and stuffy Saigon airport. Although Camp in part blamed the heat for her perspiration, she also admitted she was worried that customs officers would deny her entry into the country. She remembered hearing stories about other peace activists being turned away at the airport despite having visas.

As the line slowly moved through Customs, she watched as one of her companions gained access to South Viet Nam.[52] When her turn came, she realized what was taking so long: the customs official checked everyone's name against a list of those who should be denied entry. Camp was not on the list, so she was let in.[53] Ironically fearing more difficulty entering an allied nation of the United States than she did when she traveled to an enemy nation, North Viet Nam, just a few days later, Camp's experience highlights the perception of antiwar activists as potentially treacherous to the U.S. mission in South Viet Nam. This danger became amplified for American and Saigon officials as Camp and those who had gone before her testified to the most negative aspects of the war.

For her part, Camp lamented the social consequences of U.S. intervention. The list of nouns she scrawled down to remember her first impressions of the South illustrate this focus: "military, overcrowded, traffic . . . garbage . . . barbed wire, beautiful people."[54] She later elaborated, stating that the militarization of the society struck her as soon as she landed. Rows upon rows of helicopters and fighter-bombers filled the tarmacs; Hondas and army trucks crowded the streets in the city; rolls of barbed wire left here and there were a constant reminder of the need to fence people in or out; and people with nowhere else to go jammed onto the sidewalks.[55] Camp felt particularly sickened that much of the war materiel she saw came from the United States. For Camp, just as for Bennett before her, U.S. intervention seemed to have caused more problems for the Vietnamese, as it wrecked their way of life. Members of the Right to Live movement confirmed Camp's suspicions.

To create, solidify, and publicize the new connection between the Right to Live movement and WILPF, Ngo Ba Thanh hosted a meeting in her home during Camp's visit (see Figure 7). A broad swath of Vietnamese women's groups attended, leaving one PRG representative to tout it as one of the most significant exchanges between Americans and Vietnamese during the war.[56] In common with the 1965 Djakarta and 1968 Paris conferences, a joint statement coming out of the meeting bound women together as "mothers, wives, and sisters," defining women in terms of their familial roles.[57] But it cut short the maternalist rhetoric, making no further mention of motherhood or even children. As Thanh's story demonstrated, for women in South Viet Nam, motherhood offered very little protection from persecution. Even so, Camp told readers of WILPF's newsletter *Peace and Freedom* that, before leaving Saigon, several Right to Live members "pressed into my hand small replicas of their greatest treasures—photos of their

FIGURE 7 Kay Camp and Ngo Ba Thanh, standing. Series Accession 2006, Box 12, Folder "Photographs and Material from Binder/Scrapbook," Kay Camp Papers, Swarthmore College Peace Collection.

children."[58] Given this maternal display, Camp asked: who could doubt that what Vietnamese women most wanted was peace?[59] Yet, they faced harassment because of their opposition to the Thieu regime—a government, she was quick to point out, the United States helped to keep in power.

Subsequently, Camp made the suffering of South Vietnamese women central to WILPF's ongoing campaign against U.S. involvement in Viet Nam. In the joint statement signed by Thanh and Camp, they blamed women's loss of "dignity"—likely a reference to prostitution and prisoner abuse—on U.S. intervention in Viet Nam.[60] Camp also noted that the Vietnamese women she met placed themselves in precarious positions just by drafting a public antiwar statement.[61] But Thanh and her compatriots refused to hide even when police regularly arrested and injured protestors. In fact, Thanh informed her guests that antiwar demonstrations were becoming more prevalent despite this persecution. Showcasing the growing unrest of noncommunist Vietnamese in Saigon, Thanh accompanied the WILPF delegation to a Buddhist prayer for peace festival where thousands gathered to proclaim their desire to end the war. Standing on the street in front of an enormous, colorful "shrine bedecked with banners, palm trees, candles" and listening to "the long sing-songy speeches," Camp felt inspired.[62] In her articles about her time in Saigon, Camp underlined the political repression in the South as well as the tenacity of her Vietnamese hosts, who were determined to find a solution to the war that would result in a democratic government.[63]

Camp's visit established important ties between U.S. WILPF members and the Right to Live movement, as WILPF was now poised to aid Thanh and her fellow activists if needed. A democratic government for the RVN seemed at hand, however, as presidential candidate Duong Van Minh, who supported negotiating with the PRG, gained backing from many Saigon leaders in the upcoming fall 1971 elections.[64] Even so, Thanh kept up her public dissent, even going so far as to send a letter to the U.S. Senate Foreign Relations Committee denouncing Nixon for trying to achieve military victory. With Thanh so vocal, another arrest certainly seemed possible, and the expected soon happened when, in August 1971, police took her into custody following a demonstration outside a courthouse.[65] A judge accused her of verbally and physically abusing him, but WILPF members never doubted Thanh's innocence and quickly sprang to her defense, claiming her imprisonment was an effort to silence political dissent.[66]

WILPF's allegations may have been true, as indicated by the following proceedings. First, the attorney general upped the charges against Thanh in order to keep her incarcerated. When, in mid-September, a court ordered Thanh's release, citing lack of evidence to hold her, prison officials kept Thanh for an extra twenty-four hours.[67] Within two days of her release, Thanh was arrested once again, this time being held for a much longer period. During her two days out of prison, Thanh had joined a demonstration at the Lower House of the Senate to protest President Thieu's running for reelection unopposed. Following Thanh's August arrest, presidential candidate Minh had dropped out of the race, citing Thieu's efforts to rig the election with U.S. support as the reason.[68] When Thanh arrived to protest the one-party election, police were already on the scene, shooting tear gas into the crowd. Thanh, who had asthma, sought refuge in a nearby hotel and was subsequently arrested without being charged with a crime. Because of her exposure to the tear gas, her health was in jeopardy, but prison officials withheld medical care from her for about a week. In October, she was charged with subversion, and was held without trial for six months.[69]

During those six months, WILPF members, accompanied by WSP members and other female peace activists, took up Thanh's cause. First, in October 1971, WSP and WILPF members spoke with the RVN consul in Washington, D.C., who claimed Thanh was not being detained. They later learned that he lied. In December, women "stormed" the offices of the RVN's Mission to the United Nations in New York City, but the ambassador there declined to see them.[70] In defiance, they staged a sit-in, refusing to leave the ambassador's office until he agreed to an interview. Police forcibly removed the women but did not arrest them. Following these two failed attempts to work with South Vietnamese officials, WSP asked its members to write to the U.S. ambassador in Saigon to use his influence to secure her release.[71] This appeal also failed, and in March 1972, Thanh was brought to trial on a stretcher because her health had not yet recovered. Despite her condition, she made a speech declaring her sole desire for peace and justice. In English, she spoke directly to American women, asking them "to work together in friendship to end the war."[72] She elaborated, "True friendship is based on mutual respect for national sovereignty, not on the domination of one country by another. I believe in peaceful coexistence."[73] Informing American women of her desire to collaborate in a way that would leave Viet Nam independent from the United States, Thanh also asserted her own autonomy in her relationship with U.S. women.

WILPF members accepted this state of affairs, and when Thanh's trial was postponed indefinitely because she had had an asthma attack during the court proceedings, WILPF members protested this decision. Shortly thereafter, three WILPF members returned to the RVN embassy in D.C. for answers. Embassy officials refused to admit them, and they refused to leave. Police arrested the three women, but the charges against them were soon dropped.[74] With Thanh still in prison, female peace activists continued to advocate for her release as they also contrasted her treatment with "progressive" aspects of North Vietnamese society.

White American woman peace activists looked to North Viet Nam as an example of a society where people could live peaceably and where women could reach their full potential. White WSP member Judy Lerner, who visited Hanoi in August 1971, described Vietnamese women as "the most wonderful women I have ever met" and wanted to share their stories of triumph with the world.[75] This perspective also happened to solve a new dilemma WSP members faced. Since entering the POW debate, female peace activists had had less ability to present themselves as apolitical mothers. Contemplating the next move, white WSP member Amy Swerdlow asked herself why she should accept the VWU's recent invitation for her to visit Hanoi in October 1971. Her answer was to showcase the accomplishments of North Vietnamese society to lay to rest U.S. government officials' claims that the Vietnamese were inhumane communists. With the growing women's liberation movement in the United States as well as the VWU's persistent quantification of women's gains under socialism, disseminating stories of Vietnamese women's rights provided a way to present the North in a positive light. Swerdlow identified legal changes in the North that allowed women more freedom in marriage and pointed to improvements in women's familial responsibilities as they joined the workforce. Most notably, day care centers had spread, allowing women to work and to attend political meetings. Although Swerdlow mentioned some inconsistencies in women's rights and wondered what the postwar future would hold, her overall portrayal was one of success.[76] Citing the achievements of Vietnamese women and stating that in some ways they had actually made more progress than their American counterparts, Swerdlow adopted a new rhetorical tool for WSP members.

For activists of color, the opportunities for women in North Viet Nam were less significant than the fact that the Vietnamese were well versed on problems faced by African Americans. For African American reverend Willie Barrow, who traveled to Hanoi in October 1971 with Amy Swerdlow, Vietnamese knowledge of the Angela Davis case particularly surprised her. Davis, an activist and philosophy professor, was arrested in October 1970 after firearms she purchased were used in a hostage situation. With no solid evidence that she had conspired in the act, many activists across the nation sprang to her defense and demanded that the government "Free Angela." The Vietnamese, ever vigilant regarding strife within the United States, reported on the Davis case in *Women of Viet Nam*, the *Vietnam Courier*, and *South Viet Nam in Struggle* as an example of the U.S. government's repressive nature.[77] During Barrow's visit to Hanoi, the Vietnamese even invited her to speak at a rally to protest Davis's incarceration. The response of audience members to her speech led Barrow to declare that the Vietnamese could "identif[y] with [Davis] as a person of color, fighting for her people in [the] face of US repression."[78] For Barrow, race was the salient factor in both struggles for self-determination against a common enemy—the U.S. government. Just as Ngo Ba Thanh became a cause célèbre symbolizing the suppression of political dissent in South Viet Nam, for Vietnamese and for antiwar Americans, Angela Davis's imprisonment illustrated similar injustice still rampant in the United States.

All the while, the Vietnamese combined political, military, and diplomatic strategies to gain an advantage in peace negotiations. According to historian Robert Brigham, the NLF backed Duong Van Minh's presidential candidacy in the fall of 1971 in order to show the world the PRG's willingness to support a noncommunist leader of the South. In a seven-point agreement proffered by the PRG in July 1971, it asked the United States to cease its backing of Thieu and to set a date for troop withdrawal. In exchange, the PRG would prepare to release all POWs. When Minh dropped out of the race, PRG officials faulted Washington for supporting a corrupt government and throwing away an opportunity to make a peace deal.[79] Following the reelection of Thieu by default, Hanoi prepared for and launched a major offensive in South Viet Nam the following spring. Successfully causing ARVN soldiers to retreat and desert en masse, Hanoi showed its military strength. In retaliation, Nixon expanded and intensified the air war over North Viet Nam, striking all major cities.[80] The PRG and DRV took political advantage of the massive assault on the North, gathering evidence of the United States bombing dikes, mining ports, and blocking trade.[81] With the increased bombing, attention to women's rights in the DRV fell by the wayside. Instead, activists and Hanoi concentrated on publicizing the recent destruction in the North and blaming the Nixon administration for continuing the war.

With formal peace talks once again stalled, American women took the place of U.S. diplomats, traveling to Paris to keep lines of communication open.[82] COLIAFAM also sponsored delegations to Hanoi in May and July, increasing American scrutiny of the war and the tactics of the United States over the summer of 1972. Delegates lent credence to the DRV's depiction of indiscriminate bombing when they described the damage they had seen in the countryside. May delegate Marge Tabankin, president of the National Student Association, said that after visiting Nam Ha, Haiphong, and Hanoi, she believed the U.S. military targeted civilian areas in order to demoralize the Vietnamese. In August, Jane Fonda came back to the United States declaring that the U.S. military also targeted North Viet Nam's dike system, causing heavy flooding and the possibility of food shortages. Both women directly contradicted U.S. officials, who claimed that any bombing of civilian areas or dikes was purely "accidental."[83] Thinking ahead, Tabankin's group had borrowed recording equipment from CBS to take to Hanoi. On the news program *60 Minutes*, CBS aired footage of the bombed remains of a hospital that the Pentagon had specifically denied damaging.[84] Despite the video evidence, Pentagon officials remained steadfast in their position.

In an effort to maintain public support for the war, U.S. government officials continued to accuse the North Vietnamese of treating POWs in cruel ways. The Nixon administration clung to Hanoi's unwillingness to account for all MIAs, its obstruction of mail between POWs and their families, and its refusal to release POWs before the end of the war as reasons to carry on with U.S. involvement in Viet Nam. In reality, Hanoi did severely limit contact between POWs and American civilians following the unsuccessful Son Tay prison rescue in November 1970 and Bennett's visit that December.[85] In December 1971, right before Christmas, Hanoi released 1,001 letters to a COLIAFAM member visiting the DRV and PRG delegations in Paris and published photos of POWs receiving Christmas and New Year's packages in a January 1972 edition of the *Vietnam Courier*.[86] Although, for Hanoi, this exchange demonstrated its forthrightness, the flood of letters led U.S. officials to charge the DRV with cruelly withholding mail. Considering that POW families had received 2,646 letters in 1970 but only 499 in 1971, the allegation that Hanoi had held back letters seems plausible.[87] Even so, many activists defended Hanoi's actions as understandable.

Some activists even strategized with their Vietnamese contacts on how to gain more positive press in the United States. Peace activist Dave McReynolds wrote a letter to Viet-My leaders with recommendations on what Hanoi should do next. Stating that he now thought releasing any POWs had been a mistake because it made it seem as if Hanoi arbitrarily held the rest, McReynolds suggested the DRV be as transparent as possible with the treatment of Americans still held in North Viet Nam.[88] Perhaps taking into consideration the Nixon administration's ability to paint the North Vietnamese as cruel captors, the DRV loosened restrictions on antiwar activists visiting POWs, allowing both the May and July 1972 delegations to interview prisoners. Tabankin's group spoke with eight POWs, who claimed to have received good medical care and sufficient food. The POWs had even written a letter to Congress asking for an end to the war.[89] Fonda's group met with as many as thirteen POWs, but her statements broadcast over Voice of Viet Nam radio in Hanoi as well as a photo of her sitting on an antiaircraft gun overshadowed this aspect of her trip.[90]

Nevertheless, proving the goodwill of Hanoi remained a primary task for antiwar activists, temporarily displacing images of women's rights in the North. In regard to POWs, Nixon had demanded that the DRV provide a complete list of captives held, release all of them before the end of the war, allow inspections of detention camps by a neutral international body, and organize regular exchanges of mail. Hanoi could not prove whether it had supplied a full list of captives and would not release all POWs before the war ended, so it addressed Nixon's two other demands, albeit in its own way and with consideration to suggestions made by American activists. In his February 1972 letter, McReynolds had proposed inviting POW family members to Hanoi to visit their relatives as well as to see bomb damage. Although McReynolds discouraged freeing any more POWs until the end of the war, COLIAFAM leaders Dave Dellinger and Cora Weiss approached their Vietnamese contacts in Paris to encourage another release. Weiss argued that bringing home former POWs could demonstrate to the American public that antiwar activists were not supporting the enemy but rather were trying to reconcile the two sides.[91] Hanoi decided to combine a visit of POW family members to North Viet Nam with the release of their captured relatives in the fall of 1972.[92]

For Minnie Lee Gartley, white mother of one of the POWs, her trip in and around Hanoi cemented her conviction against the war. She had first contacted WSP member Ethel Taylor in November 1969 in an effort to find out more about her son, Mark Gartley, who had been MIA since he was shot down over North Viet Nam in August 1968. She also confided to Taylor that Mark had had mixed feelings about the war before he went MIA. Minnie Lee wanted Taylor, Weiss, and Duckles to ask the Vietnamese about him when they traveled to Hanoi in December 1969. Weiss and Taylor did indeed bring back confirmation to Minnie Lee of Mark's well-being, and Weiss even met Mark during that trip. Little did Weiss know that just three years later, she would lead a delegation that included Minnie Lee to escort Mark and two other POWs home. Following Taylor and Weiss's confirmation of Mark's condition in Hanoi, Minnie Lee remained in contact with WSP members, attending the 1971 Indochinese Women's Conference in Toronto, illustrating her own sympathy with antiwar sentiments.[93]

For the wife of another POW, African American Olga Charles, who had neither promoted nor protested U.S. involvement in Viet Nam, her trip in and around Hanoi encouraged her to see the war in a new light. At a press conference near the end of their trip to Hanoi, Minnie Lee and Olga portrayed the Vietnamese as trustworthy and called for an end to U.S. bombing. They had experienced firsthand the intensified war over North Viet Nam almost immediately upon landing in Hanoi. As the Vietnamese welcomed their guests, an air raid siren sounded and all rushed to the nearest bomb shelter.[94] The Americans' second impression of Hanoi came when they reached the Red River, which they had to cross to enter the city. Here, traffic came to a standstill because the bridge had been destroyed only a few days earlier. The Vietnamese had made a makeshift one-lane pontoon bridge to cope, but the delegates had to wait for the vehicles leaving the city to cross before making their way into the city. With the congestion, the delegates arrived late to their hotels and to the welcomes the Vietnamese had set up. Soon, another air raid siren broke off the proceedings, and everyone rushed to the hotel's bomb shelter. After this second raid, the Americans went to their hotel rooms to unpack just to be interrupted by a third siren within two hours.[95] As if experiencing the bomb raids themselves did not provide enough evidence of the intensified war in civilian areas, the Viet-My escorted the Americans to Nam Ha province, about sixty-five miles south of Hanoi, which had sustained major damage. After an arduous four-hour journey during which the driver maneuvered around and over bomb craters, the Americans reached the province. Although the roads on the way to Nam Ha bustled with activity, upon reaching Nam Dinh, the largest city in the province, the streets were eerily quiet. Seventy percent of the city had been destroyed, and the few remaining people stood in their doorways and silently watched the group pass. The Americans proceeded to a meeting with those who had been injured, widowed, or orphaned in recent bombing raids.[96] Following this interview, Minnie Lee and Olga expressed shock at the destruction they saw in Nam Dinh as well as admiration for the Vietnamese, who could show warmth, even to the recently released POWs.[97]

Olga's husband, Norris, also seemed to have come to a new outlook on the war thanks to the tours of the countryside the Vietnamese arranged. Norris had been working as an accountant when he was drafted, and he saw his enlistment in the military as part of his duty to his country. Before being captured, he had given little thought to what he was bombing below, simply seeing his missions as his job. But upon his return to the United States, Norris, with the support of his wife, admitted to having a new perspective on the war and the Vietnamese. In an interview, he stated that he believed the Vietnamese, who had shown him no animosity during his captivity, would release all POWs once the war ended.[98]

These kinds of statements worked well for COLIAFAM and the Viet-My as they argued that both antiwar activists and Hanoi wanted reconciliation and contrasted Hanoi's actions with those of the U.S. government. Weiss and her Vietnamese counterparts anticipated that the U.S. military would violate the terms of the prisoner release by coercing the pilots to return to the United States via military aircraft. Such an intervention, Weiss argued, would jeopardize the possibility of future early releases of prisoners and would reveal that the Nixon administration's real desire was to uphold the Thieu government, not ensure POWs' well-being. To prove the U.S. government's motives without actually allowing the U.S. military to gain access to the three POWs until they returned to the United States and held a press conference, Weiss and the DRV let it slip that the Americans would return to the United States via Laos on a certain date. All the while, they had made arrangements for the group to fly through China a few days later. When U.S. officials did just as Weiss and the Vietnamese expected, dispatching diplomats to the airport in Vientiane and ordering a military aircraft to stand by to take the POWs the rest of the way to the United States, Weiss took the opportunity to denounce the Nixon administration's actions. She asked the American public, "In light of [the failed intervention in Laos], how much credence can any reasonable person give to the President's professions of concern for the hundreds of American prisoners still in North Vietnam, and their families? And what does it say for the Administration's concern for the truth" when its actions demonstrated its desire to prevent the three POWs "from having a press conference upon their return to the United States from captivity in North Vietnam?"[99] Weiss implied that the Nixon administration was intent on hiding the reality of POWs' lives in North Viet Nam—a reality that would prove the humanity of the Vietnamese. To make matters worse, the U.S. government had acted in such a way as to prevent future releases until the end of the war.[100] Collaborating with the Vietnamese, Weiss hoped to undermine the Nixon administration.

The timing of this trip and these accusations should not go unremarked. Just a few weeks after this release, Nixon was up for reelection, and Weiss had set out to "embarrass" him in the hopes of reducing his chances of winning.[101] Nixon considered the political ramifications of his actions at this critical juncture as well, and, at first, he sought to reach a peace agreement with Hanoi right before the election. Although the U.S. negotiator in Paris, Henry Kissinger, came to an agreement with DRV and PRG officials in October, Saigon blocked the agreement because it undermined Thieu's total control over South Viet Nam. Foreseeing the failure of the agreement, Nixon claimed the United States could not abandon the Saigon administration at this imperative moment, and he distanced himself from Kissinger. Peace talks subsequently stalled. Nevertheless, Nixon won reelection in November and launched another intensified bombing campaign against Hanoi in December in the hopes of coercing DRV officials to renegotiate the terms of the armistice in a way that would appease Thieu.[102]

Operation Linebacker II, as it was called by the military, or the "Christmas bombings" as the media and antiwar activists dubbed it, outraged many at home and abroad. Four American eyewitnesses, including folksinger Joan

Baez, testified to the widespread and indiscriminate nature of attacks in late December 1972, as they had the misfortune of arriving in Hanoi two days before the military maneuver began. Marooned in Hanoi during twelve days of air raids, the four Americans visited ruins just after bombings took place and witnessed Vietnamese and Red Cross workers digging bodies out of the debris. For one of the visitors, the wailing of a mother as she clawed at the rubble shouting for her son spoke of the inhumanity of the U.S. military's actions. Baez released an album, *Where Are You Now, My Son*, the following May in remembrance of this scene. Another member of the delegation stopped eating for forty-eight hours after coming across the charred remains of a family of four still clutching one another. Sleeping in a bomb shelter some nights because the air raids never ceased, the four Americans could indeed testify to life "under the bombs."[103]

For Vietnamese in Paris, the Christmas bombings were almost as harrowing as they awaited news of their families. Phan Thi Minh recalled days of suspense until she heard her four children living in a heavily hit district of Hanoi had all survived.[104] But many other Vietnamese had not. In her memoir, Nguyen Thi Binh describes the Christmas bombings as a "political disaster" for the United States, as even the British government expressed "regret" at the actions of the United States.[105] The Vietnamese capitalized on world condemnation of U.S. intervention to prove Washington's disregard for POWs' well-being. In a letter to WSP member Ethel Taylor, Bui Thi Cam stated that the latest military strategy merely added more American pilots to the list of POWs as the Vietnamese shot down B-52s.[106] The Viet-My took a different tack to show the same negligence. Toward the end of its trip, Baez's group interviewed thirteen prisoners in a detention center that had been damaged by U.S. bombing. The delegation supposedly just happened to walk in on POWs fixing a roof that had caved in; although the American visitors thought it was no coincidence that they found the POWs engaged in such an activity, the damage itself was real.[107] Again, the message was clear: the U.S. government cared more about winning the war militarily than it did about the safety of POWs in the North.

Shortly after Baez's group returned to the United States, Hanoi and Washington reached a peace agreement very similar to the October agreement sabotaged by Thieu and abandoned by Nixon.[108] Although over the course of the last two years of the U.S. war the treatment of prisoners dominated press stories, U.S. female peace activists tried to redirect attention to larger issues in South Vietnamese and, by extension, U.S. society. Portraying the North Vietnamese prison system as clean and sufficient in contrast to the dirty, cramped, and sparse conditions in the South led some U.S. women to blame the U.S. government, military, and society for the limits placed on women's lives in the United States and South Viet Nam. That is, they made women's rights, including the right to protest, central to the debate over whether POWs and political prisoners were humanely treated. While for South Vietnamese women in particular these alliances provided a way to inform an international audience of their concerns, for U.S. women, it molded their feminism.

Although the intensification of bombing in the last few months of the U.S. war overshadowed concerns about women's rights in Viet Nam, the end of the war brought renewed attention to distinctions between the North and the South. Members of WILPF, WSP, the VWU, and the WUL led efforts to reconcile the United States and Viet Nam after the end of the U.S. war. For the next two years, limits to freedom in South Viet Nam continued to dominate women's stories as they kept an eye on women's rights in the North.

CHAPTER SIX

Shifting Alliances in the Postwar Period, 1973–1978

On January 19, 1973, the U.S. branch of WILPF received a telegram from the VWU inviting three women to visit Hanoi during the week of January 27. Given how long it took to get to Hanoi, whoever went would only have three days to pack, apply for visas, and receive the appropriate vaccinations. WILPF members quickly moved into action, booking flights, selecting two of the delegates—Dorothy Steffens, executive director of U.S. WILPF, who was white, and Marii Hasegawa, president of U.S. WILPF, who was Japanese American—and compiling the $3,000 to $4,000 necessary to pay for the trip. On January 20, Steffens asked her neighbor, Louise Lione, a white journalist, to suggest a photographer who could document the trip. Lione put herself forward, and before she received permission from her newspaper to go, she sent her two young children to stay with her mother and packed her suitcase. On January 23, Steffens, Hasegawa, and Lione boarded a flight to Paris without having received visas from Hanoi or Moscow and without the appropriate vaccinations. They planned to accomplish these tasks in France with the aid of the French Women's Union, but they were unsuccessful. They decided to fly on to Moscow anyway and hoped the Soviet Women's Union could help them overcome bureaucratic hurdles so that they could leave the airport. The French Women's Union cabled the Soviet Women's Union in advance to notify it of the group's arrival and asked for its assistance. Representatives of the Soviet Women's Union met the three American women at the plane in Moscow and successfully escorted them out of the airport sans visas. They went straight to the North Vietnamese Embassy, where they waited for hours for their visas to be approved. Finally, the visas came through, and the women could board the early morning indirect flight from Moscow to Hanoi. One last snag awaited them, however: they did not have seats confirmed on the fully booked once-a-week flight to Hanoi. Once again, the Soviet Women's Union stepped in and found a way to get the three women onboard. This experience, although taxing, demonstrates the coordination between American, French, Russian, and Vietnamese women that had developed over the course of the war years. But with impending changes to the role of the United States in Viet Nam, this network would face challenges.[1] The common enemy that had provided a means for U.S. and Vietnamese women to collaborate on the VWU's terms disappeared with the U.S. withdrawal from Viet Nam.

For the time being, women's organizations saw it as being in their interest to help each other without question. In fact, Steffens and Hasegawa did not even know why the VWU had invited them to Hanoi on such short notice, but they jumped at the chance to visit regardless of the reason. They supposed the invitation could have come in celebration of the fact that the United States, DRV, PRG, and RVN had finally come to an agreement for peace, or it could have been that the VWU wanted to recognize WILPF for its recent fund-raising efforts to build a hospital in Hanoi. Arriving in Hanoi on the same flight as a WIDF delegation, the WILPF group soon perceived that the VWU wanted to build stronger ties between the three organizations.[2]

Integrating the two delegations, VWU members had a clear objective for WILPF's and the WIDF's trip: to maintain the VWU's position in international women's circles. Ever vigilant about developments in the international realm, Hanoi knew that Cold War tensions were diminishing, as Washington had begun the process of détente with Moscow and Beijing the previous year. As relations between China, the Soviet Union, and the United States normalized, North Viet Nam foresaw its own isolation in the postwar period, with little aid coming from any of the major world powers. The alliance with WILPF and the WIDF could reinsert the needs of the Vietnamese into conversations in the international realm. As the WIDF and WILPF represented women's desire for peace and freedom in both the East and the West, it seemed only natural that the VWU would try to align itself with both organizations to receive maximum aid. The VWU asked both delegations to help Viet Nam in similar ways: to publicize any breaches of the armistice on the part of the United States or the RVN to an international audience, to provide evidence of the PRG's and Hanoi's compliance with the peace agreement, and to collect funds to build a Maternal and Child Health Center in Hanoi.[3] Combining women's needs with political endeavors, the VWU arranged the trip to highlight the perseverance of the Vietnamese as well as their hardships.

Arriving in Hanoi the same day that the PRG, DRV, United States, and RVN signed the Paris Peace Agreement, Steffens, Hasegawa, and Lione unexpectedly found no sign of celebration; after so many years of war, the Vietnamese were cautious to accept its end. But overnight, the streets erupted with red and yellow banners, DRV flags, and strings of lights in a combined celebration of the armistice and Tet, the lunar New Year, which began three days later. People crowded shopping districts preparing for the New Year's celebration with peach trees, the traditional decoration for Tet, strapped to the backs of their bicycles, and many returned to Hanoi and reunited with families for the first time in years.[4] Even so, the work to rebuild the city after the "Christmas bombings" continued, and the three American women saw construction crews building makeshift housing for those who had lost everything in December. As the Vietnamese took stock of their lives in preparation for the New Year, the three American women, their Vietnamese hosts, and the five WIDF members assessed the destruction in North Viet Nam and considered what they could do to fix it.

The VWU, as usual, showed the groups the devastation of the war in terms of infrastructure and human lives. Taking the delegates to damaged hospitals in Hanoi and the port city of Haiphong, the VWU demonstrated both the ingenuity of the Vietnamese, who decentralized their facilities to keep up with the needs of patients, and the obstacles facing medical staff, who had inadequate equipment to diagnose and treat afflictions. The patients themselves symbolized the need to repair Vietnamese bodies.[5] Hasegawa, who believed it best to let the Vietnamese tell WILPF what they needed and allow WILPF members to respond in ways they saw fit, appreciated this kind of information. She also saw WILPF as the perfect organization to collaborate with the Vietnamese in this manner, as it had a history of helping other groups on similar terms.

Hasegawa herself had been on the receiving end of this kind of aid upon her release from an internment camp at the end of World War II. Local WILPF chapters set up hostels where Japanese American internees could stay until they found more permanent accommodations. It was at one such residence in Philadelphia that Hasegawa first became acquainted with the organization. Joining its ranks, she brought a valuable perspective to WILPF because she had experienced firsthand the discrimination of the U.S. government. With increased militancy preached in social movements in the late 1960s as well as the military roles of Vietnamese women, some WILPF members felt at a loss as to whether and how to support these groups given their own dedication to pacifism. Hasegawa encouraged them to listen to the needs of those who called for or perpetrated acts of violence in reaction to the U.S. government because fulfilling the needs of these groups may actually prevent hostilities, she argued. She also reminded her fellow activists that the United States unleashed more violence than any civilian group could.[6]

Along this line, stories of women tortured under the Saigon regime demonstrated peace activists' obligation to continue to monitor the situation in Viet Nam. The VWU introduced the WILPF and WIDF delegations to two Vietnamese women who had been held and tortured in RVN prisons, one under Diem, the other under Thieu. Both described physical abuse, unsanitary conditions, and inadequate food, and one displayed parts of her body as evidence of the torture committed against her. To explain the relevance of the stories, VWU and PRG leaders at the meeting stated that Thieu was reopening some of the worst prisons in order to accommodate the growing number of political prisoners in the South when he should have been freeing political prisoners in accordance with the armistice. The VWU and PRG further claimed that Thieu had launched a campaign to arrest all neutralist leaders in South Viet Nam in order to block the implementation of a freely elected government that represented the PRG, neutralists, and the Thieu administration, as dictated by the peace agreement.[7]

Under these circumstances, WILPF member Ngo Ba Thanh remained imprisoned. But having heard about the peace agreement calling for the release of all political prisoners, Thanh took it on herself to begin the process of securing her own freedom. According to a 1981 interview, she packed up her few belongings and asked the guard to bring her to the warden's office. Upon entering the office, she told the warden that she was ready to go home in accordance with the peace agreement. Taken aback, the warden informed her he had heard no such news, and he politely escorted her back to her cell and offered her tea while he looked into the matter. Thanh waited days with no news until the warden told her that she was not a political prisoner but rather a criminal one, and therefore she was not eligible for release under the terms of the armistice. In response, Thanh went on a hunger strike.[8]

When WILPF members received word of Thanh's situation in April 1973, they launched a full-scale campaign calling for her release. To embarrass Thieu, who claimed that no political prisoners existed in South Viet Nam, and to pressure the U.S. government into ending its funding of Thieu's administration—at the very least of the RVN prison system—Dorothy Steffens contacted several colleges, including Thanh's alma mater, Columbia University, to ask them to invite Thanh to the United States to receive an honorary degree or to teach during the following semester. Following Steffens's suggestion, Columbia University and Bryn Mawr College extended offers to Thanh as a guest faculty member for the 1973–1974 academic year. WILPF's tactic worked: the Thieu administration yielded and offered to release Thanh to the PRG. Thanh could not accept her release under such terms, however, and neither could those working on her behalf, because it would imply that Thanh and other neutralists were communists. Part of Thanh's attraction as a cause célèbre was that she was not a communist; she was a peace activist promoting neutrality and wanted to work with both the PRG and the Thieu administration to form a truly representative South Vietnamese government. Refusing to be released under the terms offered by Thieu, Thanh remained in custody.[9]

As WILPF members continued to search for a way to secure Thanh's freedom, they decided to change tactics. While the PRG's newspaper claimed that prison officials were in the process of "liquidating" political prisoners and the WUL charged Thieu's administration with changing the status of political prisoners to that of criminal offenders in order to keep them legally incarcerated, WILPF spoke to Americans' pocketbooks rather than to their sense of morality.[10] WILPF members quoted Senator Ted Kennedy, who reported that the 1974 federal budget allocated $15,000,000 to South Viet Nam's prisons. Although a State Department official claimed any such funding was "designed to help the government of the Republic of Vietnam develop a more humane correctional system," WILPF members provided the arrest record of Ngo Ba Thanh to the House Foreign Affairs Committee to counter the depiction of the prison system as currently having any "humane" aspect to it.[11] Just five days before a congressional hearing on the treatment of political prisoners in South Viet Nam, in September 1973, Thanh was released from prison. She remained under house arrest, however, and hundreds of thousands of political prisoners remained incarcerated. Therefore, WILPF members Rosalie Riechman and Vivian Schatz asked Congress to vote against additional funding for the RVN police force and to send a congressional delegation to South Viet Nam to investigate the criminal justice system.[12]

In contrast to the treatment of political prisoners in the RVN, Hasegawa and Steffens believed Pham Van Dong when he insisted that Hanoi would release all American POWs without delay in accordance with the terms of the armistice. In fact, during the WILPF members' January 1973 visit, Hanoi had already begun the process of freeing POWs by informing them of the terms of the peace agreement and of their imminent return home. Three POWs interviewed by Steffens, Hasegawa, and Lione verified Hanoi's claims. Lione complained, however, that the Vietnamese had limited the topics of conversation that the American women could discuss with the POWs. Although she stated that all three of the POWs seemed well looked after, she felt her freedom as a journalist had been compromised by such restrictions. Steffens and Hasegawa did not share Lione's concerns and seemed satisfied with the treatment of the POWs as well as with their own ability to assess their condition.[13]

At first, Hasegawa's and Steffens's trust in the Vietnamese seemed well placed. Indeed, the last GI and POW left Viet Nam on March 29, 1973. Soon, however, some of the POWs accused their North Vietnamese captors of torture. In response, members of the press and Congress called out antiwar activists, such as Jane Fonda, Ramsay Clark, and Joan Baez, who had traveled to Hanoi during the war and attested to the well-being of POWs.[14] Some antiwar activists equivocated, whereas others tried to sideline the issue and put it into perspective. Longtime pacifist Daniel Berrigan wrote a letter to Pham Van Dong asking him to answer the recent accusations. Berrigan wanted to refute the allegations and hold up the North Vietnamese as merciful captors.[15] Cora Weiss, on the other hand, candidly stated that any imprisonment was surely difficult, but the POWs' treatment did not justify the U.S. war in Viet Nam. Neither would she admit to having done anything wrong by trying to end U.S. involvement in the war. Meeting the charges of abuse head-on, Weiss quickly moved on to the issue at hand: normalizing relations between the United States and Viet Nam.[16]

On her third trip to North Viet Nam, in October 1973, Weiss embarked on a new endeavor—medical aid—to help right the wrongs of war and to recreate the image of the United States in world opinion.[17] Just two months earlier, the FBI had decided to stop tracking her movements, as her antiwar activism had ceased. Little did its agents know that for Weiss the war was far from over.[18] Stating that Americans had "already lost our lives, money, and our sense of national unity" because of the war, Weiss feared that Americans were on the verge of losing their sense of responsibility as well.[19] Thus, she advocated humanitarian efforts in Viet Nam to reestablish American unity and to shore up American ideals. She partnered with the Viet-My and VWU to advance such activities in a way that made sense for the Vietnamese.

Throughout the U.S. war, some aid from U.S. citizens trickled into North Viet Nam and PRG-controlled areas of South Viet Nam, but not until the last few weeks of the U.S. war did appeals for humanitarian relief to these areas gain much traction. News of the December 1972 bombing of the largest hospital in North Viet Nam, Bach Mai, spurred an unprecedented outpouring of contributions. Indeed, whereas the humanitarian organization Medical Aid for Indochina (MAI), founded in 1971, solicited $100,000 in donations in the first eleven months of 1972, the newly established Bach Mai Hospital Relief Fund, a special program conducted by MAI, received $615,000 in the first six weeks of 1973, a fiftyfold increase.[20] Sending such funds to North Viet Nam without special permission, however, remained illegal, punishable under the Trading with the Enemy Act. Even after the signing of the peace agreement, the United States maintained its trade embargo against areas of Viet Nam under communist control.[21] Despite the embargo, the Bach Mai Hospital Relief Fund flourished, symbolizing some Americans' desire to help rebuild North Viet Nam. Weiss hoped she could build on this success and create long-term partnerships that would help the Vietnamese recover from war.

On her descent into Hanoi in October 1973, Weiss looked out the window and noticed two new bomb craters since her trip the previous September. But much of her arrival had become customary—North Vietnamese officials boarded the plane to check visas and passports, members of the Viet-My handed her flowers when she deplaned, and her usual interpreter greeted her.[22] This year, no air raids interrupted the welcome, and the drive into the city took only a few minutes, as the Vietnamese had repaired the bridge over the Red River. On her way to the hotel, Weiss noticed other changes in the city as well: the Vietnamese had transformed the one-person bomb shelters on the side of the road into flower beds, children laughed in the streets, and foreign visitors filled the city. Accompanying Weiss on the trip was Don Luce, who had discovered the tiger cages at Con Son prison in 1970. Together, they witnessed the reconstruction efforts, assessed medical needs in the North, and gauged whether the United States and RVN were abiding by the peace agreement in PRG-controlled areas south of the seventeenth parallel.[23]

For the first half of the trip, Weiss and Luce spent a week in Hanoi speaking with officials about U.S. responsibility to provide aid for both reconstruction and medical needs. North Vietnamese officials and humanitarian activists alike pointed to Article 21 of the peace agreement, which stipulated that the United States help "heal the wounds of war." Some activists believed the best way to persuade U.S. officials to provide relief was to show them that the American people wanted to send provisions. To find out what kind of aid the Vietnamese needed, Weiss and Luce visited the ruins of Bach Mai Hospital, met with UNICEF and Red Cross officials, and sat in on medical school classes. In these meetings, doctors and nurses identified the medical equipment most in demand. They also told Weiss that even though the war was ostensibly over, most medical problems, in-

FIGURE 8 Cora Weiss, scribbling in one of the notebooks she filled during her 1973 trip, speaking with a Son My massacre survivor. Photographs 8 × 10, Box 2, Folder "1970s—Cora in Vietnam," Cora Weiss Papers, Swarthmore College Peace Collection.

cluding tetanus, gynecological issues, and severe wounds, stemmed from the war—either as the consequence of previous war-related injuries or as new injuries caused by shrapnel, live mines, and other war materiel left in Viet Nam by the U.S. military (see Figure 8). American troops might have withdrawn, but their presence was still felt. Weiss later described seeing mounds of beer cans and barbed wire in areas of South Viet Nam that American GIs had occupied. But the real danger was in the single piece of rusted scrap metal left in the fallow fields where children played. Having left Viet Nam in such a shambles, the United States had a duty to help pick up the pieces, Weiss and her Vietnamese hosts argued. The Vietnamese also mentioned that North Viet Nam and the PRG received aid from or traded with England, Japan, Italy, Sweden, the USSR, China, and Cuba, among others, to show that the United States was one of the few nations on either side of the Cold War divide not helping with reconstruction efforts, even though its military was the main contributor to Viet Nam's current woes.[24]

With some sense of the needs in the North, a few days later, Weiss and Luce crossed the seventeenth parallel. Despite it being a foggy day, Weiss soon realized just how extensive the bombing had actually been. Every city, town, and village had been razed, and only temporary shelters dotted the landscape. The road was barely passable, and the war continued. In the "liberated zone" south of the seventeenth parallel, Nguyen Thi Binh welcomed Weiss to her native land. After a lavish lunch, Binh presented Weiss with a gift symbolizing a step in the process of reunifying the two Viet Nams: a purse made of telephone wires that had stretched across the length of the seventeenth parallel as part of the surveillance and military equipment meant to keep northerners from crossing into the South. In addition to the surveillance equipment, the U.S. military had planted mines and run a thick fence of barbed wire along the border. Despite the PRG's dismantling of this physical barrier, Binh stated that there was still much work to be done to reunite the country. She apologized that Weiss could not travel farther south because the signing of the Paris Peace Agreement had neither ended the war nor halted the persecution of Vietnamese civilians. Placing full blame on the Thieu administration, she stated that, in recent months, ARVN soldiers had regularly attacked PRG-controlled areas in an effort to seize more territory. Although she admitted that some NLF forces had retaliated, Binh and representatives of Hanoi swore that the DRV and PRG wanted reconciliation and would act with "generosity" toward those who had collaborated with "foreign enemies."[25]

Thus far, Thieu had not extended this kind of forgiveness to political prisoners or captured military personnel within the RVN. Repeating much of what Weiss and Luce already knew about the treatment of political prisoners in the South, Binh informed them that her own brother numbered among the many who had been illegally detained. Police had arrested him in 1968, shortly after Binh's selection to represent the NLF at the peace talks in Paris, and he remained incarcerated in an undisclosed location despite having been set for release in 1972.[26] For Binh, until her brother went free, the war was not over.

Many PRG and DRV representatives Weiss and Luce met reiterated this point, including DRV peace negotiator Le Duc Tho. When Tho learned in the fall of 1973 that he and U.S. negotiator Henry Kissinger would receive the Nobel Peace Prize, he knew what to do: refuse it to call international attention to the continuation of the war. Without peace, there could be no prize, he told Weiss and Luce. Pointing out the U.S. government's complicity in Thieu's violations of the armistice, he stated that Washington continued to send military assistance in the form of advisors and equipment to South Viet Nam to carry on the war effort. As summarized by Weiss, military aid meant "American planes drop[ped] American bombs using American fuel."[27] This assistance directly affected Americans' daily lives, as the U.S. Department of Defense sent fuel to South Viet Nam while Americans had to wait hours at the gas pump because of a fuel shortage. Like WILPF members before her, Weiss drew attention to people's pocketbooks to try to persuade them to protest U.S. funding of Thieu's administration. Despite the withdrawal of American GIs from Viet Nam, Weiss told audiences across the country that the United States continued to spend taxpayers' money on a war halfway around the world. She also pointed out the irony that this supposed war against communism continued during a period of détente with the two most influential communist nations.[28]

For its part, the U.S. administration argued that it needed to maintain a presence in South Viet Nam not only to uphold the anticommunist Saigon administration but also to make sure that Hanoi had actually released all POWs. In response, Weiss asserted that Hanoi had not kept any POWs hostage. Similarly, for WILPF member Phoebe Friedman, who left Hanoi the day that Weiss arrived, the idea seemed preposterous, as the Vietnamese barely had enough food to feed themselves, let alone American prisoners. Her VWU hosts showed her the primitive conditions in which many Vietnamese had to live and work—continuing to occupy damaged buildings that had tarps as roofs and missing walls. She, like many other activists, condemned what she saw as U.S. negligence toward reconstruction efforts in the North.[29]

Vietnamese and American women also denounced the U.S. government for sending funds to the Saigon administration, arguing that this interference hindered the coalition-building process in the South. In December 1973, Jacqui Chagnon, a white volunteer for the American Friends Service Committee, visited North and South Viet Nam and reported back to WILPF on her trip, which included a visit with Ngo Ba Thanh. Thanh had difficulty carrying on her activism because Saigon police kept surveillance on her and harassed those with whom she met. Even so, she remained in the public eye. From September 1973, when Thanh was released from prison, through January 1975, she gave one hundred and eleven interviews. Many of these exchanges were with journalists from the Western world—Britain, the United States, France—and humanitarian workers, peace activists, and politicians, again usually from the West, also made their way to Thanh's abode.[30] This interest in Thanh points to a desire for people in those countries that had supported U.S. involvement in Viet Nam to understand the current situation and what the South Vietnamese wanted. It also illustrates that even under house arrest, Thanh had sufficient contact with Americans and others outside Viet Nam to get her story out. Her alliance with WILPF and WSP members was of particular value, as Kay Camp became international president of WILPF, WSP supporter Bella Abzug remained in the House of Representatives, and together they pushed the UN and the U.S. Congress to make changes based on information Thanh provided.[31]

Contemplating the political advantages of Thanh's story, in the spring of 1974, WILPF members suggested she come to the United States, where she could affect U.S. policy. The time seemed ripe for change because, in the fall of 1973, the Watergate scandal erupted, corroding the Nixon administration's power. In early November, Congress voted to ban the funding of U.S. military action in Southeast Asia, marking a significant shift in U.S. policy. Nevertheless, the United States still financed the Thieu administration.[32] To prove the error of this support, WILPF members asked Thanh to testify at an upcoming congressional hearing about the political conditions in South Viet Nam.[33] Thanh wrote to Marii Hasegawa, saying that she would try to get paperwork approved that would allow her to visit the United States in March or April during the scheduled hearing.[34] Suddenly, however, communication between WILPF and Thanh broke off. Kay Camp and Marii Hasegawa waited in suspense until finally Thanh wrote, informing them that she had received their most recent letter two months after they had sent it.[35] By then, the congressional hearings had finished.

Nevertheless, women's networks sustained an alternative way for Americans and Vietnamese to communicate and shaped stories told about Viet Nam. For Thanh, the RVN government's weakness was the deteriorating economy and inflation; she asked American activists to end all assistance, including humanitarian aid, to South Viet Nam to hasten Thieu's downfall.[36] For the VWU, Saigon-controlled areas of the South were deteriorating socially. Its members told of an increased number of suicides, depravity, and inhumanity in the South. Although U.S. troops had withdrawn, prostitution abounded as women had little else to sell, pornography littered the streets, and heroin addicts wasted away in the ever-growing slums of Saigon. In the countryside, Thieu carried out "extermination" campaigns, arrested political protestors, and did nothing to help the desperately poor.[37] Once again using maternalist language, one letter signed by "A Group of Vietnamese Mothers" appealed to mothers' rights to have their children grow up in a healthy and safe environment—an environment seemingly impossible to achieve under the current administration.[38]

The U.S. government concurred that South Vietnamese children needed to be looked after in a different manner as North Vietnamese troops moved closer to Saigon in the spring of 1975. In April, the U.S. government boarded thousands of Vietnamese "orphans" onto military aircraft bound for the United States. Foreshadowing extensive problems with the project, the first flight out of Saigon crashed, killing about one hundred Vietnamese children. In dismay, activists Barbara Deming, Grace Paley, and Jacqui Chagnon, among others, denounced the campaign.[39] When it came to light that some of the children were not actually orphans and that their parents had never consented to their adoption, the project prompted even more outrage in both Viet Nam and the United States. The controversy over Operation Babylift continued for several years as relatives in Viet Nam and children in the United States asked to be reunited. But with poor adoption records, very few were. Even so, the U.S. government portrayed itself as acting in a humanitarian manner by rescuing such children.[40]

With the fall of Saigon imminent in April 1975, some antiwar activists began to contemplate what type of story would be told about the war—had it been a failed rescue mission or an act of aggression on the part of the United States? They noted that many Americans just wanted to forget the war had ever happened, whereas other Americans continued to defend U.S. intervention in Viet Nam as having been necessary in the name of democracy. Barbara Deming worried that the United States would find itself in similar situations in the future if no one "even tr[ied] to look at" what Americans had so cruelly done to the Vietnamese.[41] Like other activists who developed a feminist critique of war, Deming believed atrocities committed by U.S. military personnel revealed that U.S. society was fundamentally flawed; thus, simply ending the war would not put an end to such violence or injustice. She placed hope in feminists, however, because they seemed more inclined to criticize U.S. society, examine the brutal nature of war, and determine how to prevent such violence in the future. Comparing U.S. military strategy in Viet Nam to rape, Deming and other feminists argued that both imperialists and rapists treated people as property and expected submission. For Deming, as for anti-imperialist feminists coming out of the 1971 Indochinese Women's Conference, the way war was waged was a feminist issue. Although this was (and is) an important discussion for feminists, it also obviated communication between U.S. and Vietnamese women as it turned U.S. feminists' attention inward.

The United Nations International Women's Year in 1975 also diverted some U.S. women's attention away from the goings on in Viet Nam. Kay Camp mentioned in a note to Ngo Ba Thanh wishing her a "Happy New Year" that WILPF members were busy planning for the Mexico City conference commemorating the occasion.[42] Likewise, Ngo Ba Thanh and VWU and WUL members busied themselves preparing for the World Congress for International Women's Year hosted by the WIDF in East Berlin in the fall of 1975. There, WUL representative Ma Thi Chu informed attendees that the government had tasked her organization with aiding former prostitutes—the WUL needed to cure them of disease, train them for new jobs, and reinstate them into society. WSP and WILPF members in attendance at the conference in East Berlin supported these efforts and pledged to continue to urge Congress to normalize relations with Viet Nam, but their attention was ever more drawn to women's rights issues internationally as well as domestically.[43]

Complementing the International Women's Year, American feminists worked to secure federal funding for a national conference on women's rights in the United States. Succeeding in December 1975, U.S. women began to organize state and national meetings to take place in 1977. The significance of these meetings to female peace activists is shown through the appointment of national WSP leader Ethel Taylor to the National Commission on the Observance of International Women's Year.[44] Many other WSP and WILPF members participated in the national conference in Houston in a less visible manner either as one of the 2,000 delegates elected to represent women from their home states or as one of the 15,000 attending as observers. This participation reflected a shift in priorities for female peace activists. As more and more of them identified themselves as feminists, their previous dedication to collaborating with their Vietnamese counterparts waned.

Even so, some feminist antiwar activists continued to evaluate the strides toward women's equality made within North Viet Nam. Cora Weiss praised the advancements of Vietnamese women, who had access to birth control, abortion on demand, and two-month maternity leave—all central feminist concerns at the time.[45] Others promoted films and literature that depicted the struggles and successes of Vietnamese women as told by U.S. women.[46] Margaret Randall and Arlene Eisen Bergman, both authors, contributed to this literature after they traveled to Hanoi in August 1974. While there, they were impressed with the energy of the Vietnamese as well as the progress toward women's rights. Randall, who recalled developing a feminist consciousness in 1969, attributed women's gains to "the fact that women had to step up in Viet Nam."[47] Such responsibility "level[ed male] domination," she explained.[48] Eisen likewise asserted that revolution and independence in the North had brought women's liberation.[49] Both appreciated Vietnamese women's gains in the DRV because VWU members "talk[ed] about . . . women's opportunities . . . in a way that . . . dovetailed with our ideas of feminism."[50] For instance, just as feminists in the United States coined the title "Ms." to identify a woman as a separate entity from her father or husband, the *Vietnam Courier* asserted that "it would be an error now to address a woman by her husband's name, for this has gone out of use in Viet Nam."[51] With seemingly similar goals for women, U.S. feminists could continue to point to North Vietnamese society as inspirational.

Yet, the prescribed role of women in the DRV shifted with the fall of Saigon. During the war, women had three responsibilities—to defend their homes, produce food and goods, and care for children. After the war, women's responsibilities as mothers came to the fore as raising "good children" became their primary duty.[52] Their children, not themselves, would lead Vietnamese society to attain full equality between men and women. Through informal education at home overseen by the mother, boys and girls would learn women's worth. The VWU, promoting these new duties for women, did not see the continuation of prescribed gender roles as negating the possibility of women achieving equality. Instead, many Vietnamese argued that with Western influences out of their nation, they could get on with the task of building a socialist society that took women's rights into consideration at every level of the government.[53]

Showcasing Vietnamese women's accomplishments after peace had come to Viet Nam, the VWU invited a group of U.S. feminists to Hanoi in the summer of 1975. When VWU members asked Arlene Eisen Bergman for suggestions on who they should reach out to, she named African American scholar and activist Toni Cade Bambara. Eisen had read Bambara's 1970 book *The Black Woman*, which connected the struggles against racism, sexism, and imperialism, and she believed Bambara's perspective on what was going on in Viet Nam would be of value. Joining Bambara in the delegation was Laura Whitehorn, a white member of the radical organization Weather Underground; Pam Costain, a white socialist feminist; and Donna Futterman, a white health activist. When Bambara led the anti-imperialist feminist delegation to Viet Nam in July 1975, women's needs took center stage.[54]

Even so, Bambara identified racial connections as well, as she carried letters from black organizations declaring solidarity between African Americans and Vietnamese. Her belief that the two movements for self-determination were joined seemed confirmed when she learned that Ho Chi Minh had allegedly been reading Robert Williams's *Negroes with Guns* on his deathbed. After the trip, Bambara showed in her collection of short stories *The Sea Birds Are Still Alive* how the histories of black communities and the Vietnamese corresponded with one another.[55] Whitehorn credited Bambara, because of her activism in the African American community and her experiences with overly enthusiastic white sympathizers, with having special insight into how to tell the truth about the shortcomings of Vietnamese policies while still appreciating the heroism of the Vietnamese people—a lesson Whitehorn admitted she could not grasp at the time. Instead, Whitehorn sidestepped topics that might depict the Vietnamese negatively.[56] Although this whitewashing allowed her to avoid cultural imperialism, her overly rosy portrayal of the Vietnamese might have seemed naive at best.

Bambara's trip also provides a window on the changing nature of U.S. activists' view of their role in U.S.-Vietnamese relations as her delegation tried to redirect attention back to "the women's campaign"—providing medical aid and equipment specifically for the Maternal and Child Health Center in Hanoi.[57] Although WILPF members had donated to the project through the WIDF since Dorothy Steffens's and Marii Hasegawa's January 1973 trip, WILPF itself did not prioritize this type of fund-raising, because it saw itself as a political, not a humanitarian, organization.[58] Likewise, WSP leaders hesitated to champion these efforts, because they wanted to stop "working from crisis to crisis" and to turn the group's attention back to international nuclear disarmament.[59] Nevertheless, at the 1973 WSP National Conference, members decided to send any monies collected to Viet Nam through Medical Aid for Indochina.[60] Even though both WSP and WILPF supported humanitarian efforts and lobbied Congress to fund reconstruction, the VWU and Viet-My would have to look elsewhere for the direct and more substantial financial contributions they desired. With U.S. troop withdrawal and the victory of the DRV, cracks in the women's network that had been so painstakingly developed over the course of the war began to appear as the priorities of U.S. women's groups and the VWU diverged.

Nevertheless, some U.S. women, such as Cora Weiss, continued to concentrate on the needs of the Vietnamese. Humanitarian activists, however, had to contend with U.S. government officials who, following the fall of Saigon, had extended the trade embargo to include all of Viet Nam. The embargo had already hindered the delivery of aid collected through the Bach Mai Hospital Relief Fund. Following Weiss's October 1973 trip to Hanoi, workers for the fund spent nine months trying to obtain approval for a license to send the first two shipments of medical aid. Simultaneously, fund managers went back and forth with the IRS, which first granted and then denied tax-exempt status to the organization.[61] As many humanitarian associations faced similar difficulties, in October 1975, aid proponents, including Weiss, decided to launch Friendshipment, a coalition of thirty-five religious, peace, and civic organizations promoting aid from the American people to the Vietnamese people. Through this coalition, organizations could send supplies to Viet Nam without having to overcome bureaucratic hurdles.[62]

The promotion of "people-to-people" aid marked a discrete shift, even for women such as Weiss, who had worked in both mixed-gender and women-only groups in the past. Gone was any reference to women's or mothers' distinct needs and emotions, to be replaced by a call to all Americans to see to it that the U.S. government fulfilled its obligations. In response, U.S. officials denied the possibility that Friendshipment could truly provide people-to-people aid to communist countries—a totalitarian regime would never distribute material evenly—and accused Vietnamese officials with incarcerating political prisoners, persecuting religious persons, and concealing information regarding MIAs.[63]

As Friendshipment delegations tried to refute these accusations, they examined, evaluated, and criticized the domestic policies of North and South Viet Nam in an unprecedented manner. Delegates confirmed that donated goods were appropriately managed, and they spoke with "learners" imprisoned in reeducation camps to determine whether they were being treated justly. Shortly after the fall of Saigon, the North Vietnamese sent those who had supported the RVN's administration as military or government personnel to detention centers, where they purportedly learned the North Vietnamese perspective on the war and acquired industrial skills. American officials decried these institutions as a violation of political and civil rights, but those in Friendshipment defended them as a humane way to deal with counterrevolutionary forces—after all, the camps prevented a bloodbath, they argued.[64] Nevertheless, this debate inserted humanitarian activists into Viet Nam's domestic realm as they shifted from commenting on how U.S. intervention shaped Vietnamese society to how the Vietnamese decided to rebuild their country.

At the same time, U.S. officials wanted to move forward with promoting a new role for the United States in the world. To that end, President Jimmy Carter declared that the United States would work toward a "human rights policy" after he took office in January 1977.[65] Reacting to this declaration, in a public statement to an international audience in February 1977, Ngo Ba Thanh pointed to contradictions between the U.S. portrayal of its role in the world and its actions in Viet Nam. Referring to her imprisonment in the last years of the war, Thanh declared herself to have been "one of the most symbolic victims deprived of human rights under the so-called free world led by US imperialism" and challenged images of the United States as acting benevolently in Viet Nam.[66] She also refuted allegations of human rights abuses in reunified Viet Nam as she held up the new government of the recently unified Socialist Republic of Viet Nam (SRV) as truly representational. Two months later, when she met with a Friendshipment delegation to Saigon led by Don Luce, she beamed with excitement at the prospect of building a new society and a new government in the SRV. As a member of the National Assembly, she lent credence to claims that non-communists could participate in nation-building as she contradicted U.S. portrayals of Viet Nam. Nevertheless, Luce's delegation pointedly asked Thanh and thirteen other members of the National Assembly about human rights violations. The Vietnamese bristled at the presumption of Americans questioning them about human rights after the total war the U.S. government had just waged in their country. They also contrasted the treatment of former RVN officials and ARVN soldiers with the imprisonment and execution of Japanese high government officials during the U.S. occupation of Japan after World War II. In this way, the Vietnamese tried to undercut the right of the U.S. government or people to criticize the SRV on affairs it deemed domestic.[67]

Humanitarian activists found themselves in a precarious position as they tried to counter U.S. government charges of human rights violations without irritating their Vietnamese counterparts. In 1978, Church World Service (CWS), an umbrella religious organization, sought to overcome these challenges when it orchestrated a major campaign to provide wheat to Viet Nam in the hopes of convincing the U.S. government to send food relief as well. With the destruction of agricultural land in Viet Nam during the war compounded by recent floods and droughts, the Vietnamese were suffering a major food crisis in the fall of 1977 and spring of 1978. To combat the crisis, CWS asked farmers in a number of Midwestern states to donate their surplus wheat to the Vietnamese instead of ploughing it under, and it hired Cora Weiss as a consultant to handle the shipment of $2,000,000 worth of grain.[68] The "Ship of Wheat" campaign, as it came to be known because CWS sailed the wheat from Houston to Saigon, highlighted the contributions of churchgoers and farmers to reinforce the image of Friendshipment as a group of Americans providing aid to the Vietnamese people. Hailing the shipment as a "Christian response to need," CWS downplayed diplomatic disagreements between the United States and Viet Nam and instead emphasized the duty of the United States as a Christian nation to help those in crisis.[69] It even had the sacks of flour stamped "a gift to the Vietnamese people from American churches." Similarly demonstrating the compassion of the average American, delegation member and Kansas farmer Harvey Schmidt received the limelight in many news stories as an unlikely traveler to socialist Viet Nam. Described as a "conservative farmer, who rarely strayed from Kansas," Schmidt represented the desire of the average American for reconciliation.[70]

Taken together, promotions of people-to-people aid, discussions of human rights, and portrayals of the United States as a Christian nation obscured gendered aspects of humanitarian deeds as well as the usefulness of women's networks. Even so, WSP member and feminist Cora Weiss time and again was central to these proceedings, and VWU members continued their efforts to sustain people's diplomatic ties with American women. In December 1977, the VWU hosted another U.S. women's group to Viet Nam to showcase the accomplishments of Vietnamese women since reunification in July 1976.[71] Because the "rehabilitation of women's dignity" remained a central concern for the VWU, it took the women's group to a center where the VWU trained former prostitutes in cottage industries.[72] In an unprecedented manner, delegate and white WSP member Judy Lerner commented on the shortcomings of such a training program. Coming from the National Women's Conference in Houston, Lerner was primed to analyze Vietnamese gender roles. Contrasting rehabilitation centers for female prostitutes and male drug addicts, she pointed out sexist assumptions about men's and women's work—men learned "more practical" manual labor skills, whereas women learned how to sew and weave.[73] As Lerner asserted which labor was more valuable, she inserted U.S. feminist views into the SRV's domestic policies—a space she and other peace activists had so painstakingly preserved during the war years.

The new roles of women in Hanoi's government, formerly praised by American women, also received denigration. Both Judy Lerner and Cora Weiss recalled telling Nguyen Thi Binh of their disappointment when they learned of her "demotion" from foreign minister of the PRG to minister of education of the SRV following reunification. Binh did not openly share in Lerner's and Weiss's dissatisfaction, however, and did not seem to appreciate their assessment of her new post or the new SRV government, which they implied continued to subordinate women.[74] Whereas Weiss and Lerner had abstained from such criticism during the war years, instead focusing on the U.S. government's faults, once the war ended, little by little, they and other U.S. activists started to scrutinize Vietnamese domestic policy. Even so, Weiss and Lerner simultaneously supported their Vietnamese contacts; Lerner even lent out her house about twenty miles north of New York City as a place of retreat for members of the SRV mission to the UN, and Weiss helped them find lodging within walking distance of the UN.[75] Lerner also saw her December 1977 trip as a renewal of women's concern for Viet Nam.[76] Thus, relationships between Vietnamese and Americans did not abruptly end but instead transformed in a way that allowed Americans to opine on the inner workings of the Socialist Republic of Viet Nam.

Some Americans successfully resisted this shift, however. Marilyn Clement, director of the Center for Constitutional Rights and white, visited Hanoi with Lerner in December 1977. Instead of speaking about Vietnamese policy or gender roles, she declared that Americans could not recover from the war until the United States reconciled with Viet Nam. Contributing to reconstruction efforts and thereby acknowledging the damage done by the U.S. military would help Americans heal psychologically. Clement set aside the issue of human rights to make a critical shift in whose war wounds needed healing. In doing so, she refused to engage in the new U.S. foreign policy rhetoric that would reinsert the United States into the domestic issues of Viet Nam.[77]

Organizations providing humanitarian aid became invested in monitoring the inner workings of Viet Nam. Just as during the war the Vietnamese had constantly assured American visitors that they recognized the American government, but not the American people, as their enemy, after the war, the American people, not the U.S. government, came to the aid of the Vietnamese. But with increased monetary contributions on behalf of the American public came increased scrutiny of Viet Nam's domestic affairs. American government officials diverted attention away from the responsibility of the United States to support reconstruction efforts by raising issues of human rights abuses in Viet Nam, vilifying Vietnamese officials. Some U.S. activists entered into these debates in such a way as to cause indignation among Vietnamese. Although other activists tried to sidestep the issue of human rights, the universal nature of human rights discourse made maintaining Viet Nam's autonomy difficult regardless.

By contrast, many U.S. feminists, including women in peace organizations, turned their attention to international and domestic women's rights. With the United Nations declaring 1975 International Women's Year, feminists were drawn away from what was going on in Viet Nam to consider women's issues in a wide array of contexts. Even so, some continued to praise what they saw as women's advancements in North Viet Nam, whereas others began to criticize the limits placed on Vietnamese women, particularly after reunification. With U.S. troop withdrawal, American and Vietnamese women found themselves redefining their relationships with one another in a way that projected some U.S. feminists' views onto Vietnamese society.

Conclusion

It seems remiss not to end a book ostensibly about the Viet Nam war with the acknowledgment that the memory of the war still divides U.S. society.[1] Yet, evaluating American and Vietnamese women's relationships leads to a different conclusion. By war's end, women had created networks such that, despite national, social, political, and economic differences, they collaborated on terms dictated by those asking for assistance—the Vietnamese. Although these alliances did not continue in this manner, this story provides an example of women from the East and West or the Global South and Global North forming cooperative relationships against a common enemy, the U.S. government. They formed these alliances primarily for informational purposes at first, but soon the reasons on both sides for maintaining contact with one another expanded beyond these initial desires. As more and more Americans came to describe U.S. actions in Viet Nam in terms similar to those the Vietnamese used, groups of American activists identified more closely with the Vietnamese people. With this shift came new perspectives on U.S. society and multiple versions of feminism.

American women from many backgrounds believed U.S. intervention in Viet Nam only exacerbated injustice, and they sought to join efforts with Vietnamese to end the war. As images of state-sponsored atrocities in Viet Nam caused public outrage, U.S. activists looked for faults within U.S. society to explain U.S. foreign policy. Women of color in rights-based movements pointed to restrictions on economic and social rights at home and abroad in a way that linked their community struggles with that of the Vietnamese. They charged that heinous U.S. foreign policy stemmed directly from pernicious white American culture, which oppressed all peoples of color. Female peace activists similarly found faults with U.S. society after visiting North and South Vietnam. They identified negative aspects of U.S. society reflected in Saigon and contrasted South Vietnamese society with the orderly and dignified people in Hanoi. Blaming the United States for social ills in the South, female peace activists reconsidered their own situation in the United States.

WSP members discerned limits placed on themselves as women as they sought to claim expertise on Viet Nam. At first, they tried to overcome these boundaries through maternalist rhetoric, but they could not succeed in changing U.S. policy. Through this experience, some female peace activists developed a feminist consciousness. For some WSP and WILPF members, their first hand observations of Vietnamese women's lives also encouraged a rethinking of maternal instincts because they came to appreciate that mothers' violence, if not justified, could at least be comprehended. These transformations of WSP and WILPF members' own thinking about women's roles paralleled those of other U.S. women who also found fault with their own gender roles. Women of color often wanted to claim their ability to remain authentic to their culture while taking on revolutionary roles, and young white women sought liberation from both restrictive white American culture and its gender roles. For white women's liberationists, their abhorrence of the war and desire to center feminism in their activism created a fruitful environment for rethinking the relationship between war and gender as they came to criticize the destructive performance of American masculinity at home and abroad.

Despite divergent views on women's roles, by the early 1970s, countless women around the world looked to Vietnamese women as paragons of revolutionary womanhood. American women in peace, women's liberation, and "Third World" organizations alike overlooked the complexities of North Vietnamese gender roles and largely agreed that North Vietnamese society benefited women. They claimed that Vietnamese women had gained women's liberation as they found that their own rights did not measure up to those of their Vietnamese counterparts.[2] Regardless of their race, class, ethnicity, or politics, many U.S. activists viewed Vietnamese women as embodying a new womanhood, albeit in ways that spoke to American women's own social, political, and economic statuses. For many female activists, their representations of Vietnamese provided a means to discuss their own subordination within their communities and U.S. society more broadly. As the Vietnamese pointed to a common enemy—the U.S. government—that united women's groups, the details of what constituted women's rights remained immaterial. That is, female antiwar activists did not have to subscribe to a particular brand of feminism to relate to the Vietnamese.

Recognizing the VWU and WUL as drivers of international women's collaboration, this study suggests the significance of their efforts to people's diplomacy and the political front for Hanoi and the PRG. Vietnamese women spread propaganda about the U.S. war, its effect on women's lives, and women's rights under socialism through networks they built and maintained. Condemning the nature of the war as maternal figures, they mobilized women's international organizations, particularly WSP, WILPF, and the WIDF, which in turn publicized civilian deaths. Making known the guerrilla roles young women took on in the fight for independence, the VWU and WUL also gained sympathy from those women who believed these duties were an undue burden, and they elicited reverence in those desiring to revolutionize gender roles. Providing statistics on women's gains since the DRV's independence, they advanced a counternarrative to the discourse on women's freedom and equality in the West as they pointed to the degradation of women in South Viet Nam under U.S. influence. In the name of both motherhood and revolutionary womanhood, members of the VWU and WUL proved themselves good Vietnamese women by standing up for both family and nation.

The VWU and WUL also paid attention to the internal dynamics of the United States, gathering information during international conferences and delegation visits to Hanoi. Reaching out to particular groups of Americans, the Vietnamese learned more about activists' and communities' dissatisfactions with U.S. domestic policies and could capitalize on these discontents. They created rhetorical ties to various communities within the United States, blaming the U.S. government for social ills at home as well as in South Viet Nam. In this way, the Vietnamese collaborated with American activists to make connections between Americans and Vietnamese in their common struggles against the U.S. government. When speaking to people of color, in particular, Vietnamese portrayed the U.S. administration as the common enemy suppressing social, economic, and cultural freedoms. Separating the American people from the U.S. government, Vietnamese encouraged their American counterparts to enter the international realm as people's diplomats who could reestablish the role of the United States in the world in a way that better fit "true" American ideals. The Vietnamese considered women particularly effective antiwar advocates, as their testimonies would stand out in U.S. society; therefore, the VWU and WUL received support to attend countless international women's conferences and to invite women's delegations to Hanoi.

Efforts to build a women's people's diplomacy continued in the postwar period, but with less success. The 1976 winter issue of the VWU's *Women of Viet Nam* published an article titled "How Women the World over Feel about Their Vietnamese Sisters," indicating the continued efforts of the VWU to promote international ties between women. Indeed, the accounts of female diplomats at a few international conferences over the course of 1975 described the support women from all over the world pledged to Viet

Nam after the fall of Saigon and portrayed women's international networks as growing ever stronger in the postwar period. One Palestinian woman at the Congress of Arabian Women in Kuwait had even stopped the Vietnamese delegates to tell them what an inspiration a 1968 photograph of a young Vietnamese woman capturing an American pilot had been to her years before.[3] What seems to have been lost on the Vietnamese women, however, was the underlying implication that unless their revolution continued to challenge imperialism, sexism, and racism in such visible ways, their influence on the world stage would quickly diminish. Indeed, by 1979, when the VWU wrote an "Appeal to Women over the World" to denounce Chinese invasion, the depreciation of Vietnamese status was clear, as no mass international movement sprang to their defense.[4] On the one hand, the Chinese could not represent the same common enemy as the U.S. government had, and on the other, the Vietnamese could not command the same kind of positive publicity they had just a few short years before because of recent charges of human rights abuses in the postwar reeducation camps and during the border war with Cambodia in the late 1970s.

The loss of the U.S. government as the symbol of mass repression in Viet Nam significantly altered the relationships between American and Vietnamese women. Indeed, even as many U.S. woman peace activists remained focused on international relations, they lost sight of the specific needs of the Vietnamese. Cora Weiss, who had spent years trying to reconcile the United States and Viet Nam, turned her attention to a new project following the success of the CWS food relief program in 1978—ending the nuclear arms race. For many WSP and WILPF members, nuclear armament resumed its place as the preeminent threat to their vision of peace as they continued to try to realign the trajectory of U.S. foreign policy.[5] For other U.S. woman activists, issues of racism and sexism remained of the utmost concern, and changing domestic policy often took precedence. Even so, some continued to push for normalization of relations between the two countries until President Bill Clinton ended the embargo against Viet Nam in 1994.

Although this story demonstrates the possibility of fruitful cooperation between "Western" and "Eastern" women, more recently, U.S. feminists have been charged with ignoring the ways in which U.S. foreign policies detracted from women's rights in other countries.[6] Washington successfully harnessed feminist support for wars waged in such places as Afghanistan in the name of "saving" women.[7] In light of this recent history, the fact that both Vietnamese and U.S. women blamed a Western entity, not an Eastern

Notes

Archival Abbreviations Used in Notes

AAM 1805
    Steve Louie Asian American Movement Collection (Collection
    Number 1805)
AMBC   Anne McGrew Bennett Collection, GTU 89-5-017
ARWM   Anne Roberts Women's Movement Fond
BDP   Barbara Deming Papers
BOP   Bobbye S. Ortiz Papers
CBAP   Charlotte Bunch Additional Papers
CBP   Charlotte Bunch Papers
CHS   Chicago Historical Society
COLIAFAM records
    Committee of Liaison with Families of Servicemen Detained in North
    Vietnam Records
CSWR   Center for Southwest Research
CWP   Cora Weiss Papers
DAP   Donna Allen Papers, M92-226
Duke   Rare Book, Manuscript, and Special Collections Library, Duke University
Friendshipment
    Friendshipment/Bach Mai Hospital Relief Fund Records
HBLP   Helen Boyden Lamb Papers
Hoover   Hoover Institution Archives
JBC   Joan Biren Collection
JBMP   J. B. Matthews Papers
KCP   Kay Camp Papers
KHWB   Kathleen Hudson Women's Bookstore Collection
MFH   Martin Florian Herz Collection, propaganda leaflets
MHP   Marianne Hamilton Papers
NOP   Nancy Osterud Papers
PC   Peace Collection
Schlesinger
    Schlesinger Library
SCPC   Swarthmore College Peace Collection
SFU   Simon Fraser University Archives and Records Management Department
SLP   Shirley Lens Papers
SSC   Sophia Smith Collection
UCLA   Department of Special Collections, Charles E. Young Research Library,
    UCLA

UNC   Underground Newspaper Collection
VOP   Victoria Ortiz Papers
VWU   Vietnam Women's Union Records
WILPF   Women's International League for Peace and Freedom Papers
WLC   Women's Liberation Collection
WSPR   Women Strike for Peace Records

Introduction

1. Although WSP called itself a "communication network," not an organization, and did not have membership lists or dues, I have chosen to use the term "members" to describe WSP activists. Women who were part of WSP most often referred to themselves as "WSPers."

2. Unknown, Hanoi, Pham Van Dong, Lorraine Gordon, and Mary Clarke, Photograph, May 1965, Photograph Collection, Box "Dated Images/Billboards, etc.," WSPR, SCPC.

3. Trinh Ngoc Thai, interview with author. Some have dated the reliance on these three fronts of foreign relations back to the fourteenth century. See Nguyen Thi Binh, *Family, Friends and Country*, footnote 17 on 126, 177–78.

4. Brocheux, *Ho Chi Minh*, 78.

5. Pham Van Chuong, interview with author.

6. Burton, "The White Woman's Burden"; Burton, *Burdens of History*; Davin, "Imperialism and Motherhood"; Jacobs, *White Mother to a Dark Race*; Newman, *White Women's Rights*; Midgley, *Feminism and Empire*; Pascoe, *Relations of Rescue*; Sneider, *Suffragists in an Imperial Age*.

7. Laville, *Cold War Women*.

8. Olcott, "Empires of Information."

9. For other works similarly complicating this scholarship, see Prevost, "Assessing Women, Gender, and Empire in Britain's Nineteenth-Century Protestant Missionary Movement"; Pripas-Kapit, "Piety, Professionalism and Power."

10. Wu, *Radicals on the Road*, 4.

11. Gluck, "Whose Feminism, Whose History?"; Roth, *Separate Roads to Feminism*. See also Springer, *Living for the Revolution*; Enke, *Finding the Movement*; Hewitt, *No Permanent Waves*; Hesford, *Feeling Women's Liberation*; Cobble, *The Other Women's Movement*; Ezekiel, *Feminism in the Heartland*. Sara Evans wrote an historiographical essay on women's liberation calling for studies that grapple with challenges that conversations about race and class brought to the fore as well as for studies that consider the international realm. See Evans, "Women's Liberation."

12. In her dissertation, Caitlin Casey researched transnational 1960s social movements. See Casey, "Vanguards of Globalization." For an historiographical overview of transnational feminism, see De Haan, "Eugenie Cotton, Pak Chong-ae, and Claudia Jones." For more on the changing nature of the international feminist organizing of British and American women over the course of the twentieth century, see Bolt, *Sisterhood Questioned?*

13. In some ways, this finding echoes that of Rhodri Jeffreys-Jones, who claimed that antiwar activists succeeded in ending the war via serial protests undertaken by

people in different social movements—workers, women, students, and African Americans. The present work, however, disagrees with the serial nature of the protests. See Jeffreys-Jones, *Peace Now!*

14. Oropeza, *¡Raza Sí!, ¡Guerra No!*; Maeda, *Chains of Babylon*; Wu, *Radicals on the Road*. See also Mariscal, "Mexican Americans and the Viet Nam War"; Young, *Soul Power*.

15. Nguyen, *Hanoi's War*. Nguyen Thi Binh remembers people's diplomacy as of significance; see ibid., 183–84, 296.

16. Quoc Thich, "The Women Who Assume the 'Three Responsibilities' at Haiphong Port," *Women of Vietnam*, no. 3 (1965): 12–13, 28; "Quang Binh, a Heroic Province," *Women of Vietnam*, no. 3 (1965): 6–8. See also Turner, *Even the Women Must Fight*, 26–27; Anderson, "Fighting for Family."

17. In some ways, this project parallels that of Marian Mollin as she sought to expose the practices of radical pacifists that underlay their claims to promote an egalitarian society. See Mollin, *Radical Pacifism in Modern America*.

18. Brigham, *Guerrilla Diplomacy*; Turner, *Even the Women Must Fight*; Taylor, *Vietnamese Women at War*; The Military History Institute of Vietnam, *Victory in Vietnam*; Nguyen, *Hanoi's War*; Anderson, "Fighting for Family."

19. Recently, Lien-Hang Nguyen has called for more research along these lines. See Nguyen, "Revolutionary Circuits."

20. Nguyen, *Hanoi's War*; Nguyen Thi Binh, *Family, Friends and Country*, 158–60.

21. Young, *The Vietnam Wars*, 38–42, 116–23, quotation from Resolution on 119.

22. Frances Herring, "American and Vietnamese Women Join Hands for Peace," 1965, Series B, 2, Box 2, Folder "1965, Djakarta—WSP Delegation to Vietnamese Women," WSPR, SCPC, 1.

Chapter One

1. Shirley Lens, "Issues for Discussion," *Memo* 3, no. 2 (1964): 11.

2. Indonesia was chosen because it was one of a limited number of countries that would allow the entrance of Vietnamese women on such short notice. Other possible locations were India, Japan, Burma, Ceylon, and Cambodia. Some WSP members were concerned about having Indonesia as the location because it had pulled out of the United Nations to protest Malaysia becoming a member state. See Mary Clarke and Lorraine Gordon, "WSP's Project Meeting with Vietnamese Women," *Memo* 3, no. 21 (June 14, 1965): 1–3, 10; Women Strike for Peace, "Concerning the Jakarta Meeting" (Washington, D.C., June 28, 1965), Series A, 2, Box 2, Folder "Literature: 1965," WSPR, SCPC; Mary Clarke, "The Realities of the World Are at Odds with Our Foreign Policy," Report (ca. 1965), Series B, 1, Box 3, Folder "Orig Folder—Trip to Djakarta (1965)," WSPR, SCPC; "Discussions between WISP and Vietnamese Women" (Jakarta, July 1965), Box 26, Folder "Sidney Lens Papers—Shirley Lens Material," SLP, CHS.

3. Swerdlow, "Ladies' Day at the Capitol"; Swerdlow, *Women Strike for Peace*. For more on women's use of maternalism, see, among many other examples, Alonso, *Peace as a Women's Issue*; Brookfield, *Cold War Comforts*; Castledine, *Cold War Progressives*;

Koven and Michel, *Mothers of a New World;* Michel and Rosen, "The Paradox of Maternalism"; Sklar, " 'Some of Us Who Deal with the Social Fabric.' " According to historian Landon Storrs, in the 1940s and 1950s, "government and private actors manipulated the fear of espionage toward ends that included shoring up social hierarchies." Along this line, WSP members hoped to mask the potentially subversive nature of their protests by highlighting their dedication to women's maternal responsibilities. See Storrs, *The Second Red Scare and the Unmaking of the New Deal Left*, 4.

4. See, for example, Alonso, *Peace as a Women's Issue;* Bussey and Tims, *Pioneers for Peace;* Fischer, "Addams's Internationalist Pacifism and the Rhetoric of Maternalism"; Foster, *Women for All Seasons;* Loyd, " 'War Is Not Healthy for Children and Other Living Things.' " For other examples of works on women's peace activism, see Early, *A World Without War;* Goosen, *Women against the Good War;* Plastas, *A Band of Noble Women;* Schneidhorst, *Building a Just and Secure World;* Schott, *Reconstructing Women's Thoughts;* Sharer, *Vote and Voice.*

5. Swerdlow, *Women Strike for Peace*, 27 and chapter 3.

6. FBI, "FBI File: Mary Clarke, 100-HQ-395252, Section 1" (Los Angeles, 1952–1961).

7. Taylor, *We Made a Difference*, 30.

8. Bui Thi Cam, "To Margaret Russell" (May 16, 1964), Box 8, Folder 6, DAP.

9. Ibid. See also Bui Thi Cam, "To Helen Lamb (Enclosure: Open Letter to American Mothers)," March 2, 1965, Box 9, Folder 125, HBLP, Schlesinger; Nguyen Thi Thuc Vien, "Nguyen Thi Thuc Vien to American Mothers," December 1, 1965, Series A, 3, Box 2, Folder "International Correspondence 1965," WSPR, SCPC; Vietnamese Women's Union, "Vietnam Women's Union to American Mothers," June 21, 1966, Series A, 3, Box 2, Folder "International Correspondence 1966," WSPR, SCPC; Le Thi Xuyen, "To Friends," February 9, 1965, Box 9, Folder 125, HBLP, Schlesinger; Le Thi Xuyen, "To Friends," September 23, 1963, Box 8, Folder 6, DAP; Women's Union of Liberation, "Open Letter to the Women of Various Countries on the Occasion of Women's International Day," February 20, 1964, Box 8, Folder 6, DAP; Chien si, "Open Letter to the Women of the U.S.A.," March 8, 1964, Box 8, Folder 6, DAP; Nguyen Thi Tu, "To Women Strike for Peace," April 3, 1964, Box 8, Folder 6, DAP; Phan Thi An, "Speech by Mrs. Phan Thi An" (Hanoi, March 28, 1963), Box 4, Folder 53, HBLP, Schlesinger.

10. "A Fighting Mother or The Story of Nguyen Thi Ut," in *Vietnamese Women*, 84–110, quotation on 88.

11. "A National Socialist Culture Promoted," *Vietnam Courier*, August 24, 1970, 7.

12. Clarke and Gordon, "WSP's Project Meeting," 3.

13. Ibid., 2.

14. Ibid., 3. Clarke and Gordon presented no evidence that the Johnson administration was planning to use nuclear weapons, but their statement was a common one for WSP members.

15. Also included on the trip were Beverly Axelrod, a white lawyer who later defended members of the Black Panther Party, from San Francisco; Aline Berman, an Asian American WSP member and writer from Washington, D.C.; Nanci Gitlin

[Hollander], a white member of Students for a Democratic Society (SDS) from Ann Arbor; Frances Herring, a white WSP member and Berkeley professor of governmental studies; Esther Cooper Jackson, an African American civic worker from California and editor of the civil rights periodical *Freedomways*; Shirley Lens, a white WSP member and teacher from Chicago; Phyllis Schmidt, a white WSP member and teacher from Long Beach, California; and Bernice Steele, a white WSP member and social worker from Washington, D.C.

16. Other members representing the VWU included Nguyen Khoa Dieu Hong, president of the Hanoi branch of the VWU; Bui Thi Cam, a lawyer who drafted legislation pertaining to women's rights; Vo Thi The, a professor of literature in Hanoi; Nguyen Thi Truc, a medical doctor; and Bui Boi Anh, a news editor and interpreter.

17. The two other WUL members in attendance were Nguyen Ngoc Dung, executive in the Student's Liberation Movement; and Le Thi Cao, a teacher. See Gilbert Benjamin, "Mary Leona Clarke," FBI file (Los Angeles, July 11, 1966), 12–13; Phyllis Schmidt, "Speaking Notes of Phyllis Schmidt Re Trip to Djakarta," July 1965, Series B, 1, Box 3, Folder "Orig Folder—Phyllis Schmidt, Trip to Djakarta (1965)," WSPR, SCPC; "Notes on Vietnamese Women," July 1965, Series B, 1, Box 3, Folder "Orig Folder—Trip to Djakarta (1965)," WSPR, SCPC; " 'Peace' Women and the Viet Cong," *Tocsin* 6, no. 27 (July 15, 1965): 1, 3; Unknown, "To Mary [Clarke]," August 20, 1965, Series B, 1, Box 3, Folder "Correspondence—Mary Clarke, Trip to Djakarta (1965)," WSPR, SCPC; "Press Release about Djakarta Trip," July 1965, Series B, 1, Box 3, Folder "Orig Folder—Trip to Djakarta (1965)," WSPR, SCPC.

18. South Vietnamese women who were part of the NLF were "the enemy" and were already in danger when in the South. See Frances Herring, "Statement of Frances Herring to Some Members of Parliament, London," July 19, 1965, Series B, 2, Box 2, Folder "1965, Djakarta—WSP Delegation to Vietnamese Women," WSPR, SCPC; Ann Arbor Women for Peace, "Memo Concerning the Jakarta Proposal," June 1965, Series D, 3, Box 1, Folder "Michigan," WSPR, SCPC; Women Strike for Peace, "Concerning the Jakarta Meeting" (Washington, D.C., June 28, 1965), Series A, 2, Box 2, Folder "Literature: 1965," WSPR, SCPC.

19. "Notes on Vietnamese Women"; Unknown, "To Mary [Clarke]"; Mary Clarke, "Meeting in Djakarta," October 1965, Series A, 2, Box 2, Folder "Literature: 1965," WSPR, SCPC.

20. Women Strike for Peace, "Draft: Call from Women Strike for Peace to the Women of America," July 1965, Series B, 1, Box 3, Folder "Orig Folder—Phyllis Schmidt, Trip to Djakarta (1965)," WSPR, SCPC. The "call" was distributed through WSP's periodical, *Memo*.

21. Delegation of the South Vietnam Liberation Women's Union and Delegation of the American Women, "Joint Appeal to the Women of the United States from the Women Who Assembled at Jakarta, Indonesia in July 1965 from North Vietnam, the National Liberation Front of South Vietnam and the United States," 18 July 1965, Box 26, Folder "Jakarta July 1965," SLP, CHS. Initially, one woman from each delegation, the VWU, the WUL, and WSP, wrote a joint proposal for distribution in the United States. The WSP delegation, however, rejected the entire statement and

wrote a different version of the statement overnight. Although I have found references to the original statement, I have yet to locate it in the archives. For information about the original statement, see Frances Herring, "Statement of Frances Herring to Some Members of Parliament, London," July 19, 1965, Series B, 2, Box 2, Folder "1965, Djakarta—WSP Delegation to Vietnamese Women," WSPR, SCPC; Phyllis Schmidt, "North Still Has the Floor . . . ," July 1965, Series B, 1, Box 3, Folder "Orig Folder—Trip to Djakarta (1965)," WSPR, SCPC. The VWU published the joint communiqué in its quarterly periodical *Women of Vietnam*. See "Joint Appeal to the Women of the United States from the Women Who Assembled at Jakarta, Indonesia in July 1965 from North Vietnam, the National Liberation Front of South Vietnam and the United States," *Women of Vietnam*, no. 3 (1965): 24–25.

22. Delegation of the South Vietnam Liberation Women's Union and Delegation of the American Women, "Joint Appeal," 1.

23. Ibid.

24. Ibid., 2.

25. Ibid., 3.

26. "Notes on Vietnamese Women"; Nguyen, *Hanoi's War*, 182–84; Nguyen Thi Binh, *Family, Friends and Country*, esp. 56–59, 101–15, 124–28.

27. Mary Clarke, "WSPers Return from Jakarta," *Memo* 3, no. 24 (July 31, 1965): 4.

28. Ibid.

29. Aline Berman, "To Mary Clarke," October 26, 1965, Series B, 1, Box 3, Folder "Correspondence—Mary Clarke, Trip to Djakarta (1965)," WSPR, SCPC; Bernice Steele, "To Mary Clarke," October 27, 1965, Series B, 1, Box 3, Folder "Correspondence—Mary Clarke, Trip to Djakarta (1965)," WSPR, SCPC; Shirley Lens, "To Mary Clarke," November 2, 1965, Series B, 1, Box 3, Folder "Correspondence—Mary Clarke, Trip to Djakarta (1965)," WSPR, SCPC; Nanci Gitlin, "To Mary Clarke," November 3, 1965, Series B, 1, Box 3, Folder "Correspondence—Mary Clarke, Trip to Djakarta (1965)," WSPR, SCPC; Mary Clarke, "To Jakarta Ten," November 8, 1965, Series B, 1, Box 3, Folder "Correspondence—Mary Clarke, Trip to Djakarta (1965)," WSPR, SCPC.

30. Lens, "To Mary Clarke."

31. Bernice Steele, Margaret Russell, and Aline Berman, "Report of American Women Who Met with the Women of Vietnam" (Washington, D.C., 1966), Series A, 2, Box 2, Folder "Literature: 1966," WSPR, SCPC, 1.

32. Ibid., 7–8.

33. Ibid., cover letter.

34. Dagmar Wilson, "WSPers Return from Jakarta," *Memo* 3, no. 24 (July 31, 1965): 2.

35. Milward Simpson, "An Incisive Look at Women Strike for Peace," *Congressional Record—Senate* 111, no. 17 (September 2, 1965): 22759–65, quotation on 22759.

36. Vietnamese Women's Union, "Vietnam Women's Union to American Mothers," June 21, 1966, Series A, 3, Box 2, Folder "International Correspondence 1966," WSPR, SCPC.

37. Union of Australian Women, "Union of Australian Women to WISP," June 1965, Series B, 1, Box 3, Folder "Correspondence—Mary Clarke, Trip to Djakarta (1965)," WSPR, SCPC; Phyllis Latona, "Report on Discussions between the Austra-

lian Delegation and Delegations of Women from North and South Vietnam," July 1965, Series B, 1, Box 3, Folder "Orig Folder—Trip to Djakarta (1965)," WSPR, SCPC.

38. "The Whole World Supports Us," *Vietnam Courier*, January 23, 1967, 6.

39. "1966: Landmarks of the Vietnamese People's Patriotic Struggle against U.S. Aggression," *Vietnam Courier—Supplement*, January 9, 1967, esp. 10–12. Delegations from Cuba, Czechoslovakia, Italy, Japan, Romania, and the Soviet Union visited Hanoi in 1966.

40. "A Negro Mother Tells Why U.S. Cannot Win in Asia," *Muhammad Speaks*, February 10, 1967, 18.

41. Diane Nash Bevel, "Journey to North Vietnam," *Freedomways* 7 (Spring 1967): 118–28. See also Gill, "From Maternal Pacifism to Revolutionary Solidarity."

42. "Mrs. Bevel Gives Minority Press Viet Trip Exclusive," *The Afro American*, February 4, 1967, 13; "3 Women, Home, Say North Vietnam Won't Capitulate," *New York Times*, January 11, 1967, 6; "4 U.S. Women Get Visas from Hanoi: They Want to See If Civilian Targets Are Bombed," *New York Times*, December 17, 1966, 5; "Arrival of 4 U.S. Women in North Vietnam Reported," *New York Times*, December 24, 1966, 8; Leroy Aarons, "Mother Sees Another View of the War," *St. Petersburg Times*, January 24, 1967, 1-D; Jean Hailey, "Woman Visits Hanoi, Says U.S. Should Quit," *Washington Post*, January 17, 1967, A-6; "U.S. Woman, Home, Reports on Trip to Hanoi," *New York Times*, January 9, 1967, 11; "U.S. Women's Flight to Hanoi Is Delayed," *New York Times*, December 18, 1966, 4. See also Duberman, *A Saving Remnant*, esp. chapter 6. A statement made by the VWU to the American women implies that it did invite Nash in order to learn more about the African American movement and to gain access to an African American audience. See Barbara Deming, "Saturday, December 24," diary entry, Hanoi, December 24, 1966, Box 70, Folder 1362, BDP, Schlesinger, 1.

43. Le Mai, interview with author.

44. Pham Ngac, interview with author.

45. "A Crime of Genocide: Systematic Bombing of North Viet Nam Dykes," *Vietnam Courier*, July 31, 1967, 1–2; Special Correspondent, "On a Dyke Section of the Red River Bombed by U.S. Aircraft," *Vietnam Courier*, July 31, 1967, 2.

46. Nash Bevel, "Journey to North Vietnam"; Barbara Deming, "Calendar [of North Viet Nam Trip]," December 1966, Box 70, Folder 1362, BDP, Schlesinger.

47. Barbara Deming, "Notes on North Vietnam Trip," December 1966, Box 70, Folder 1358, BDP, Schlesinger; "U.S. Woman, Home."

48. Deming, "Saturday, December 24."

49. Nash Bevel, "Journey to North Vietnam," 120.

50. Ibid.

51. Ibid.

52. Deming, "Saturday, December 24," 6.

53. "Bộ Trưởng Lê Văn Hiến qua Lời Kể Của Cháu Ngoại (phần 1) (Minister Le Van Hien through the Testimony of Grandchild (Part 1))," *Kien Thuc*, March 5, 2013, http://kienthuc.net.vn/chuyen-nha/bo-truong-le-van-hien-qua-loi-ke-cua-chau -ngoai-phan-1-194299.html (April 20, 2015); "Những Cái Nhất Của Phụ Nữ Việt Nam (The Best of Viet Nam's Women)," *Truong THCS Dien Hai*, October 19, 2013,

http://thcs-dhai.phongdien.thuathienhue.edu.vn/tin-tuc/tin-van-hoa-xa-hoi/nhung
-cai-nhat-cua-phu-nu-viet-nam.htm (April 20, 2015).

54. Barbara Deming, "Thursday, December 29," December 29, 1966, Box 70, Folder 1362, BDP, Schlesinger, 1–2.

55. Barbara Deming, "It Is Very Hard . . ." (Monticello, N.Y., April 7, 1975), Box 71, Folder 1381, BDP, Schlesinger.

56. Deming, "Thursday, December 29"; Deming, "Saturday, December 24"; Barbara Deming, "December 28, Wednesday," Box 70, Folder 1362, BDP, Schlesinger, esp. 1; Barbara Deming, "Sunday, December 25" (Phu Ly and Nam Dinh, December 25, 1966), Box 70, Folder 1362, BDP, Schlesinger, 6.

57. Deming, "Saturday, December 24," 5.

58. "Two U.S. Women Report Hanoi Bomb 'Horrors,'" New York Post, January 9, 1967, Box 565, Folder 2, JBMP, Duke, n.p.

59. "3 Women, Home"; Barbara Deming, "Friday, December 23" (Hanoi, December 23, 1966), Box 70, Folder 1362, BDP, Schlesinger; Barbara Deming, "Friday, December 30," December 30, 1966, Box 70, Folder 1362, BDP, Schlesinger; Barbara Deming, "Sunday, January 1," January 1, 1967, Box 70, Folder 1362, BDP, Schlesinger, esp. 4–5; Barbara Deming, "January 2—Monday," January 2, 1967, Box 70, Folder 1362, BDP, Schlesinger; Paul McCloskey, "Our Bombs Fall on People," Congressional Record—House 118, no. 22 (September 6, 1972): 29635–36; "Pentagon Concedes and Denies Queries on Bombs," Palm Beach Post, May 3, 1972, A4.

60. Deming, "Sunday, December 25," 13.

61. Barbara Deming, "Ullman of Cape Codder Asks . . . ," Lecture, Cape Cod, January 1967, Box 70, Folder 1364, BDP, Schlesinger; Deming, "Sunday, January 1."

62. Barbara Deming, "Talk: The Temptations of Power," Lecture, Spring 1967, Box 70, Folder 1362, BDP, Schlesinger, 8.

63. Ibid., 5.

64. Ibid.

65. Ibid., 6.

66. Deming, "January 2—Monday," 1.

67. "New Lies Are Invented," Vietnam Courier, January 9, 1967, 3; "Salisbury's Reports on Bombing of Civilians: Anatomy of an Exposure," Mobilizer 1, no. 2 (February 6, 1967): 1–2, 7.

68. Committee on Foreign Relations, Harrison E. Salisbury's Trip to North Vietnam, 3.

69. Committee on Foreign Relations, Harrison E. Salisbury's Trip to North Vietnam; William Ryan, "Harrison Salisbury Reports from Hanoi," Congressional Record—House 113, no. 1 (January 11, 1967): A35–A36, A39–A40, A42–A43, A43–A45, A46–A47, A48–A49, A51, A53–A54, A55, A58–A60.

70. Deming, "Saturday, December 24—Hospital"; "U.S. Woman, Home."

71. Nash Bevel, "Journey to North Vietnam," 119. See also Deming, "January 2—Monday," 1.

72. "A Negro Mother Tells Why U.S. Cannot Win in Asia."

73. Ibid. See also, for example, "Mrs. Bevel Gives Minority Press"; "Woman Reports on Trip," New York Times, January 21, 1967, 3.

74. "U.S. Woman, Home." See also, among other examples, Hailey, "Woman Visits Hanoi"; "Woman Reports on Trip"; "North's Civilians Called Targets," *New York Times*, January 10, 1967, 5.

75. Louis Wyman, "Should There Be a Declaration of War in Vietnam?" *Congressional Record—House* 113, no. 9 (May 4, 1967): 11689-90, quotation on 11689. See also Deming, "Ullman of Cape Codder Asks . . . ."

76. John Finney, "U.S. Acts to Revoke Passports of 4 More for a Visit to Hanoi," *New York Times*, February 4, 1966, 7; Fred Graham, "Passport Denial Curbed by Court," *New York Times*, December 21, 1967, 1; "U.S. Unit Sends Mission to Hanoi in Behalf of Colloquy on Peace," *New York Times*, January 8, 1967, 22; Benjamin Welles, "U.S. to Lift Passports of Lynd and 2 Others for Hanoi Visit," *New York Times*, February 3, 1966, 1; "4 Women Who Visited Hanoi Will Lose U.S. Passports," *New York Times*, January 18, 1967, 9. See also Hershberger, *Traveling to Vietnam*, 66.

77. Hammond, *Reporting Vietnam*, esp. 2-3, 39; "U.S. Unit Sends Mission to Hanoi."

78. Dagmar Wilson, "To Talk about Vietnam Today . . . ," ca. 1967, Series A, 3, Box 14, Folder "Speeches by Dagmar Wilson (c. 1967)," WSPR, SCPC, 2.

79. Ha Giang, "To Friends," February 27, 1967, Series A, 3, Box 2, Folder "International Correspondence 1967," WSPR, SCPC; Ha Giang, "To Women Strike for Peace," June 7, 1967, Series A, 3, Box 2, Folder "International Correspondence 1967," WSPR, SCPC.

80. Ruth Krause, "The Trip," *Memo* 5, no. 12 (October 1967): 7-10.

81. Judith Martin, "A Visit to Vietnam Stirs Impulse to 'Strike Back,'" *Memo* 5, no. 12 (October 1967): 5-6. Originally published in the *Washington Post*. See Krause, "The Trip"; "Girl Sniper Bags 25 GI's," *L.A. Free Press*, October 20, 1967, n.p.

82. Hershberger, *Traveling to Vietnam*, esp. chapter 5. See also Allen, *Until the Last Man Comes Home*.

83. Committee on Internal Security, *Investigation of Students for a Democratic Society Part 7-A*, esp. 2267-70. Carol McEldowney and Vivian Rothstein met with the sailor along with Tom Hayden. For more on their trip, see chapter 4.

84. Unknown, Dagmar Wilson and Vietnamese Woman during Bombing, Photograph, 1967, Photograph Collection, Box "Demonstrations/Protests; Billboards; Delegations," WSPR, SCPC.

85. Unknown, Dagmar Wilson, Ruth Krause, and Vietnamese Militiawoman, Photograph, 1967, Photograph Collection, Box "Demonstrations/Protests; Billboards; Delegations," WSPR, SCPC.

86. Unknown, Girls' Militia North of Hanoi, Photograph, 1967, Photograph Collection, Box "North Vietnam: Misc. Vietnam/Cambodia/Laos/Injured & Dead," WSPR, SCPC.

87. Krause, "The Trip."

88. Pham Ngac, interview with author. Pham Ngac could not recall the name of the woman who made this statement, but it seems likely that it was Dagmar Wilson.

89. Quoted in Martin, "A Visit to Vietnam," 5. See J. T. Waggonner, "'Strike Three' on Peacenik Women's Group," *Congressional Record—House* (September 26, 1967): 12496-97. J. T. Waggonner, a representative from Alabama, provided a disapproving

editorial from the *Washington Post* as evidence that WSP was no longer effective. He further argued that WSP's leaders had "obvious Communist leanings."

90. Martin, "A Visit to Vietnam," 5.

91. FBI, "Memo: Dagmar Wilson" (Washington, D.C., February 5, 1968). See also S. A. Philip H. Wilson, "Succinct Summary," FBI file, October 28, 1968; FBI, "Supplemental Correlation Summary: Dagmar Wilson," February 24, 1971.

92. Krause, "The Trip," 9.

93. "Girl Sniper Bags 25 GI's."

94. Martin, "A Visit to Vietnam," 6.

95. "The Conference . . . ," *Memo* 5, no. 12 (October 1967): 11–14, quotation on 11.

96. Krause, "The Trip," 10.

97. Gail Eaby, "In Memoriam," *Memo* 6, no. 1 (November 1967): 15; Gail Eaby, "To Cora," January 12, 1970, Box 1, Folder "WSP," CWP, SCPC.

Chapter Two

1. Susan Sontag, "Trip to Hanoi," *Esquire*, December 1968, http://www.viet-studies.info/TripToHanoi_Sontag.htm (June 14, 2013); Anderson, *Imagined Communities*. Lady Borton explains this aspect of Vietnamese language in Nguyen Thi Binh, *Family, Friends and Country*, footnote 1, 53–54.

2. Cora Weiss, "I Was in Vietnam," Typescript (New York, N.Y., 1970), Box 2, Folder "Hanoi Article 1969," CWP, SCPC, 9.

3. Swerdlow, "'Not My Son, Not Your Son, Not Their Sons.'"

4. Larry Gates, *Girls Say Yes to Boys Who Say No*, Poster, 1968.

5. Young, *The Vietnam Wars*, 211.

6. Hendrick Smith, "Leaders in Hanoi Favor Cambodia as Site for Talks," *New York Times*, April 7, 1968, 1, 3, quotation on 3.

7. Ibid., 1, 3; Young, *The Vietnam Wars*, 192–231; Robert Trumbull, "2 Novelists Tell of Visit to Hanoi," *New York Times*, April 8, 1968, 3. For more on McCarthy's trip, see McCarthy, *Hanoi*.

8. Lynda Barrett, "Minutes of the National Consultative Committee" (Washington, D.C., January 17, 1968), Series A, 1, Box 1, Folder "National Consultative Committee Minutes and Memos (1965–July 1970)," WSPR, SCPC, n.p.

9. Ibid.; Ruth Meyers, "Report" (New York, February 1968), Series A, 2, Box 2, Folder "Literature: 1968," WSPR, SCPC. Support included letting the United States set up military bases in that country, sending troops to Viet Nam, and financially supporting the U.S. military endeavor in Viet Nam. See Young, *The Vietnam Wars*, 192–231.

10. Yvonne Dumont, "Speech by Mrs. Yvonne Dumont, General Secretary of the Union of French Women" (Paris, April 1968), Series A, 4, Box 3, Folder "Paris Conference of Women to End the War in Vietnam (Apr. 1968)," WSPR, SCPC, 3.

11. Dumont, "Speech by Mrs. Yvonne Dumont"; Voice of Women, Canada, "Paris Conference of Women Working to End the War in Vietnam Report from Voice of Women, Canada" (Paris, April 1968), Series A, 4, Box 3, Folder "Paris Con-

ference of Women to End the War in Vietnam (Apr. 1968)," WSPR, SCPC; "Joint Communique" (Paris, April 1968), Series A, 4, Box 3, Folder "Paris Conference of Women to End the War in Vietnam (Apr. 1968)," WSPR, SCPC; "List of Participants" (Paris, April 1968), Series A, 4, Box 3, Folder "Paris Conference of Women to End the War in Vietnam (Apr. 1968)," WSPR, SCPC; Andree Audoin, "At the Reception Organized by the U.F.F. American and Vietnamese Women Said to Me: 'We Want to Save Our Children,'" April 27, 1968, Series A, 4, Box 3, Folder "Paris Conference of Women to End the War in Vietnam (Apr. 1968)," WSPR, SCPC; "Faith, Love & Compassion: Common Bond for American & Vietnamese Women's Peace Talks" (New York, N.Y., May 1968), Box 4, Folder 62, HBLP, Schlesinger; Ruth Meyers, "Report" (New York, February 1968), Series A, 2, Box 2, Folder "Literature: 1968," WSPR, SCPC.

12. "Report of the Anti-Draft Workshop," Typescript (Paris, April 1968), Box 2, Folder "Paris Air 1968 Conference of Women to End War," CWP, SCPC; "Women from 10 Countries Call for End of 'Unjust War,'" *New York Times*, April 28, 1968, 24; Lynda Barrett, "Minutes of the National Consultative Committee" (Washington, D.C., January 17, 1968), Series A, 1, Box 1, Folder "National Consultative Committee Minutes and Memos (1965–July 1970)," WSPR, SCPC; Lorna Brown, "Opposition to the Vietnam War in New Zealand" (Paris, April 1968), Series A, 4, Box 3, Folder "Paris Conference of Women to End the War in Vietnam (Apr. 1968)," WSPR, SCPC; Meyers, "Report"; Ellen Reiser, "'It Was a Love-In That Lasted One Week,'" *Journal News*, June 28, 1968, Box 566, Folder 1, JBMP, Duke; Voice of Women, "Paris Conference of Women Working to End the War."

13. "Nữ Dũng Sĩ 7 Lần Được Gặp Bác Hồ (Female Warrior Saw Uncle Ho Seven Times)," *Dantri*, May 19, 2013, http://dantri.com.vn/xa-hoi/nu-dung-si-7-lan-duoc -gap-bac-ho-732255.htm (April 20, 2015); "O Du Kích 'Dũng Sĩ Diệt Mỹ' Được 7 Lần Gặp Bác (Guerrilla 'Valiantly Killed Americans' Met Uncle 7 Times)," *Nguoi Dua Tin*, June 3, 2013, http://www.nguoiduatin.vn/chuyen-chua-ke-cua-o-du-kich -dung-si-diet-my-duoc-7-lan-gap-bac-a82650.html (April 20, 2015); "Kỷ Niệm 123 Năm Ngày Sinh Chú Tịch Hồ Chí Minh: Dũng Sĩ Bảy Lần Gặp Bác (Celebrating 123rd Anniversary of President Ho Chi Minh's Birth)," *Cong An*, May 16, 2013, http://cadn.com.vn/news/122_97269_ky-nie-m-123-nam-nga-y-sinh-chu-ti-ch-ho -chi-minh-du-ng-si-ba-y-la-n-ga-p-ba-c.aspx (April 20, 2015).

14. Ngo Thi Tuyet, interview with author. Photos in possession of Ngo Thi Tuyet.

15. Nguyen Thi Binh, "Speech by Mrs. Nguyen Thi Binh, Head of the Delegation of the South Vietnamese Women's Union for Liberation at the Meeting with Women from the USA and Countries Helping It in the Vietnam War" (Paris, April 1968), Series A, 4, Box 3, Folder "Paris Conference of Women to End the War in Vietnam (Apr. 1968)," WSPR, SCPC, 5.

16. Ibid.

17. "Faith, Love & Compassion."

18. Commission de Travail, "Rapport de La Commission de Travail Sur L'Echange d'Informations Sur Les Methodes et Activites Concernant Les Actions Pour La

Paix, Contre La Guerre Au Vietnam, La Coordination Des Actions Futures" (Paris, April 1968), Series A, 4, Box 3, Folder "Paris Conference of Women to End the War in Vietnam (Apr. 1968)," WSPR, SCPC.

19. Audoin, "At the Reception Organized by the U.F.F."

20. Phan Thi An, "Message Taped by Mrs. Phan Thi An," April 1968, Box 4, Folder 62, HBLP, Schlesinger.

21. "Joint Communique" (Paris, April 1968), Series A, 4, Box 3, Folder "Paris Conference of Women to End the War in Vietnam (Apr. 1968)," WSPR, SCPC.

22. Voice of Women, "Paris Conference of Women Working to End the War," 2.

23. Ethel Taylor, "Paris in the Spring: Report of the Paris Conference of Concerned Women to End the War April 23–26, 1968" (Paris, April 1968), Series A, 4, Box 3, Folder "Committee of Liaison with Families (1969–1972)," WSPR, SCPC.

24. Reiser, "'It Was a Love-In That Lasted One Week.'"

25. Ha Giang, "To Cora Weiss," September 1, 1968, Box 2, Folder "Vietnamese Women Visit Canada, 1968," CWP, SCPC; Phan Thi An, "To Ethel Taylor," October 19, 1968, Series A, 3, Box 1, Folder "Ethel Taylor Files: Vietnam (1968–1979)," WSPR, SCPC; Phan Thi An, "To Irma Zigas," October 22, 1968, Series C, 2, Box 8, Folder "Vietnam," WSPR, SCPC; Ha Giang, "A Letter to American Women on the Occasion of March 8" (February 15, 1969), Box 1, Folder "Paris Conference of Women to End War, 1968," CWP, SCPC.

26. Women's Union of Liberation, "Open Letter to the Women of Various Countries on the Occasion of Women's International Day" (February 20, 1964), DAP.

27. "Women's International Democratic Federation Delegation to Official Talks in Paris," *Vietnam*, no. 10 (October 1968): 1–8, quotation on 3.

28. Ibid., 7.

29. Phan Thi An, "Report of the Viet Nam Women's Union," *Documents and Information 7*, Congress Special, II (1969): 15–32, quotation on 29. See also Women's International Democratic Federation, *The Situation in the Countries of Indochina and Solidarity with Their Peoples* (Berlin: International Viet Nam Solidarity Committee, Women's International Democratic Federation, 1970).

30. Phan Thi An, "Report of the Viet Nam Women's Union," 21.

31. Duckles, Nguyen Thi Binh: Pacifica Radio Archive, http://archive.org /details/MadelineDucklesInterviewsNguyenThiBinh.

32. Cora Weiss, "A Message to All WSPers" (New York, N.Y., February 1969), Box 2, Folder "Paris Air 1968 Conference of Women to End War," CWP, SCPC. See also "CCC Minutes: Cora Weiss Reports from Paris" (New York, N.Y., February 5, 1969), Box 2, Folder "Paris Air 1968 Conference of Women to End War," CWP, SCPC.

33. Cora Weiss, "The Face of the Enemy," *Memo* (Fall 1969): 4–7; "Montreal Plans for the Vietnamese Women," 1969, Box 2, Folder "Vietnamese Women Visit Canada, 1968," CWP, SCPC; Kay Macpherson, "Visit of Vietnamese Women Meetings in Toronto Area" (Toronto, June 1969), Box 2, Folder "Vietnamese Women Visit Canada, 1968," CWP, SCPC; Voice of Women, Canada, "We Acknowledge with Thanks" (Toronto, June 1969), Box 2, Folder "Vietnamese Women Visit Canada, 1968," CWP, SCPC; Women Strike for Peace, "Vietnamese Women Visit Canada

Will Meet Americans" (New York, June 1969), Series A, 7, Box 1, Folder "WSP Literature Copied by FBI (1965–1972)," WSPR, SCPC; Women Strike for Peace, "Good News!," Memorandum (Washington, D.C., June 16, 1969), Box 2, Folder "Vietnamese Delegation Visit Canada Women Strike for Peace, 1969 (June–July)," CWP, SCPC; Voice of Women, Canada, "Vietnamese Women Visit Canada," Pamphlet (Toronto, July 1969), Box 2, Folder "Canada Vietnam Women Visit," CWP, SCPC; "'Peace' Women to Meet Viet Reds," *Long Island Press*, July 7, 1969, Box 2, Folder "Canada Vietnam Women Visit," CWP, SCPC; Mark Starowicz, "Canada Delays U.S. Women Seeking to Meet North Viets," *Toronto Daily Star*, July 8, 1969, 1–2; "Women's Confab: From Rochester and Vietnam," *Democrat & Chronicle*, July 17, 1969, Box 566, Folder 2, JBMP, Duke.

34. Cora Weiss, "To NCC," Memorandum (Washington, D.C., May 6, 1969), Box 2, Folder "Vietnamese Delegation Visit Canada Women Strike for Peace, 1969 (June–July)," CWP, SCPC.

35. Cora Weiss, "Report from Canada" (Report, Toronto, 1969), Box 2, Folder "Canada Vietnam Women Visit," CWP, SCPC; Huynh Ngoc An, interview with author.

36. Nguyen Thi Binh, *Family, Friends and Country*, footnote 28, 139.

37. "Notes on Vietnamese Women," July 1965, Series B, 1, Box 3, Folder "Orig Folder—Trip to Djakarta (1965)," WSPR, SCPC; Mark Starowicz, "She Stared at America—and It Made Her Cry," *Toronto Daily Star*, July 9, 1969, 3.

38. Weiss, "Report from Canada," 3.

39. Richard Fernandez, "To Clergy and Laymen Concerned about Vietnam," Memorandum (New York, N.Y., July 2, 1969), Box 2, Folder "Vietnamese Delegation Visit Canada Women Strike for Peace, 1969 (June–July)," CWP, SCPC; Ellin Hirst, "Several Women Who Have . . ." (Boston, ca. 1970), Carton 1, Folder 34, CBAP, Schlesinger; Starowicz, "Canada Delays U.S. Women"; "Vietnamese Women Visit Canada Will Meet Americans"; "Pullout Dooms Saigon—Cong Visitor," July 10, 1969, Box 1, Folder "WSP," CWP, SCPC; "FBI File: WSP," 1970, Box 24, Folder "WSP FBI File," CWP, SCPC; Cora Weiss, "Notes on Conference in Toronto, Canada, Monday, July 7, 1969" (Toronto, July 7, 1969), Box 2, Folder "Canada Vietnam Women Visit," CWP, SCPC.

40. Sontag, "Trip to Hanoi." Also see McEldowney, *Hanoi Journal*.

41. Weiss, "Notes on Conference in Toronto."

42. Voice of Women, Canada, "Vietnamese Women Visit Canada," Pamphlet (Toronto, July 1969), Box 2, Folder "Canada Vietnam Women Visit," CWP, SCPC, 3; Weiss, "The Face of the Enemy," 1. See also Cora Weiss, "Report from Canada" (Toronto, 1969), Box 2, Folder "Canada Vietnam Women Visit," CWP, SCPC, 1.

43. Elizabeth Shelton, "Women and the War," *Washington Post*, July 16, 1969, B1, B3; Starowicz, "She Stared at America"; Mora Armour, Amy Swerdlow, and Cora Weiss, "American Women Cross Canadian Border for Face to Face Meeting with Vietnamese Women in Gesture of Friendship and Peace," Press Release (New York, N.Y., July 7, 1969), Box 2, Folder "Vietnamese Delegation Visit Canada Women Strike for Peace, 1969 (June–July)," CWP, SCPC.

44. Hirst, "Several Women Who Have . . . ," 1.

45. Weiss, "Report from Canada," 1.

46. Weiss, "The Face of the Enemy," 4–7; "FBI File: WSP," (1970), Box 24, Folder "WSP FBI File," CWP, SCPC.

47. Ronald Koziol, "Communists Praise Role of Pacifists: Ask Them to Keep Up Their Protests," *Chicago Tribune*, July 27, 1969, Section 1A, 4.

48. "Pullout Dooms Saigon"; "To Have Us Believe . . . ," n.d., Box 2, Folder "Canada Vietnam Women Visit," CWP, SCPC.

49. Chong, *The Girl in the Picture*; Young, *The Vietnam Wars*; Turse, *Kill Anything That Moves*.

50. "A Housewife Goes to Hanoi," *Manhattan Tribune*, February 14, 1970, 3. See also "A Letter from Daddy," *Philadelphia Daily News*, December 24, 1969, 1–2.

51. Hershberger, *Traveling to Vietnam*, 142–50, 47–48; John Rarick, "POWs at Christmastime—What Are We Doing for Them?," *Congressional Record—House* 115, no. 29 (December 17, 1969): 39791–93; Committee on Internal Security, *New Mobilization Committee to End the War in Vietnam Part II*; Harry F. Byrd Jr., "The Plight of American Prisoners in North Vietnam," *Congressional Record—Senate* 116, no. 23 (September 14, 1970): 31512–13; Clinton, "Ethel Taylor," in *The Loyal Opposition*, 148–64.

52. Stewart Meacham, "The Release and Escort Mission for Three American Pilots" (August 1968), Box 2, Folder "Returned POWs," COLIAFAM, SCPC; Clinton, "Anne Weills," in *The Loyal Opposition*, 118–35.

53. Meacham, "Release and Escort Mission," 5.

54. Richard Ottinger, "American Prisoners of War—The Forgotten Americans of the Vietnam War," *Congressional Record—House* 114, no. 17 (September 29, 1969): 27376–85. A quick search of the *Congressional Record* reveals that the number of items mentioning POWs tripled from the calendar years of 1967 and 1968 to 1969 and 1970.

55. "3 U.S. Servicemen Released by Hanoi," *New York Times*, August 5, 1969, 1; John Kifner, "Court Backs Plan to Free POWs," *New York Times*, July 16, 1969, 7; "North Viet Journey," *The Great Speckled Bird*, August 25, 1969, 16.

56. Grace Paley, "Report from the DRV," *WIN*, September 15, 1969, 8.

57. Ibid., 8–9.

58. Ibid., 7.

59. Ibid. See also "North Viet Journey"; Grace Paley, "I Guess It Must Have Been Someone Else," *WIN*, May 15, 1971, 30–33.

60. Paley, "Report from the DRV," 8.

61. Committee on Internal Security, *Investigation of Students for a Democratic Society Part 7-A*; "3 U.S. Servicemen Released by Hanoi"; Ottinger, "American Prisoners of War—The Forgotten Americans of the Vietnam War."

62. "North Vietnam Politburo Resolution No. 194-NQ/TW, On Policy Toward Captured American Pilots in North Vietnam," November 20, 1969, History and Public Policy Program Digital Archive, Nguyen Quy, editor, Van Kien Dang Qoan Tap, 30, 1969 [Collected Party Documents, Volume 30, 1969] (Hanoi: National Political Publishing House, 2004), 303–5, translated for Cold War International History Project by Merle Pribbenow, http://digitalarchive.wilsoncenter.org/document/113936 (May 4, 2015).

63. Ibid.

64. Tran Minh Quoc, interview with author.

65. Betty Donovan, "To Peter Weiss with Enclosed CIA File," June 18, 1976, Box 22, Folder "FOIA 1976," CWP, SCPC; Federal Bureau of Investigation, "Women Strike for Peace Delegation to North Vietnam December 1, 1969" (Philadelphia, December 13, 1969), Series A, 7, Box 1, Folder "WSP literature copied by FBI (1965-1972)," WSPR, SCPC; Cora Weiss, "Detention Camp Inspected," 1970, Box 1, Folder "WSP, 1962-1972," CWP, SCPC.

66. Clinton, "Cora Weiss," in *The Loyal Opposition*, 165-82; "Captives' Letters Brought," *New York Times*, December 24, 1969, 7; "List of 132 POWs Brought from Hanoi," *Washington Post*, December 24, 1969, Box 22, Folder "CIA File," CWP, SCPC; "Names of 132 POWs Released," *Miami Herald*, December 24, 1969, 8-A; "U.S. Women Release POW List," *Everett Herald*, December 24, 1969, Box 3, Folder "Newspaper Clippings: Cora Weiss 1960s-mid 1970s," CWP, SCPC; "5 POWs Reported Dead," *New York Times*, December 25, 1969, 2; "Messages from 131 POWs," December 25, 1969, Box 22, Folder "CIA File," CWP, SCPC; "Group Reports First Letter from 18 POWs to Families," *Philadelphia Bulletin*, January 19, 1970, 10.

67. Cora Weiss, interview with author; Jen Darr, "20 Questions: Ethel Barol Taylor," *Philadelphia City Paper*, December 10, 1998, http://citypaper.net/articles /121098/20q.shtml (May 28, 2013); Taylor, *We Made a Difference*, 41-57; Adams, "Ethel Barol Taylor," in *Peacework*, 10-18.

68. Hang Phuong, "To American Mothers," December 15, 1969, Series A, 3, Box 1, Folder "Ethel Taylor Files: Vietnam (1968-1979)," WSPR, SCPC.

69. Cora Weiss, "I Was in Vietnam" (New York, N.Y., 1970), Box 2, Folder "Hanoi Article 1969," CWP, SCPC.

70. Taylor, *We Made a Difference*, 56.

71. Young, *The Vietnam Wars*, 217-19, 243-44; Turse, *Kill Anything That Moves*.

72. "Letters from Survivors of U.S. Mass Killing in Son My," ca. 1969, Series A, 3, Box 1, Folder "Ethel Taylor Files: Vietnam (1968-1979)," WSPR, SCPC; Vo Thi Lien, "Testimony of Vo Thi Lien, Survivor of Song Mai [sic] Massacre," ca. 1969, Series A, 3, Box 1, Folder "Ethel Taylor Files: Vietnam (1968-1979)," WSPR, SCPC; Vo Thi Lien, "Son My Massacre Girl Survivor Vo Thi Lien's Letter to American and World Women," November 30, 1969, Series A, 3, Box 1, Folder "Ethel Taylor Files: Vietnam (1968-1979)," WSPR, SCPC.

73. Taylor, *We Made a Difference*, 53.

74. See also "Mass Slaying at Son My Denounced by Local Women's Committee," ca. 1969, Series A, 3, Box 1, Folder "Ethel Taylor Files: Vietnam (1968-1979)," WSPR, SCPC; Nguyen Thi Thuc Vien, "A Letter from Vietnamese Mothers to American Mothers," December 12, 1969, Series A, 2, Box 2, Folder "Literature: 1969," WSPR, SCPC; Weiss, "I Was in Vietnam"; Ethel Taylor, "Inquiry into War Crimes," March 26, 1971, Series A, 4, Box 3, Folder "Committee of Liaison with Families (1969-1972)," WSCP, SCPC; Cora Weiss, "The Next Time I Am a Tourist" (New York, N.Y., 1970), Box 2, Folder "Hanoi Article 1969," CWP, SCPC; "Son My," *Vietnam*, no. 8 (1969): 1-3; Patitucci, *Chronology of Developments in Vietnam*.

75. Donovan, "To Peter Weiss"; William Ryan, "Eaton's Hanoi Trip Helps Peace Cause," *Congressional Record—Senate* 115, no. 30 (December 23, 1969): 41429-30.

76. See, for example, "A Letter from Daddy"; "Glad Tidings from American POWs," *The Sun-Journal*, December 1969, Box 3, Folder "Newspaper Clippings: Cora Weiss 1960s–mid 1970s," CWP, SCPC; "At Last—Word from Our POWs," *San Francisco Examiner*, December 23, 1969, 1; "Lyndon POW's Wife Due First Letter Since 1965," *Courier-Journal*, December 24, 1969, A1–A2, Box 2, Folder "Hanoi Article 1969," CWP, SCPC; Steve Emmons, "6 Lines Tell Wife POW Husband Is Alive," *Los Angeles Times*, December 27, 1969, Box 2, Folder "Hanoi Article 1969," CWP, SCPC; "U.S. Women Release POW List"; "5 POWs Reported Dead"; "Messages from 131 POWs"; "Woman Says U.S. Plays Cruel Game," *Arkansas Gazette*, December 28, 1969, Box 6, Folder "Trips," COLIAFAM records, SCPC.

77. "A Missing Flier's Wife Softly Begged to Differ," *Philadelphia Daily News*, January 25, 1970, Box 22, Folder "CIA File," CWP, SCPC.

78. Committee on Armed Services, *Problems of Prisoners of War and Their Families.*

79. John Rarick, "Congressional Hearing Room Provided Hanoi Agents," *Congressional Record—House* 116, no. 2 (January 28, 1970): 1749-50; Howard Shapiro, "Pacifists Prey on POW Wives," *Pittsburgh Press*, February 4, 1970, Series A, 4, Box 3, Folder "Committee of Liaison with Families (1969–1972)," WSPR, SCPC; "Rep. Scherle Assails POW Liaison Group," *Washington DC Star*, June 11, 1970, Box 3, Folder "Newspaper Clippings: Cora Weiss 1960s–mid 1970s," CWP, SCPC; Jim Lucas, "POW Wives Show Their Ire," *Washington Daily News*, February 5, 1970; "2 to Reject Peace Group POW Letters," *Washington Post*, April 15, 1970.

80. Clinton, "Ethel Taylor," 155-56; Adams, "Ethel Barol Taylor," 16.

81. "CCC Minutes: Cora Weiss Reports from Paris" (New York, N.Y., February 5, 1969), Box 2, Folder "Paris Air 1968 Conference of Women to End War," CWP, SCPC.

Chapter Three

1. Elizabeth Martínez, "Looking for the Truth in North Vietnam—with Our Own Eyes," *El Grito del Norte* 3, no. 10, August 29, 1970, 4–5, 14, quotation on 14.

2. Ibid.

3. A note on terminology: "Mexican American" broadly includes people of Mexican descent living in the United States. "Chicano" is a political term adopted by some Mexican American activists beginning in the 1960s. For Martínez and other activists of color, "Third World" included people of color living in the United States.

4. Wu, *Radicals on the Road.* See also Young, *Soul Power*; Pulido, *Black, Brown, Yellow, and Left*; Gore, *Radicalism at the Crossroads*; Jung, *The Rising Tide of Color.*

5. In terms of the Cold War, this meant focusing on people's economic and social needs. See Burke, "From Individual Rights to National Development."

6. Anderson, *Eyes off the Prize*; Borstelmann, *The Cold War and the Color Line*; Dudziak, *Cold War Civil Rights*; Von Eschen, *Race against Empire.*

7. See, for example, Kelley and Esch, "Black Like Mao"; Frazier, *The East Is Black.*

8. See, for example, Roth, *Separate Roads to Feminism*; Springer, *Living for the Revolution*; Chow, "The Development of Feminist Consciousness among Asian American Women"; Blackwell, *¡Chicana Power!*; Chavez, "'We Have a Long, Beautiful History.'"

9. Martínez, "Looking for the Truth." For the perspectives of Martínez's travel companions, see Frank Joyce, "Back from Hanoi," *Rat*, June 5, 1970, 2–3, 27; Charlotte Bunch-Weeks, "Back from Hanoi," *off our backs* 1, no. 7 (June 26, 1970): 2–4; Charlotte Bunch, "Asian Women in Revolution," *Women: A Journal of Liberation* 1, no. 4 (1970): 9.

10. For more on the Chicano antiwar movement, see Oropeza, *¡Raza Sí! ¡Guerra No!* Oropeza also argues that Chicanos connected to the Vietnamese through the issue of land. See also Mariscal, "Mexican Americans and the Viet Nam War."

11. Martínez, interview by Loretta Ross, 3.

12. Ibid., 4.

13. Ibid.

14. Ibid., 5.

15. Ibid.

16. Ibid., 11.

17. Ibid. See also Martínez, interview by Anselmo F. Arellano.

18. Martínez, interview by Loretta Ross, 11.

19. Ibid.; "We Are Not Alone: A Survey of Movements around the World," *El Grito Del Norte*, March 20, 1969, 5–7; Enriqueta Longeaux y Vásquez, "The Woman of La Raza, Part I," *El Grito Del Norte*, July 6, 1969, 8–9; Enriqueta Longeaux y Vásquez, "The Woman of La Raza, Part II," *El Grito Del Norte*, July 26, 1969, 13; Enriqueta Longeaux y Vásquez, "La Chicana: Let's Build a New Life," *El Grito Del Norte*, November 15, 1969, 11.

20. Busto, *King Tiger*, 3.

21. Busto, *King Tiger*.

22. Martínez, "Looking for the Truth," 4.

23. Namely, Valdez related stories from Wilfred Burchett and Felix Greene. Burchett lived in Viet Nam for a number of years and wrote a book called *Vietnam: Inside Story of a Guerrilla War*. Greene toured the United States after reporting in North Viet Nam for a number of years and wrote the book *Vietnam! Vietnam!* See Valentina Valdez Martínez, "Hermanos: Who Are These People?," *El Grito Del Norte*, August 10, 1969, 6–8; Valentina Valdez Martínez, "Vietnam Story: The People Fight Using Nature and Courage," *El Grito Del Norte*, September 14, 1969, 8–9; Valentina Valdez Martínez, "Viet Nam: Schools and Hospitals for People," *El Grito Del Norte*, November 15, 1969, 13; Valentina Valdez Martínez, "Vietnam: Part 4, Who Is Fighting?" *El Grito Del Norte*, January 17, 1970, n.p.

24. Valdez, "Hermanos," 7.

25. Ibid., 8.

26. Ibid.

27. Ibid.

28. Valdez, "Viet Nam," 13. See also Martínez, "Looking for the Truth."

29. See, for example, Vásquez, "La Chicana"; Valentina Valdez Martinez, "Our Land and Our Culture," *El Grito Del Norte*, November 27, 1968, 5; Vásquez, "The Woman of La Raza, Part I."

30. Valdez, "Our Land and Our Culture," 5.

31. Ibid.

32. Martínez, *500 Years of Chicana Women's History*; Trujillo, *Chicano Empowerment and Bilingual Education*; Raul Ruiz, "Sal to Be Removed . . . Again," *Chicano Student Movement*, Los Angeles, Calif., August 1969, 1, 6; Raquel Tijerina, "Chicana Student Speaks Her Mind," *El Grito Del Norte*, October 5, 1968, 3; La Coronela, "Cultural Nationalism: A Fight for Survival—The Culture," *Chicano Student Movement*, Los Angeles, Calif., August 1969, 3.

33. Martínez, "Looking for the Truth"; Valdez, "Hermanos."

34. Martínez, "Looking for the Truth"; Bunch-Weeks, "Back from Hanoi."

35. Vásquez, "La Chicana"; Oropeza, "*Viviendo y Luchando*," in Espinoza and Oropeza, *Enriqueta Vasquez and the Chicano Movement*, xix–liii.

36. Vásquez, "The Woman of La Raza, Part II," 13.

37. Ibid.

38. Ibid. See also Vásquez, "The Woman of La Raza, Part I"; "Our Unknown Revolucionarias," *El Grito Del Norte*, June 5, 1971, C; Cotera, "Our Feminist Heritage," in García, *Chicana Feminist Thought*, 41–44, originally a speech given by Cotera in 1973; Rincón, "La Chicana," in García, *Chicana Feminist Thought*, 24–28, originally published in *Regeneración* 1, no. 10 (1971): 15–18.

39. "Special Section: La Chicana," *El Grito Del Norte*, June 5, 1971, A–P.

40. Valdez, "Vietnam: Part 4, Who Is Fighting?" n.p.

41. Ibid.

42. Enriqueta Longeaux y Vásquez, "Soy Chicana Primero!" *El Grito Del Norte*, April 26, 1971, 11.

43. Ibid.

44. Martínez, "Looking for the Truth," 15; Bunch, "Asian Women in Revolution," 9; Martínez, interview by Loretta Ross.

45. "Front Matter: Vietnam War—Why?" *El Grito Del Norte*, August 29, 1970, 1.

46. "Los Angeles—3 Raza Murdered," *El Grito Del Norte*, September 16, 1970, 5–7. For more on the Chicano Moratorium, see Oropeza, *¡Raza Sí! ¡Guerra No!*, esp. chapter 5.

47. Kimball, "Richard M. Nixon and the Vietnam War."

48. Gumbo Albert, "CounterPunch."

49. "In Brief," *South Viet Nam in Struggle*, September 20, 1970, 8; "Social Unrest in United States over Indochina," *South Viet Nam in Struggle*, July 1, 1970, 8.

50. William Scherle, "Question of Separation of Powers," *Congressional Record—House* 116, no. 29 (December 2, 1970): 39521–22, quotation on 39522.

51. Ibid.; Committee on the Judiciary, *Extent of Subversion in "New Left."*

52. The members of the delegation included Jan Austin, a white editor at *Ramparts*; Regina Blumenfeld, a white women's liberation activist; Elaine Brown, an African American and deputy minister of information for her chapter of the Black Panther Party in Los Angeles; Eldridge Cleaver, an African American and minister

of information for the Black Panther Party; Ann Froines, a white woman involved in the defense of the Chicago 8, including her husband; Alex Hing, an Asian American and minister of information for the Red Guards; Janet Kranzberg, a white representative of the Newsreel Alternative Media Collective; Randy Rappaport, a white member of the women's liberation group Bread and Roses in Boston; Robert Scheer, a white journalist and co-leader of the delegation; Hideko "Patricia" Sumi, an Asian American participant in the Movement for a Democratic Military; and Andy Truskier, a white member of the Peace and Freedom Party.

53. Brown, *A Taste of Power*, 228.

54. Elaine Brown, "The End of Silence," song from the album *Seize the Time* (Rhino Entertainment Company, 1969).

55. Giddings, *When and Where I Enter*, esp. 315; Sugrue, *Sweet Land of Liberty*.

56. For more on the history of Black Power, see, among many others, Joseph, *Waiting 'Til the Midnight Hour*; Joseph, *The Black Power Movement*; Lazerow and Williams, *In Search of the Black Panther Party*; Ogbar, *Black Power*; Tyson, *Radio Free Dixie*.

57. Kelley and Esch, "Black Like Mao"; Elbaum, *Revolution in the Air*; Rafalko, *MH/Chaos*, esp. 98.

58. "Report Hanoi Offer of PW-Panther Swap," *Chicago Sun-Times*, October 22, 1969, Box 65, Folder 1, JBMP, Duke.

59. Rafalko, *MH/Chaos*, 117–18; "Cleaver and Black Panther Group Attend Hanoi Observance," *New York Times*, August 19, 1970, 13.

60. "A Cause Whose Triumph Is a Certainty," *Vietnam Courier*, August 24, 1970, 2.

61. "Victory Belongs to the Afro-Americans in the US," *South Viet Nam in Struggle*, August 20, 1970, 11.

62. See, for example, South Vietnam National Liberation Front, "To Afro-American G.I.'s!," ca. 1968, Box 1, MFH, Hoover; South Vietnam National Liberation Front, "American Negro Soldiers!," ca. 1969, Box 1, MFH, Hoover; South Vietnam National Liberation Front, "US Armymen—Negro Armymen," ca. 1969, Box 1, MFH, Hoover; South Vietnam National Liberation Front, "Black GI's!," n.d., Box 1, MFH, Hoover.

63. Elaine Brown, "In North Korea, North Vietnam, Peking China, We Were Greeted as the Anti-Imperialist Delegation and Treated as Human Beings, as Respected Members of the Human Race," *The Black Panther*, October 3, 1970, C.

64. Ibid., D.

65. Brown, *A Taste of Power*, 189.

66. Ibid., 191.

67. Brown recruited Ericka Huggins, Evon Carter, Gwen Goodloe, and Joan Kelley to join her pursuit to expose sexist attitudes.

68. Brown, *A Taste of Power*, 191.

69. Ibid., 192. For more on how the shift to Black Power reshaped women's activism, see Cleaver, "Women, Power, and Revolution"; Springer, "Black Feminists Respond to Black Power Masculinism"; Ward, "The Third World Women's Alliance"; Williams, "Black Women, Urban Politics, and Engendering Black Power."

70. Myrna Hill, "Feminism and Black Nationalism," *The Militant*, April 2, 1971, 10.

71. Bobby Seale, "Women & B.P.P.," *Quicksilver*, March 3, 1970, Box 86, Folder 12, JBC, SSC.

72. Daniel Patrick Moynihan studied the causes of African American poverty for the Labor Department at the request of the Johnson administration. See Moynihan, *The Negro Family*.

73. White, *Too Heavy a Load*, 200.

74. Ibid., 201; Giddings, *When and Where I Enter*, 329. According to activists, women in black nationalist movements also demoted themselves to make room for men. See Political Education Committee, "Position Paper on Women," n.d., Box 6, Folder "Black Women," VOP, Duke.

75. White, *Too Heavy a Load*, 200, 203.

76. Brown, "In North Korea, North Vietnam, Peking China," B.

77. Brown, *A Taste of Power*.

78. Springer, "Black Feminists Respond to Black Power Masculinism," 108.

79. Giddings, *When and Where I Enter*, 311.

80. Quoted in Pam Newman, "Black Feminist Replies to Ultraleftist," *The Militant*, December 11, 1970, Box 5, Folder 4, WLC, SSC. See also Giddings, *When and Where I Enter*, 310; Anderson-Bricker, "'Triple Jeopardy.'"

81. Springer, "Black Feminists Respond to Black Power Masculinism," 108.

82. Maxine Williams, "Women's Liberation and Nationalism," *The Second Wave* 1, no. 1 (Spring 1971): 18–20. See also Harris, "From the Kennedy Commission to the Combahee Collective."

83. Quoted in Kelley and Esch, "Black Like Mao," 25.

84. Frances Beal, "Black Women: The Struggle for Liberation," New York City, n.d., Box 22, Folder "United States—Women of Color/Black Women," BOP, Duke, 171.

85. Patricia Haden, Donna Middleton, and Patricia Robinson, "A Historical and Critical Essay for Black Women," *The Spectator*, May 21, 1970, 6–12, quotation on 11.

86. Ibid.

87. Brown, "In North Korea, North Vietnam, Peking China," D.

88. Ibid.; Brown, *A Taste of Power*, 231.

89. Evelyn Yoshimura, "GIs and Asian Women," *Feminist Liberation Newsletter*, no. 28 (June 1971): 18.

90. Cited in Maeda, *Chains of Babylon*, 10.

91. Takemoto, "Pat Sumi," in *Asian Women*, 108.

92. Yokota, "Interview with Pat Sumi," in Louie, *Asian Americans*, 16–31.

93. "White Male Qualities," in Tachiki, Wong, and Odo, *Roots*, 44, originally published in *Gidra* (January 1970).

94. Ibid.

95. Discrimination against Asians often targeted only one ethnic group, making collaboration among Asian Americans less attractive. These conditions underlay Chinese American inaction when the U.S. government interned Japanese Americans during World War II and highlight that there was no natural alliance among peoples of Asian descent. Long before the Japanese bombed Pearl Harbor in 1941, Chinese Americans saw Japan as an enemy because it had invaded China. After Japan attacked

Pearl Harbor, the United States and China became allies, and Chinese Americans benefited from this alliance when the U.S. government revoked the Chinese Exclusion Act in 1943, allowing more immigration from China. In addition, Chinese Americans gained inroads into employment previously reserved for white male Americans because of the labor shortage caused by men going to war. Whereas Japanese Americans faced internment and the loss of their livelihoods during World War II, Chinese Americans won favor. See Wong, "War Comes to Chinatown." See also Tachiki, Wong, and Odo, "Success Story of One Minority Group in U.S.," in Tachiki, Wong, and Odo, *Roots*, 6–9, originally published in *U.S. News and World Report*, December 26, 1966.

96. Espiritu, "Panethnicity and Asian American Activism," 442.

97. Hsiao, "The Hidden History of Asian-American Activism in New York City"; Liu, Géron, and Lai, *The Snake Dance of Asian American Activism*; Maeda, *Chains of Babylon*, 3, 6–7; Wei, *The Asian American Movement*, 2.

98. Bay Area Asian Coalition Against the War, "Hiroshima Nagaski Indochina," ca. 1972, Box 5, Folder 5, AAM 1805, UCLA.

99. Ibid.

100. UCLA Asian Strike Committee, "My Lai–Hiroshima—No Real Loss" (Los Angeles, Calif., n.d.), Box 5, Folder 5, AAM 1805, UCLA.

101. Ibid.

102. Kerry, "American Policy Makers," 40.

103. Yoshimura, "GIs and Asian Women."

104. "Sam Choy: Asian American Solider," in Louie, *Asian Americans*, 19–25, quotation on 21, originally printed in *Getting Together*, April 1970. At one point, Choy was so fed up with being taunted with racial slurs that he refused to obey orders, grabbed his rifle, fired warning shots at the Military Police and his commanding officers, and started for the perimeter of the base. He was captured by the Military Police, however, and was held in custody at Long Binh Stockade for four months while awaiting a court martial hearing. Following the hearing, Choy was sentenced to eighteen months of hard labor at Fort Leavenworth in Kansas. He was released after serving nine months.

105. Kerry, "American Policy Makers," 38.

106. Ibid., 36.

107. Nakamura, "The Nature of G.I. Racism," in Tachiki, Wong, and Odo, *Roots*, 24–26, esp. 26, originally published in *Gidra* (June/July 1970).

108. Peggy Saika, interview by Loretta Ross, 7.

109. Ibid.

110. Chan, "The Exclusion of Chinese Women, 1870–1943," 97.

111. Encarguez Perez, "Woman Warrior Meets Mail-Order Bride"; Kwan, "Invention, Inversion and Intervention."

112. Kerry, "American Policy Makers," 33.

113. Quoted in Ling, "The Mountain Movers: Asian American Women's Movement in Los Angeles," *Amerasia* 15, no. 1 (1989): 53.

114. Editorial Staff of *RODAN*, "Asian Women as Leaders," in Tachiki, Wong, and Odo, *Roots*, 297–98, quotation on 298, originally published in *RODAN*, April 1971.

115. Wei, *The Asian American Movement*, 76.

116. "Asian Women as Leaders," 298.

117. Takemoto, "Pat Sumi," 109.

118. Quoted in Iwataki, "The Asian Women's Movement—A Retrospective," 38–39. Mirikitani's poem was originally published in *Third World Women*, ed. Janice Mirikitani (San Francisco: Third World Communications: 1972).

119. Chow, "The Development of Feminist Consciousness among Asian American Women"; Chow, "The Feminist Movement"; Ling, "The Mountain Movers"; Shah, *Dragon Ladies*.

120. Takemoto, "Pat Sumi," 108.

121. Ibid.

122. "Asian Women: Outlook in a Changing Society," *Wei Min*, ca. 1971, 4, 10, quotation on 4.

123. Ibid.

124. May Chen, interview with Karen Harper.

125. "Life in New Asia," *Getting Together*, December 1970, 15–16.

126. Takemoto, "Pat Sumi," 111.

127. Ibid.

128. Sumi's claim that all of these traditions continued into the 1940s is not accurate. Nor did she explain that, for example, the tradition of binding feet was a mark of class status. See Ko, *Cinderella's Sisters*.

129. Patrell, "Glad They're Back," *Gidra*, October 1970, 4. The author's full name was not provided in the publication.

130. Brown, "In North Korea, North Vietnam, Peking China," D.

131. Ibid.; "Life in New Asia," 16. See also Sanche de Gramont, "Our Other Man in Algiers," *New York Times Magazine*, November 1, 1970, 30, 112–19, 126.

132. "A National Socialist Culture Promoted," *Vietnam Courier*, August 24, 1970, 3, 7, quotation on 3.

133. Patrell, "Glad They're Back," 4.

134. Brown, "In North Korea, North Vietnam, Peking China," G.

135. "Life in New Asia," 15.

136. Brown, *A Taste of Power*, 240.

137. Brown, "In North Korea, North Vietnam, Peking China," E–F.

138. Brown, *A Taste of Power*, 242.

139. Ibid., 258.

Chapter Four

1. Renee Blakkan, "Women Meet Indochinese in Canada," *Guardian*, April 17, 1971, 5.

2. Rothstein, telephone interview with author.

3. Ibid.; Kathleen Gough, "An Indochinese Conference in Vancouver," n.d., Folder "Indo-Chinese Women's Conference," #1, ARWM, SFU; Anne Roberts and Barbara Todd, "Murmurings after the Indochinese Conference," *The Pedestal*, May 1971, 6–7; "Indochinese Sisters: We Met in Toronto," *off our backs*, May 27, 1971,

14; Vivian [Rothstein], "To Charlotte Bunch," ca. 1970, Carton 1, Folder 35, CBAP, Schlesinger; Anne Van Heteren, "Vancouver Conference," *Voice of Women*, supplement, July 1971, n.p.

4. Wu, "Rethinking Global Sisterhood"; Wu, *Radicals on the Road*; Casey, "Vanguards of Globalization."

5. The six Southeast Asian women included Vo Thi The, a professor of literature who had attended the Djakarta conference in 1965, and Nguyen Thi Xiem, a medical researcher, of the VWU; Phan Minh Hien, a teacher, and Dinh Thi Huong, a housewife, of the WUL; and Khampheng Boupha and Khemphet Pholsena, primary school teachers of the Laos Women's Union (LWU). Women from Cambodia and Saigon could not attend the conference because of "internal issues." It is unclear why women from Cambodia could not attend the conference, but the minutes of a meeting in early March assert that it had nothing to do with the Canadian government. South Vietnamese women representing the Saigon-based group Right to Live could not attend because the South Vietnamese government denied them passports.

6. Rupp, *Worlds of Women*. This contradicts the depiction of this conference by Caitlin Casey. See Casey, "Vanguards of Globalization," 252.

7. Echols, *Daring to Be Bad*. See also Berkeley, *The Women's Liberation Movement*; Evans, *Personal Politics*; Rosen, *The World Split Open*. Sara Evans reconsiders the stark contrast between liberal and radical feminists in her description of women's liberation, which she defines as a movement that grew "so fast and with such intensity that it swept up liberal feminist organizations such as the National Organization for Women (NOW) in a wildfire of change." See Evans, "Women's Liberation," 139.

8. Although I realize that not all feminists were women's liberationists, I use the two terms interchangeably to avoid repetition.

9. Thank you to Tom Dublin and Kitty Sklar for helping me formulate the question of how organized feminism contributed to antiwar arguments. I would also like to thank Sarah King for highlighting the potential contribution of my work on women's liberationists in antiwar organizations.

10. Nguyen Thi Binh, *Family, Friends and Country*, 144. For the Vietnamese more broadly, this meeting held particular significance because it brought together a large number of Americans and Vietnamese (about forty Americans attended). Pham Van Chuong, interview with author; Trinh Ngoc Thai, interview with author.

11. Rothstein, telephone interview with author. For more on McEldowney, see McCormack, "'Good Politics Is Doing Something.'"

12. Rothstein, telephone interview with author.

13. Osterud, interview with author. Ellin Hirst also tells a version of this story in her recollections of meeting with Vietnamese women in Canada in July 1969. See Ellin Hirst, "Several Women Who Have . . ." (Boston, ca. 1970), Carton 1, Folder 34, CBAP, Schlesinger. See also McEldowney, *Hanoi Journal*, 12.

14. Rothstein, telephone interview with author.

15. Osterud, interview with author.

16. Charlotte Bunch-Weeks, "Women's Liberation Movement and the MOBE Spring Offensive," ca. January 1970, Carton 1, Folder 29, CBP, Schlesinger.

17. This finding complicates the assumptions of previous works. See Adams, "The Women Who Left Them Behind"; Echols, "'Women Power' and Women's Liberation."

18. Jan Fenty, Charlotte Bunch-Weeks, and Celia Slattery, "To Sisters," February 10, 1970, Carton 1, Folder 33, CBAP, Schlesinger; Susan Myerberg, "To Sisters and Brothers," January 23, 1970, Carton 1, Folder 33, CBAP, Schlesinger.

19. Bunch, "Asian Women in Revolution"; Bunch-Weeks, "Back from Hanoi"; Federal Bureau of Investigation, "FBI Report on WLM May 1–October 30, 1970," 1970, Carton 2, Folder 55, CBAP, Schlesinger.

20. The Collective has also been referred to as the Women's Anti-Imperialist Collective and the Women and Imperialism Collective in various reports and articles.

21. The two WSP members were Trudi Young and Cora Weiss. Both women attended the IWC in Toronto, but in an interview, Weiss did not remember it—a sign that it was not an event that carried as much significance for her as it did for others. Weiss, interview with author.

22. "Can Radical Young Women Work in WSP?" *Memo*, Summer 1970, 12–14; "Women's Strike for Equality and Peace," *Memo*, Summer 1970, 1–2. See also Estepa, "Taking the White Gloves Off."

23. D.C. Conference Committee, "An Evaluation of the Canadian Conference Process" (Washington, D.C., 1971), Box 1A, Folder 3, PC, SSC; Vivian Rothstein, "Anti-Imperialist Program for WLM," ca. 1970, Box 73, Folder 16, JBC, SSC; Vivian [Rothstein], "To Charlotte Bunch"; Nancy Williamson, "The Antiwar Movement and Female Liberation" (Washington, D.C., 1970), Box 1A, Folder 2, PC, SSC; "Projected Conference in North America with Indochinese Women," n.d., Box 73, Folder 16, JBC, SSC; Muriel Duckworth, "To Ethel Taylor," February 17, 1970, Box 11, Folder "Correspondence and COL files 1970s," COLIAFAM records, SCPC.

24. Ellin Hirst and Alice Wolfson, "Budapest Report," ca. 1970, Carton 1, Folder 34, CBAP, Schlesinger; WSP International Committee, "Memo Regarding Proposed Conference of Women on Indo China—Canada 1971" (New York, October 6, 1970), Series A, 1, Box 1, Folder "National Consultative Committee Minutes & Memos (August 1970–1973)," WSPR, SCPC; "Projected Conference in North America with Vietnamese, Laotian and Cambodian Women," October 9, 1970, Box 73, Folder 16, JBC, SSC; "Packet: Schedule and Information about the Indochinese Conference," January 1971, Box 1A, Folder 3, PC, SSC; Alice Wolfson, "Budapest Journal," *off our backs*, December 14, 1970, n.p.

25. Swerdlow, *Women Strike for Peace*, 228.

26. Ibid.

27. Hirst and Wolfson, "Budapest Report." See also Wolfson, "Budapest Journal."

28. Wolfson, "Budapest Journal." See also "They Embody the Struggle . . . ," *The Mole*, November 20, 1970.

29. Wolfson, "Budapest Journal."

30. Ibid.

31. Buffalo Women's Liberation, "Tenth Anniversary of the NLF," *Rat*, December 17, 1970–January 6, 1971, 17.

32. Sharon Rose and Marilyn Albert, "Minutes—Meeting of Anti-Imperialist Education Committee" (New York, November 7, 1970), Carton 1, Folder 35, CBAP, Schlesinger.

33. "Sexism and Imperialism," in *People's Peace Treaty and Women*, ed. Women's Caucus of New University Conference (Chicago, 1971), Box 1A, Folder 2, PC, SSC.

34. Ibid., 1.

35. Cynthia Fredrick, "Women Play Key Role in Growing Saigon Peace Movement," in *People's Peace Treaty and Women*, ed. Women's Caucus of New University Conference (Chicago, 1971), Box 1A, Folder 2, PC, SSC. See also Buffalo Women's Liberation, "To Sisters," 1970, Box 1A, Folder 2, PC, SSC; Laura Dertz, Ruth Getts, and Jacquiline Rice, "Women's Liberation and the Fight against the War," n.d., Carton 1, Folder 33, CBAP, Schlesinger; Women about Prisoners of War, "Pamphlet: Women about Prisoners of War" (Boston, December 20, 1970), Box 1A, Folder 2, PC, SSC; Chicago Women's Liberation Union, "Women and Imperialism," December 20, 1970, Carton 1, Folder 35, CBAP, Schlesinger.

36. Alonso, *Peace as a Women's Issue*, 226.

37. Buffalo Women's Liberation, "To Sisters."

38. Ellin Hirst, "What Is an 'Anti-Imperialist Women's Movement'?" (Boston, December 1970), Carton 1, Folder 35, CBAP, Schlesinger, 1.

39. Ibid. See also "Women's Liberation Front," *EVO*, July 23, 1969, Box 564, Folder 4, JBMP, Duke, n.p.

40. "Minutes from Meeting with Women Strike for Peace, WILPF, Third World Caucus and Women's Liberation," New York City, March 3, 1971, Box 1A, Folder 3, PC, SSC.

41. See "Minutes from Meeting with Women Strike for Peace"; "Some Notes on the Springfield Conference," January 1971, Box 1A, Folder 3, PC, SSC; "Canadian Conference Nationwide Contacts," ca. 1971, Carton 1, Folder 34, CBAP, Schlesinger; "Minutes: Dayton Regional Conference" (Dayton, February 1971), Box 1A, Folder 3, PC, SSC; Canada Conference Committee, "Canada Conference for Women on Indo-China (East Coast)"; FBI Director, "Memo Regarding the TWWA to SAC, New York and Legat, Ottawa," February 14, 1971, FBI File on the Third World Women's Alliance; DC Conference Committee, "An Evaluation of the Canadian Conference."

42. "Canadian Conference Nationwide Contacts"; "Minutes: Dayton Regional Conference."

43. Boston Area Conference Group, "To Women's Conference Project," March 2, 1971, Box 1A, Folder 3, PC, SSC; DC Conference Committee, "An Evaluation of the Canadian Conference."

44. Burris, *Fourth World Manifesto*, 6.

45. Ibid.; "Meeting of the D.C. Anti-Imperialist Collective about Celebrating the Vietnamese Struggle" (Washington, D.C., November 3, 1970), Carton 1, Folder 35, CBAP, Schlesinger; DC Conference Committee, "An Evaluation of the Canadian Conference"; DC WLM Anti-Imperialist Collective, "Thoughts about the Women's Proclamation" (Washington, D.C., November 28, 1970), Carton 1, Folder 35, CBAP, Schlesinger; Rose and Albert, "Minutes—Meeting of Anti-Imperialist Education

Committee"; "This Letter Is for Women in the Women's Movement" (Chicago, December 1970), Carton 1, Folder 35, CBAP, Schlesinger.

46. "We as Third World Women," n.d., Subject Files, Folder "Indochinese Women Conference," KHWB, SFU, 2.

47. "Statement from a Number of the White Women in Los Angeles Who Are Working on the Indochinese Women's Conference," n.d., Subject Files, Folder "Indochinese Women Conference," KHWB, SFU; Gough, "An Indochinese Conference in Vancouver."

48. Canada Conference Committee, "Canada Conference for Women on Indo-China"; "Minutes from Meeting with Women Strike for Peace"; "Indochinese Sisters: We Met in Toronto"; DC Conference Committee, "An Evaluation of the Canadian Conference."

49. DC Conference Committee, "An Evaluation of the Canadian Conference," 13.

50. Ibid.; "Summary of Decisions Made by the Format Committee" (New York City, March 1971), Box 1A, Folder 3, PC, SSC.

51. "Indochinese Women's Conference," 80.

52. Donna, "Chicanas Meet Indo-Chinese: The Enemy Is Imperialism," *El Grito Del Norte*, Special Section: La Chicana (June 5, 1971), K. Donna's last name was not provided.

53. Gough, "An Indochinese Conference in Vancouver," 31, 32.

54. DC Conference Committee, "An Evaluation of the Canadian Conference," 16.

55. Ibid.

56. Ibid.

57. "Indochinese Sisters: We Met in Toronto," 14.

58. Blakkan, "Women Meet Indochinese in Canada."

59. A few articles referred to Huong as a housewife in their accounts of her story. See Gough, "An Indochinese Conference in Vancouver," 6; Elizabeth Dingman, "Waves of Peace and Domesticity," *Toronto Telegram*, April 12, 1971, reprinted in the *Voice of Women* supplement, July 1971; "Six Years in a Tiger Cage," in *Asian Women*, 83–84.

60. "Six Years in a Tiger Cage," 84.

61. Blakkan, "Women Meet Indochinese in Canada"; Gough, "An Indochinese Conference in Vancouver," 6–7; "Six Years in a Tiger Cage," 83–84; *Voice of Women* supplement, July 1971; "Their Stories," *The Pedestal*, May 1971, 8–9.

62. Blakkan, "Women Meet Indochinese in Canada," 5.

63. Ibid.

64. Rowbotham, *Women, Resistance and Revolution*, 211.

65. Gough, "An Indochinese Conference in Vancouver"; "Their Stories"; "Tiger Cages," *Getting Together*, June 1971, 7; Judy Thaman, "Nguyen Thi Xiem," *off our backs*, May 6, 1971, 7.

66. All three essays were published in Women's Caucus of New University Conference, ed., *People's Peace Treaty and Women* (Chicago, March 30, 1971), Box 1A, Folder 2, PC, SSC.

67. Women's Anti-Imperialism Committee, "Indochinese Conference Speech" (Chicago, 1971), Box 1A, Folder 3, PC, SSC; "Packet: Schedule and Information about

the Indochinese Conference"; "Our Indochinese Sisters," *The Pedestal*, March 1971, 4–5; Gough, "An Indochinese Conference in Vancouver"; "Learning How to Do It," *The Pedestal*, May 1971, 10–11; Interim Work Committee, "To Sisters," December 1970, Carton 1, Folder 34, CBAP, Schlesinger; Marlene Voorhees, "Report of Minutes of the Mid-Atlantic Subregional Meeting of January 23, 24, 1971" (Washington, D.C., January 28, 1971), Carton 1, Folder 34, CBAP, Schlesinger. See also the work of women of color on the connection between "U.S. imperialism" at home and abroad: "Indochinese Women's Conference," in *Asian Women*; "Sisters Meet across 10,000 Miles," *Getting Together*, May 1971, 2; "Tiger Cages"; "Six Years in a Tiger Cage"; Dolores Varela, "Chicanas Meet Indo-Chinese: We Are People of the Land," *El Grito Del Norte* Special Section: La Chicana (June 5, 1971), K; Donna, "Chicanas Meet Indo-Chinese."

68. Quoted in "Sexism and Imperialism," 1, and Fran Ansley and Linda Gordon, "Women and Imperialism: A Speech Originally Given at a Women's Rally in Boston on Nov. 1, 1969, as Part of the November Action Coalition's Week of Actions against MIT's Imperialism" (Boston, November 1, 1969), Box 1, Folder 4, NOP, Schlesinger, 2. See also "Draft: On the Relationship between Capitalism and the Family," n.d., Box 1, Folder 11, NOP, Schlesinger.

69. "U.S. Govt. Blamed for My Lai Deaths," *Winnipeg Free Press*, March 31, 1971, reprinted in the *Voice of Women* supplement, July 1971; Kay Camp, "Notes from Meetings in Toronto" (Toronto, April 18, 1971), Series Accession 2006, Box 12, Folder "Vietnam Related Material," KCP, SCPC; DC Women's Liberation Conference Collective, "To Third World Sisters," ca. 1971, Carton 1, Folder 34, CBAP, Schlesinger; Thaman, "Nguyen Thi Xiem"; "They Embody the Struggle . . ."; "Indo-Chinese Conference," *The Pedestal*, February 1971, 3; "Our Indochinese Sisters"; "Sisters Meet across 10,000 Miles"; Ansley and Gordon, "Women and Imperialism"; Women's Anti-Imperialism Committee, "Indochinese Conference Speech."

70. For example, see Yang Yung-Ching, "Cover Image: A Militia Woman," *The Pedestal*, March 1971, 1; "Our Indochinese Sisters"; "Stories from Vietnam," *The Pedestal*, March 1971, 6; "Mother's Day," May 19, 1970, Box 1, Folder 5, NOP, Schlesinger; "They Embody the Struggle . . ."; Women's Caucus of New University Conference, *People's Peace Treaty and Women*.

71. "Sisters Meet across 10,000 Miles," 2.

72. Ibid.

73. Blakkan, "Women Meet Indochinese in Canada," 5.

74. Gough, "An Indochinese Conference in Vancouver," 8.

75. Osterud, interview with author.

76. "Questions Given to South Vietnamese as Examples of What Women in US Movement Might Ask," ca. 1971, Carton 1, Folder 34, CBAP, Schlesinger; "Summary of Decisions Made by the Format Committee" (New York City, March 1971), Box 1A, Folder 3, PC, SSC.

77. Gough, "An Indochinese Conference in Vancouver," 16.

78. See also "Summary of Decisions Made by the Format Committee"; "Sisters Meet across 10,000 Miles"; Thaman, "Nguyen Thi Xiem."

79. Gough, "An Indochinese Conference in Vancouver."

80. "Sisters Meet across 10,000 Miles," 2.

81. Gough, "An Indochinese Conference in Vancouver," 4. See also "Nguyen Thi Xiem," *Voice of Women* supplement, July 1971.

82. Gough, "An Indochinese Conference in Vancouver,"19.

83. Ibid.

84. Scholarship on gender and war has blossomed over several decades. Some works in this field include Goldstein, *War and Gender*; Hoganson, *Fighting for American Manhood*; Stur, *Beyond Combat*; Vuic, *Officer, Nurse, Woman*.

85. "Questions Given to South Vietnamese as Examples of What Women in US Movement Might Ask."

86. Bread and Roses, "Bread & Roses Speaks on Revolutionary Feminism," May 8, 1970, Box 1, Folder 5, NOP, Schlesinger, 3.

Chapter Five

1. Nguyen Thi Binh, *Family, Friends and Country*, 152–62.

2. Ibid., 168.

3. Ibid., 170–71.

4. Ibid., 182–83; Trinh Ngoc Thai, interview with author.

5. Phan Thi Minh, interview with author.

6. Nguyen Thi Binh, *Family, Friends and Country*, 268.

7. Wu, *Radicals on the Road*, 210.

8. Charlotte Bunch-Weeks, "To Madame Nugyen [*sic*] Dung," September 24, 1970, Carton 1, Folder 34, CBAP, Schlesinger; Maria Jolas, "For Your Information" (Typescript, Paris, April 1972), Box 3, Folder "Trip April 1972," CWP, SCPC.

9. Marsha Steinberg, "Women of the South: An Interview with Vietnamese Women," *The Second Wave* 2, no. 2 (1972): 9–12, quotation on 12.

10. Ibid., 10.

11. "Blood in Support of Viet Nam Fighting against American Aggression," *Women of Viet Nam*, nos. 3–4 (1970): 47–49.

12. "A Quarter Century of Struggle," *Women of Viet Nam*, nos. 3–4 (1970): 45–47, quotation on 46.

13. "We Have Matured with Our Land," *Women of Viet Nam*, nos. 3–4 (1970): 7–11, quotation on 11.

14. The four committee members were Congressmen Augustus Hawkins and William Anderson, congressional aide Thomas Harkin, and former head of the International Voluntary Services in Vietnam Don Luce. These cages were about five feet wide and ten feet long, with concrete floors and walls and a barred opening in the ceiling, and each held three to five prisoners, who had little room to lie down and no comforts whatsoever. The only "furnishings" in each cell included a bucket for waste and an iron bar about a foot off the ground to which prisoners could be shackled. See Don Luce, "Statement on Visit to Con Son Prison" (1970), Box 22, Folder "CIA File," CWP, SCPC; "We Demand the Immediate Dismantling of the 'Tiger Cages,'" *South Viet Nam in Struggle*, July 20, 1970, 4; Don Luce, "The Tiger Cages of Poulo Condor," *South Viet Nam in Struggle*, August 20, 1970, 2–3.

15. Strobel, "Gender, Sex, and Empire"; Midgley, "Anti-Slavery and the Roots of Imperial Feminism"; Pascoe, *Relations of Rescue*; Newman, *White Women's Rights*; Thomas, *Politics of the Womb*; Burton, "The White Woman's Burden"; Sylvester, *Feminist International Relations*.

16. Hirschkind and Mahmood, "Feminism, the Taliban, and Politics of Counter-insurgency"; Farrell and McDermott, "Claiming Afghan Women"; Fernandes, "The Boundaries of Terror."

17. "Where Lies Social Corruption," *South Viet Nam in Struggle*, August 10, 1970, 4. "U.S. Puppet Crimes against South Viet Nam Women and Children in Two Years of Nixon's Rule," *Women of Viet Nam*, no. 2 (1971): 22–24, 37.

18. Anne McGrew Bennett, "Visit to North Vietnam" (Berkeley, January 9, 1971), Box 4, AMBC, both quotations on 2.

19. Anne McGrew Bennett, "Visit with Five American Servicemen Detained in North Vietnam" (Berkeley, January 1971), Box 4, AMBC; Abraham Ribicoff, "U.S. Study Team on Religious and Political Freedom in Vietnam," *Congressional Record—Senate* 115, no. 99 (June 17, 1969): 6572–80.

20. Bennett, "Visit to North Vietnam."

21. Ribicoff, "U.S. Study Team," 6578.

22. Anne McGrew Bennett, "Women's Involvement in the Peace Movement" (Manhasset, N.Y., April 21, 1969), Box 1, Folder 5, AMBC, 5.

23. Phong Vu, "Not a Word," *Women of Viet Nam*, no. 1 (1971): 24–26; Bennett, "Visit to North Vietnam"; "Committee Delegation Speaks to American Pilots at Christmas," *American Report: Review of Religion and American Power*, January 15, 1971, 1. In some American versions, Kien's name is given as Huyng Thi Giong or Huynh Thi Kieng.

24. Bennett, "Visit to North Vietnam," 4.

25. Phong Vu, "Not a Word."

26. John Schmitz, "War Criminals and Reparations," *Congressional Record—House* 117, no. 2 (February 11, 1971): 2673–75, quotation on 2673.

27. Bennett, "Visit to North Vietnam," 1. During the Son Tay raid on November 21, 1970, U.S. forces landed at a POW camp in North Viet Nam only to find the prisoners had been relocated some time earlier.

28. Anne McGrew Bennett and Madeline Duckles, "Facts on Prisoners of War Detained in North Vietnam," *Freedom News*, March 1971, 3.

29. Quoted in Bennett, "Visit with Five American Servicemen," 2. For more on the visit, see also Lynne Fitch, "Congressman Is Told Hanoi Gave P.O.W.s Special Holiday Privileges," *New York Times*, December 27, 1970, Box 4, Folder 17, AMBC; Lynne Fitch, "She Gave POWs Mail from Home," *Catholic Voice*, January 7, 1971, Box 4, Folder 13, AMBC; Lynne Fitch, "U.S. Uses POW Families' Anguish to Escalate War," *National Catholic Reporter*, January 15, 1971, 1, 16; Schmitz, "War Criminals and Reparations"; Ronald Young, "Prisoners of War and Our Hanoi Trip," *Fellowship*, February 1971, 1–2; "Strangers' Letters to P.O.W.s Assailed," *New York Times*, January 8, 1971, 36; "Committee Delegation Speaks to American Pilots at Christmas."

30. Bennett, "Visit to North Vietnam," 5.

31. Fitch, "She Gave POWs Mail"; Young, "Prisoners of War"; "Committee Delegation Speaks to American Pilots at Christmas."

32. Bennett, "Visit to North Vietnam." The routine that Bennett described is the same as a routine described in a congressional report on POWs. See Committee on Foreign Relations, *American Prisoners of War in Southeast Asia*, 498.

33. Bennett, "Visit with Five American Servicemen."

34. Bennett, "Visit to North Vietnam."

35. "U.S. Puppet Crimes against South Viet Nam Women and Children in Two Years of Nixon's Rule."

36. Le Mai, interview with author.

37. Anne McGrew Bennett, "Journal Notes" (Hanoi, December 1970), Box 4, AMBC, 3. Barbara Deming also remarked on this kind of propaganda. See Barbara Deming, "Sunday, December 25" (Phu Ly and Nam Dinh, December 25, 1966), Box 70, Folder 1362, BDP, Schlesinger, 5.

38. Fitch, "U.S. Uses POW Families' Anguish to Escalate War"; "Committee Delegation Speaks to American Pilots at Christmas." Photographs outside the cathedral in Hanoi confirm Bennett's description. They are available in Box 4, Folder 9, AMBC.

39. Quoted in "Anne Bennett, Christian Feminist Voice, Dies at 82," *Los Angeles Times*, October 25, 1986, http://articles.latimes.com/1986-10-25/news/mn-7158_1_commencement-address (June 10, 2013).

40. This organization has also been referred to as the Association of International Women.

41. Ngo Thi Phuong Thien, interview with author; Gloria Emerson, "A Biographical Profile of Madame Ngo Ba Thanh" (Philadelphia, June 1973), Series G, Box 20, Folder "Vietnam: Mme Ngo ba Thanh," KCP, SCPC; "CV: Madame Ngo Ba Thanh," June 1973, Part III, Series H, 4, Box 20, Folder "Correspondence, etc. re: Freeing Vietnamese Political Prisoners, 1972–1975," WILPF, SCPC; Thieu Son, "Who Is Mrs. Ngo Ba Thanh?," *Vietnam Courier*, March 1975, 22–23.

42. "Interview with Mrs. Ngo Ba Thanh, 1981," http://openvault.wgbh.org/catalog/vietnam-0bb668-interview-with-mrs-ngo-ba-thanh-1981; Ngo Thi Phuong Thien, interview with author.

43. Pham Van Huyen, "Lai Mot Mua Don Xuan . . . Luu Vong (Another Spring and Tet . . . in Exile)," in Ngo Ba Thanh, *Thuc the Chinh Tri Thu Ba Tai Mien Nam Viet-Nam Dong Gop Vao Cham Dut Chien Tranh va Lap Lai Hoa Binh O Viet Nam (The Third Political Force in Viet Nam Contributing to the End of the War and the Restoration of Peace in Viet Nam)*, vol. 1, 44b.

44. Emerson, "A Biographical Profile of Madame Ngo Ba Thanh"; "CV: Madame Ngo Ba Thanh"; Thieu Son, "Who Is Mrs. Ngo Ba Thanh?"

45. Ngo Ba Thanh in sweater she made while in prison, Photograph, ca. 1973, in possession of Ngo Thi Phuong Thien; "Moi Ngay 1 Nhan Vat: Ba Ngo Ba Thanh (One Person per Day: Mrs. Ngo Ba Thanh)," September 25, 1973, in possession of Ngo Thi Phuong Thien.

46. Ngo Thi Phuong Thien, interview with author.

47. Ibid.

48. Also translated as the Right to Life in some documents.

49. "Townswomen Blame the Americans and Their Stooges," *South Viet Nam in Struggle*, August 20, 1970, 5.

50. Committee of Woman Action for the Right to Live and Ngo Ba Thanh, "A Letter Refused in Saigon but Accepted in Washington," *Women of Viet Nam*, no. 1 (1971): 24–26; Cynthia Fredrick, "Women Play Key Role in Growing Saigon Peace Movement," *Memo*, 1, no. 3 ca. 1971, 12–14.

51. Ngo Ba Thanh, "Opening Speech Delivered in the Special Meeting Held at Ngoc Phuong Pagoda, Gia-Ding on October 19, 1970, by Mrs. Ngo Ba Thanh, Chairwoman of the Presidium of the Vietnamese Women's Movement for the Right to Life" (October 18, 1970), Series Accession 2006, Box 12, Folder "Vietnamese-Related Material," KCP, SCPC.

52. Camp traveled to Saigon with three other WILPF members: Lois Hamer of Los Angeles, Patricia Shannon of Wellington, New Zealand, and Marguerite Loree of Paris, France.

53. Katherine Camp, "First Draft of Notes from Saigon" (Saigon, January 3, 1971), Series Accession 2006, Box 12, Folder "Photographs and Material from Binder/Scrapbook," KCP, SCPC.

54. Katherine Camp, "Handwritten Notes on Reason to Go to Vietnam," 1971, Series Accession 2006, Box 12, Folder "Vietnam-Related Material," KCP, SCPC, 2.

55. Kay Camp, "WILPF Mission Welcomed in Saigon and Hanoi," *Peace and Freedom*, March 1971, 1–2; Kay Camp, "Visit to Saigon and Hanoi by Six Delegates from 18th Triennial Congress of Women's International League for Peace and Freedom, New Delhi, Jan 1 1971," January 1971, Series Accession 2006, Box 12, Folder "Photographs and Material from Binder/Scrapbook," KCP, SCPC.

56. Pham Van Chuong, interview with author.

57. Katherine Camp and Ngo Ba Thanh, "Joint Resolution of the Women's International League for Peace and Freedom U.S. Section and the Vietnamese Women's Movement for the Right to Life" (Saigon, January 1971), Series Accession 2006, Box 12, Folder "Vietnam-Related Material," KCP, SCPC.

58. Katherine Camp, "Mission to Vietnam" (Philadelphia, 1971), Series Accession 2006, Box 12, Folder "Vietnam-Related Material," KCP, SCPC, 2.

59. Ibid.; Katherine Camp, "Typed Notes on Trip," 1971, Series Accession 2006, Box 12, Folder "Photographs and Material from Binder/Scrapbook," KCP, SCPC; Camp, "WILPF Mission Welcomed in Saigon and Hanoi," 2.

60. Camp and Thanh, "Joint Resolution." See also Committee of Women Action for the Right to Live and Ngo Ba Thanh, "To Spiro Agnew," August 1970, Carton 1, Folder 35, CBAP, Schlesinger; Ngo Ba Thanh, "To Foreign Relations Committee," May 7, 1971, Series Accession 2006, Box 12, Folder "Vietnam-Related Material," KCP, SCPC.

61. Kay Camp and Pat Samuel, "Indochina Lives: A Separate Peace," *off our backs* 1, no. 18 (February 26, 1971): 2.

62. Katherine Camp, "We are part of a 6-woman team . . . ," 1971, Series Accession 2006, Box 12, Folder "Vietnam-Related Material," KCP, SCPC, n.p.

63. Ibid.; Katherine Camp, "Ah well...," January 1971, Series Accession 2006, Box 12, Folder "Vietnam-Related Material," KCP, SCPC; Camp, "Mission to Vietnam."

64. Brigham, *Guerrilla Diplomacy*, 96–101.

65. Ngo Ba Thanh, "Ngo to Foreign Relations Committee"; Young, *The Vietnam Wars*, 263–66.

66. Women's International League for Peace and Freedom, "For Publication" (Geneva, September 27, 1971), Series G, Box 20, Folder "Vietnam: Mme Ngo ba Thanh," KCP, SCPC.

67. "To Secretary of State William Rogers," August 11, 1972, Part III, Series H, 4, Box 20, Folder "Correspondence, etc. re: Freeing Vietnamese Political Prisoners, 1972–1975," WILPF, SCPC; Ngo Thi Phuong Thien, interview with author.

68. Brigham, *Guerrilla Diplomacy*, 99.

69. "US-Thieu Scheme to Liquidate Prisoners and Detained Patriots," *South Viet Nam in Struggle*, October 30, 1972, 3; Women's International League for Peace and Freedom, "Your Tax Dollars at Work," Flyer (Washington, D.C., July 1973), Part III, Series H, 4, Box 20, Folder "Correspondence, etc. re: Freeing Vietnamese Political Prisoners, 1972–1975," WILPF, SCPC; Emerson, "A Biographical Profile of Madame Ngo Ba Thanh"; Vivian Schatz and Rosalie Riechman, "Statement by Vivian Schatz and Rosalie Riechman on Mistreatment in South Vietnam's Prisons and U.S. Responsibility on Behalf of the United States Section, Women's International League for Peace and Freedom before the Subcommittee on Asian and Pacific Affairs" (Washington, D.C., September 26, 1973), Part III, Series H, 4, Box 20, Folder "Correspondence, etc. re: Freeing Vietnamese Political Prisoners, 1972–1975," WILPF, SCPC.

70. "American Women Demand the Release of Mrs. Ngo Ba Thanh," *Memo* 2, no. 2 (Winter 1971): 27.

71. Ibid.

72. Quoted in Thomas Fox, "Woman Peace Leader Collapses in Saigon Courtroom," *Memo* 2, no. 3 (Spring 1972): 18.

73. Ibid.

74. "Three American Women Arrested in Ngo Ba Thanh Protest," *Memo* 2, no. 3 (Spring 1972): 18.

75. Lerner, interview with author.

76. Patricia Weiner, "Amy Swerdlow Reports on Her Trip to Hanoi," *Great Neck Record*, November 18, 1971, n.p.; Amy Swerdlow, "Up From the Mud," *WIN*, December 15, 1971, 6–10; Jean Murphy, "Woman-to-Woman Talk in Hanoi," *Los Angeles Times*, November 1, 1971, 1, 6.

77. "Angela Davis Must Be Set Free," *Women of Viet Nam*, no. 2 (1971): 31; "The Release of Angela Davis—A First Success of the American and World Peoples and Women," *Women of Viet Nam*, no. 1 (1972): 21; "The Angela Davis Case," *Vietnam Courier*, March 13, 1972, 6; "Complete Freedom for Angela Davis," *South Viet Nam in Struggle*, March 13, 1972, 8.

78. Willie Barrow, "Willie Barrow Brings Greeting to Angela from Vietnam," *Memo* 2, no. 2 (Winter 1971): 22–23, quotation on 22.

79. Brigham, *Guerrilla Diplomacy*, 98–100; Nguyen Thi Binh, *Family, Friends and Country*, 206.

80. Young, *The Vietnam Wars*, 269–72; Nguyen, *Hanoi's War*, 231–56; Kimball, "Richard M. Nixon and the Vietnam War," 231–32.

81. Nguyen Thi Binh, *Family, Friends and Country*, 210–11.

82. Amy Swerdlow, "'Our Children Have Never Lived a Single Day of Peace': A Report from the Paris Meeting between Congresswomen Bella Abzug, Patsy Mink, and Ministers Nguyen Thi Binh and Xuan Thuy," *Memo* 2, no. 3 (Spring 1972): 30–31; Marsha Steinberg, "Women of the South: An Interview with Vietnamese Women," *The Second Wave* 2, no. 2 (1972): 9–12.

83. "Jane Fonda: I Accuse," *Vietnam Youth*, August 1972, 14. See also Frances Lang, "It's a Women's War Too," *off our backs*, September 30, 1972, 26; "Jane Fonda Visits Bombed City, Dikes," *War Bulletin*, ca. 1972, Box 88, UNC, CSWR, 1, 4.

84. "CBS News Contract" (New York, N.Y., May 16, 1972), Box 8, Folder "TV Contracts," COLIAFAM records, SCPC.

85. John Schmitz, "Committee of Liaison," *Congressional Record—House* 117, no. 4 (March 3, 1971): 5010–12; Graham Purcell, "National Week of Concern for Prisoners of War," *Congressional Record—House* 117, no. 6 (March 18, 1971): 7112–15; Alphonzo Bell, "Our Prisoners in Southeast Asia," *Congressional Record—House* 117, no. 9 (April 21, 1971): 11201; John Schmitz, "'The Second Front of the Vietnam War': Communist Subversion in the Peace Movement," *Congressional Record—House* 117, no. 9 (April 21, 1971): 11156–201; "Department of Defense Appropriations," *Congressional Record—House* 117, no. 32 (November 17, 1971): 41799–841; Richard Ichord, "Woman-to-Woman Talk in Hanoi," *Congressional Record—House* 117, no. 36 (December 17, 1971): 47702–4.

86. Marilyn Berger, "Communists Release 1,001 POW's Letters," *Washington Post*, December 23, 1971, A1, A8; "Xmas and New Year Parcels Delivered to Captured US Pilots," *Vietnam Courier*, January 31, 1972, n.p.

87. Berger, "Communists Release 1,001 POW's Letters."

88. David McReynolds, "To Tran Trong Quat" (February 9, 1972), Box 7, Folder "DRV Correspondence," COLIAFAM records, SCPC.

89. "American Antiwar Activist Tells of POW Peace Pleas," *Plainfield Courier News*, June 12, 1972, Box 3, Folder "Newspaper Clippings: Cora Weiss 1960s–mid 1970s," CWP, SCPC.

90. Stephanie Nielson, "To Cora Weiss" (September 21, 1972), Box 8, Folder "Jane Fonda," COLIAFAM records, SCPC; Hershberger, *Jane Fonda's War*; Lembcke, *Hanoi Jane*.

91. Tran Minh Quoc, interview with author.

92. McReynolds, "To Tran Trong Quat."

93. Minnie Lee Gartley, "To Ethel Taylor," November 1969, Series A, 4, Box 3, Folder "Committee of Liaison with Families (1969–1972)," WSPR, SCPC; Bennett, "Visit with Five American Servicemen"; Bennett, "Visit to North Vietnam"; Voice of Women, Canada and Women Strike for Peace, "List of Attendees in Toronto" (Toronto, April 5, 1971), Box 3, Folder "VOW Canada Conference," COLIAFAM records, SCPC.

94. Much of the information about the trip itself comes from the diary of Marianne Hamilton, who traveled to Hanoi on the same flights as the POW escorts to confer with Vietnamese Catholics. Although the two delegations were ostensibly on two separate trips—the Vietnamese booked them in separate hotels and created staggered schedules for the two groups—they had similar experiences and common impressions. See Marianne Hamilton, "Hanoi Diary," September 1972, Box 3, "Hamilton Hanoi Diary, 1972," MHP; Marianne Hamilton, "To Norm and Children," September 17, 1972, Box 3, "Hamilton and Bury in North Viet Nam, 1972," MHP.

95. Hamilton, "Hanoi Diary."

96. Ibid.

97. Vietnam News Agency, "American Pilots' Relatives Shocked by Senseless Destruction by US Forces" (Hanoi, September 18, 1972), Box 7, Folder "DRV Statements," COLIAFAM records, SCPC; Vietnam News Agency, "Released American Pilots Relatives Visit Bombed Areas" (Hanoi, September 21, 1972), Box 7, Folder "DRV Statements," COLIAFAM records, SCPC; Vietnam News Agency, "American Christians Delegation Holds Press Conference" (Hanoi, September 22, 1972), Box 7, Folder "DRV Statements," COLIAFAM records, SCPC.

98. Steve Jaffee, "Freed POW Tells of His Life after Capture in North Vietnam," *Los Angeles Times*, November 23, 1972, 7.

99. "Statement Re: POW Release" (September 1972), Box 7, Folder "Trips—Itineraries," COLIAFAM records, SCPC, 1–2.

100. "FBI File: COLIAFAM More" (1970), Box 24, Folder "WSP FBI File," CWP, SCPC; "FBI File: Cora Weiss" (1971–1973), Box 24, Folder "FBI File 4," CWP, SCPC; Cora Weiss, "Vietnam 1972 POW Release Materials," Notebook (1972), Box 3, Folder "Cora Weiss Notebooks, Trips 1973," CWP, SCPC; Cora Weiss, "Notes Regarding POW Release" (Paris, September 1, 1972), Box 8, Folder "Paris Sept 1 1972 Re: Release," COLIAFAM records, SCPC; "US Endangers POW's," *United Justice Train*, October 1972, Box 90, UNC, CSWR; "Priest Says Fliers Definitely Coming Out," *Greensboro Daily News*, September 25, 1972, Box 5, Folder "Bury/Hamilton Trip Newspaper Clippings," CWP, SCPC.

101. "FBI File: Cora Weiss," n.p.

102. Cora Weiss, "To Steve Jaffee," November 8, 1972, Box 6, Folder "Jaffee," COLIAFAM records, SCPC; John Duncan, "Peaceniks Use PW's to Aid McGovern Campaign," *Congressional Record—House* 118, no. 25 (October 3, 1972): 33555; Young, *The Vietnam Wars*, 272–77; Kimball, "Richard M. Nixon and the Vietnam War," 233–34; Nguyen, *Hanoi's War*, 279–86.

103. Tim Cahill, "Joan Baez in Hanoi: 12 Days under the Bombs," *Rolling Stone*, February 1, 1973, 1, 18–19. See also Diedre Carmody, "4 Who Visited Hanoi Tell of Destruction," *New York Times*, January 2, 1973, Late City Edition, 1, 4; "Visitors in Hanoi Saw Civilian Facilities Hit," *Spartanburg Herald*, January 2, 1973, 1; Richard Briffault, "Taylor Assails Bombing of Hanoi," *Columbia Spectator*, January 23, 1973, 1, 6.

104. Phan Thi Minh, interview with author.

105. Nguyen Thi Binh, *Family, Friends and Country*, 217.

106. Bui Thi Cam, "To Ethel Taylor," December 21, 1972, Series A, 3, Box 1, Folder "Ethel Taylor Files: Vietnam (1968–1979)," WSPR, SCPC.

107. Telford Taylor, "The Treatment of U.S. Prisoners," *New York Times*, January 10, 1973, Box 9, Folder "COL Articles," COLIAFAM records, SCPC.

108. Young, *The Vietnam Wars*, 279.

Chapter Six

1. "Itinerary," January 1973, Part III, Series H, 4, Box 20, Folder "WILPF Delegation to Hanoi (Vietnam) Feb. 1973," WILPF, SCPC; "WILPF Delegation to Hanoi" (Philadelphia, January 1973), Part III, Series H, 4, Box 20, Folder "Visit to Hanoi (Vietnam) Jan. 1973," WILPF, SCPC; Viet Nam Women's Union, "Cable Received Washington, D.C.," Telegram (January 19, 1973), Part III, Series H, 4, Box 20, Folder "WILPF Delegation to Hanoi (Vietnam) Feb. 1973," WILPF, SCPC; Dorothy Steffens, "Delegation to the Vietnam Women's Union" (Philadelphia, February 1973), Part III, Series H, 4, Box 20, Folder "Report 'Delegation to the Vietnam Women's Union' by Steffens, Feb. 1973," WILPF, SCPC.

2. Steffens, "Delegation to the Vietnam Women's Union"; "WILPF Delegation to Hanoi"; Women's International League for Peace and Freedom, "Steffens Returns from Hanoi," Press Release (Philadelphia, January 31, 1973), Part III, Series H, 4, Box 20, Folder "WILPF Delegation to Hanoi (Vietnam) Feb. 1973," WILPF, SCPC; Dorothy Steffens, "Statement of Dorothy R. Steffens, National Director of Women's International League for Peace and Freedom, on Her Return from Hanoi, February 7, 1973," February 7, 1973, Part III, Series H, 4, Box 20, Folder "Visit to Hanoi (Vietnam) Jan. 1973," WILPF, SCPC; Marii Hasegawa and Dorothy Steffens, "WILPF to Vietnam Women's Union," Telegram (February 13, 1973), Part III, Series H, 4, Box 20, Folder "WILPF Delegation to Hanoi (Vietnam) Feb. 1973," WILPF, SCPC.

3. Steffens, "Delegation to the Vietnam Women's Union"; Women's International Democratic Federation, *Vietnam*; "Itinerary"; Nguyen, *Hanoi's War*, 231–56.

4. Laura Murray, "Peace Delegate Tells of War's End in Hanoi," *Bulletin*, 1973, Part III, Series H, 4, Box 20, Folder "WILPF Delegation to Hanoi (Vietnam) Feb. 1973," WILPF, SCPC; Louise Hickman Lione, "Hanoi Celebrates 'Victory' after a Day of Caution," *Philadelphia Inquirer*, January 30, 1973, 1-A, 3-A.

5. Steffens, "Delegation to the Vietnam Women's Union"; Louise Hickman Lione, "North Vietnamese Band Together in Rebuilding Homes, Lives," *Philadelphia Inquirer*, February 5, 1973, 1-A–2-A; Bruce Dallas, "Hanoi Report: Joy and Rubble," *Germantown Courier*, February 15, 1973, Part III, Series H, 4, Box 20, Folder "WILPF Delegation to Hanoi (Vietnam) Feb. 1973," WILPF, SCPC; Women's International Democratic Federation, *Vietnam*.

6. Wu, *Radicals on the Road*, 212; Marii Hasegawa, "Statement by Marii Hasegawa on Racism," June 30, 1969, Part III, Series A, 2, Part 3A, Box 2, Folder "Hasegawa, Marii," WILPF, SCPC. For more on race and WILPF, see Blackwell, *No Peace without Freedom*.

7. Louise Hickman Lione, "Hanoi's Premier Irked by Nixon Remark, Insists on Reunification," *Philadelphia Inquirer*, February 6, 1973, 1-A, 3-A; Steffens, "Delegation to the Vietnam Women's Union"; Lione, "North Vietnamese Band Together"; Dallas, "Hanoi Report"; Women's International Democratic Federation, *Vietnam*; Young, *The Vietnam Wars*, 278.

8. "Interview with Mrs. Ngo Ba Thanh, 1981," http://openvault.wgbh.org/catalog/vietnam-0bb668-interview-with-mrs-ngo-ba-thanh-1981.

9. Vo Thi The, "To Dorothy Steffens," April 30, 1973, Part III, Series H, 4, Box 20, Folder "Correspondence with Vietnamese Women's Union, 1972–1975," WILPF, SCPC; Dorothy Steffens, "Telephone Conversations Concerning Madame Ngo Ba Thanh," May 1973, Part III, Series H, 4, Box 20, Folder "Correspondence to/from/about Women in Vietnam, 1972–1975," WILPF, SCPC; Dorothy Steffens, "To Yvonne See," May 15, 1973, Part III, Series H, 4, Box 20, Folder "Correspondence to/from/about Women in Vietnam, 1972–1975," WILPF, SCPC; Dorothy Steffens, "To Adelaide Baker," May 21, 1973, Part III, Series H, 4, Box 20, Folder "Correspondence to/from/about Women in Vietnam, 1972–1975," WILPF, SCPC; "Mme Ngo Ba Thanh's Case—Living Indictment against Saigon Regime," *South Viet Nam in Struggle*, May 21, 1973, 3; Dorothy Steffens, "To Fanny Edelman," June 19, 1973, Part III, Series H, 4, Box 20, Folder "Correspondence to/from/about Women in Vietnam, 1972–1975," WILPF, SCPC.

10. "US-Thieu Scheme to Liquidate Prisoners and Detained Patriots," *South Viet Nam in Struggle*, October 30, 1972, 3. See also Women's Union of Liberation, "Statement by the South Viet Nam Liberation Women's Union of the Saigon Administration's Continued Delay in Returning and Acts of Terror against Patriots and Peace-Loving People Still Detained in South Viet Nam" (South Viet Nam, July 31, 1973), Part III, Series H, 4, Box 20, Folder "Correspondence, etc. re: Freeing Vietnamese Political Prisoners, 1972–1975," WILPF, SCPC.

11. Vivian Schatz and Rosalie Riechman, "Statement by Vivian Schatz and Rosalie Riechman on Mistreatment in South Vietnam's Prisons and U.S. Responsibility on Behalf of the United States Section, Women's International League for Peace and Freedom before the Subcommittee on Asian and Pacific Affairs" (Washington, D.C., September 26, 1973), Part III, Series H, 4, Box 20, Folder "Correspondence, etc. re: Freeing Vietnamese Political Prisoners, 1972–1975," WILPF, SCPC, 1.

12. Ibid.; Young, *The Vietnam Wars*, 278; Women's International League for Peace and Freedom, "Your Tax Dollars at Work" (Flyer, Washington, D.C., July 1973), Part III, Series H, 4, Box 20, Folder "Correspondence, etc. re: Freeing Vietnamese Political Prisoners, 1972–1975," WILPF, SCPC; "Prisoner: WILPF Member Mme Thanh in a South Vietnam Prison," *The Churchman*, September 1973, Part III, Series H, 4, Box 20, Folder "Correspondence, etc. re: Freeing Vietnamese Political Prisoners, 1972–1975," WILPF, SCPC; House Committee on Foreign Affairs, *The Treatment of Political Prisoners in South Vietnam by the Government of the Republic of South Vietnam*; "Conference Report on H.R. 9286, Military Procurement Authorization," *Congressional Record—House* 119, no. 27 (October 31, 1973): 35545–67; Marii Hasegawa, "To the Vietnam Women's Union," 1973, Part III, Series H, 4, Box 20, Folder "Correspondence to/from/about Women in Vietnam, 1972–1975," WILPF, SCPC.

13. Steffens, "Delegation to the Vietnam Women's Union"; Louise Hickman Lione, "PWs Interviewed: We're Well Fed," *Philadelphia Inquirer*, February 4, 1973, 1-A-2-A; "Women's Page Reporter Sees Peace Celebrated in Hanoi," *Editor & Publisher*, February 17, 1973, Part III, Series H, 4, Box 20, Folder "Visit to Hanoi (Vietnam)

Jan. 1973," WILPF, SCPC; Dorothy Steffens, "To Nguyen Khanh Phong," March 15, 1973, Part III, Series H, 4, Box 20, Folder "Correspondence with Vietnamese Women's Union, 1972–1975," WILPF, SCPC.

14. Bob Wilson, "The Truth Jane Fonda Can't See," *Congressional Record—House* 119, no. 12 (May 9, 1973): 15079; William Scherle, "Lest We Forget," *Congressional Record—House* 119, no. 13 (May 17, 1973): 16182–84.

15. Daniel Berrigan, "To Pham Van Dong" (April 10, 1973), Box 4, Folder "Requests for Travel," COLIAFAM records, SCPC.

16. Edward Derwinski, "Hanoi's Heinous POW Treatment," *Congressional Record—Senate* 119, no. 10 (April 13, 1973): 12311.

17. In some ways, this work builds on Justin Hart's *Empire of Ideas*, but instead of examining how and why U.S. officials shaped the United States' image abroad, it finds that humanitarian activists tried to exploit U.S. officials' and the American public's concern for the United States' image in order to force a change in U.S. foreign policy.

18. "FBI File: Cora Weiss" (1971–1973), Box 24, Folder "FBI File 4," CWP, SCPC.

19. Rose DeWolf, "Critic Finds Aid on Wane in Vietnam," *Focus*, November 28, 1973, 1.

20. Early in the U.S. war in Viet Nam, Quakers, in particular, sent medical aid to both North and South Viet Nam. Another organization, the Committee of Reconciliation, even brought wounded Vietnamese children to the United States to receive medical treatment during the war. Toward the end of the war, in 1971, antiwar activists founded Medical Aid for Indochina, which sent medical equipment to North Viet Nam, PRG-controlled areas of South Viet Nam, Cambodia, and Laos, where the U.S. military had launched offensives, as a form of protest. For more on Quaker trips to Viet Nam during the U.S. war, see Hershberger, *Traveling to Vietnam*; "Medical Aid to Indochina," ca. 1971, Box 1, Folder "History," Friendshipment, SCPC; "Bach Mai," *Medical Aid for Indochina News*, February 1973, 3; Bella Abzug, "Bach Mai Hospital Emergency Relief Fund," *Congressional Record—House* 119, no. 1 (January 6, 1973): 499–500; Ronald Dellums, "Bach-Mai, Truth, and Bombing of Civilian Targets," *Congressional Record—House* 119, no. 3 (February 5, 1973): 3409–10.

21. Schulzinger, "The Legacy of the Vietnam War."

22. Cora Weiss, "S. DRV," Notebook (ca. 1973), Box 5, Folder "Cora Weiss—Notebooks, Vietnam Trips, 1976," CWP, SCPC, 3–4.

23. Ibid.; Cora Weiss, "Vietnam: Postwar or Prewar?," *University Review*, January 1974, Box 3, Folder "Newspaper Clippings: Cora Weiss 1960s–mid 1970s," CWP, SCPC, 11–16.

24. Cora Weiss, "Vietnam 1973 Oct/Nov with Don Luce and Sam Normoff," Notebook (November 1973), Box 3, Folder "Cora Weiss Notebooks, Trips 1973," CWP, SCPC; Cora Weiss, "Scrapbook" (November 1973), Box 4, Folder "Cora Weiss Notebooks, Trips 1973," CWP, SCPC; Crocker Snow Jr., "Observers Predict 'Harsh Fighting' in Vietnam," *Boston Globe*, November 19, 1973, 8; Peggy Eastman, "Cora Weiss: Still Pushing," *Montgomery Journal*, February 7, 1974, B1–B2; Weiss, "Vietnam: Postwar or Prewar?"; Weiss, "S. DRV"; "You Have Come during the Rainy Season"

(North Viet Nam, ca. 1973), Box 3, Folder "WSP Vietnam Trip, 1972," CWP, SCPC; "Viets May Renew War, Activists Say," *Miami Herald*, November 19, 1973, n.p.

25. Duong Gia Thoai, "An Imperative National Requirement," *Vietnam Courier*, March 1973, 3. See also Van Tan, "The Policy of Reconciliation and National Concord in Various Reigns in Vietnamese History," *Vietnam Courier*, March 1973, 4; "When the Vietnamese Are among Themselves," *Vietnam Courier*, April 1973, 16–17.

26. Nguyen Thi Binh, *Family, Friends and Country*; Young, *The Vietnam Wars*, 278; Kathy Kucera, "Peace Activist Recounts Vietnam Visit," *Register-Guard*, December 6, 1973, 3B, http://news.google.com/newspapers?id=lKtVAAAAIBAJ&sjid =A-EDAAAAIBAJ&pg=5263%2C1778500 (June 28, 2013); N.V., "What Does the Saigon Administration Want?," *Vietnam Courier*, March 1973, 6, 10.

27. Quoted in Diane Sherman, "No Peace in Vietnam, Weiss Says," *Capital Times*, January 25, 1974, Box 8, Folder "CW Press 1973–1974," Friendshipment, SCPC, n.p.

28. Cora Weiss, "To WSP Sisters" (December 1973), Box 2, Folder "Vietnamese Women Visit Canada, 1968," CWP, SCPC; Weiss, "Vietnam: Postwar or Prewar?"; Roy McHugh, "NY Housewife Keeps Viet Vivid," *Pittsburgh Press*, January 30, 1974, 2; Kathryn Roberts, "Many S. Viets in Jail, Woman Says," *Post Gazette*, January 30, 1974, Box 8, Folder "CW Press 1973–1974," Friendshipment, SCPC; Eastman, "Cora Weiss: Still Pushing"; Vietnamese Women's Union, "Vietnam Women's Union to Friends," January 17, 1974, Folder "Vietnam Women's Union, 1973–1974," VWU, SCPC; A Group of Vietnamese Mothers, "To American Mothers," April 20, 1974, Folder "Vietnam Women's Union, 1973–1974," VWU, SCPC; A Group of Vietnamese Mothers, "An Open Letter to American Mothers," June 20, 1974, Folder "Vietnam Women's Union, 1973–1974," VWU, SCPC; Vietnamese Women's Union, "The Real Tragic Life of South Vietnamese Women in Saigon-Held Areas," September 15, 1974, Folder "Vietnam Women's Union, 1973–1974," VWU, SCPC; Vietnamese Women's Union, "To American Women," December 19, 1974, Folder "Vietnam Women's Union, 1973–1974," VWU, SCPC; "FBI File: Cora Weiss"; Weiss, "Scrapbook"; "The Anti-Communist Crusade of a Phantom Front," *Vietnam Courier*, April 1973, 17.

29. Kucera, "Peace Activist Recounts Vietnam Visit"; Phoebe Friedman, "Life Today in North Vietnam," *The Nation*, December 10, 1973, 626–28.

30. Ngo Ba Thanh, "111 Cuoc Phong van (111 Interviews)," in Ngo Ba Thanh, *Thuc the Chinh Tri Thu Ba Tai Mien Nam Viet-Nam (The Third Political Force of Southern Viet Nam)*, 101–6, in possession of Ngo Thi Phuong Thien.

31. "Third Force in Vietnam," *Common Sense*, September 15, 1974, Part III, Series H, 4, Box 20, Folder "Correspondence, etc. re: visit of Mme. Ngo ba Thanh, 1974–1976," WILPF, SCPC; Marii Hasegawa, "To Ngo Ba Thanh," October 31, 1974, Part III, Series H, 4, Box 20, Folder "Correspondence, etc. re: visit of Mme. Ngo ba Thanh, 1974–1976," WILPF, SCPC; Bella Abzug, "Rep. Abzug's Preliminary Reaction to Recent Trip in Indochina" (Washington, D.C., March 3, 1975), Series B, 1, Box 11, Folder "Vietnam 1975," WSPR, SCPC.

32. Young, *The Vietnam Wars*, 285, 291.

33. Marii Hasegawa, "To Ngo Ba Thanh," January 7, 1974, Part III, Series H, 4, Box 20, Folder "Correspondence, etc. re: Visit of Mme. Ngo ba Thanh, 1974–1976," WILPF, SCPC.

34. Ngo Ba Thanh, "To Marii Hasegawa," February 4, 1974, Part III, Series H, 4, Box 20, Folder "Correspondence, etc. re: Visit of Mme. Ngo ba Thanh, 1974–1976," WILPF, SCPC.

35. Ngo Ba Thanh, "To Kay Camp and Marii Hasegawa," June 1, 1974, Part III, Series H, 4, Box 20, Folder "Correspondence, etc. re: Visit of Mme. Ngo ba Thanh, 1974–1976," WILPF, SCPC.

36. "Notes on Meeting with Jacki [sic] Chagnon," February 26, 1974, Part III, Series H, 4, Box 20, Folder "Correspondence, etc. re: Visit of Mme. Ngo ba Thanh, 1974–1976," WILPF, SCPC.

37. Vietnamese Women's Union, "To Friends," January 17, 1974, Folder "Vietnam Women's Union, 1973–1974," VWU, SCPC.

38. A Group of Vietnamese Mothers, "To American Mothers"; A Group of Vietnamese Mothers, "An Open Letter to American Mothers"; Vietnamese Women's Union, "The Real Tragic Life of South Vietnamese Women in Saigon-Held Areas"; Thi Vui Nguyen, "Letter of Denunciation from Mrs Nguyen Thi Vui, 34 Years Old" (South Vietnam, October 13, 1974), Folder "Vietnam Women's Union, 1973–1974," VWU, SCPC; Vietnamese Women's Union, "To American Women"; "About U.S.-Saigon Observance of the Paris Agreement," *Vietnam Courier*, April 1973, 19–20, 30. For more on the repressive nature of the Thieu administration in these years, see Ngo Vinh Long, "Legacies Foretold."

39. Barbara Deming, "It Is Very Hard . . ." (Monticello, N.Y., April 7, 1975), Box 71, Folder 1381, BDP, Schlesinger; "Stop the Babylift," *South Viet Nam in Struggle*, April 28, 1975, Box 8, Folder "Newsclippings Jan 1974–Jan 1978," Friendshipment, SCPC; Grace Paley, "Other People's Children," *Ms.*, September 1975, 68–72, 102; "Group Opposes 'Exporting' Vietnam Children to U.S.," *Morning Record*, April 8, 1975, 11, http://news.google.com/newspapers?id=H_pHAAAAIBAJ&sjid=CgANAAAAIBAJ&pg=3010%2C934180 (June 28, 2013); Grace Paley, "The Baby Myth," *Liberation* 19, no. 3 (May 1975): 19, 22.

40. Deming, "It Is Very Hard . . . ," 2.

41. Ibid., 1.

42. Kay Camp, "To Ngo Ba Thanh," in Ngo Ba Thanh, *Thuc the Chinh Tri Thu Ba Tai Mien Nam Viet-Nam*, 97.

43. Carol Goertzel and Sally Simmons, "WILPF Pledges Support for Vietnamese Women," *Peace and Freedom* 35, no. 9 (December 1975): 1, 3; "Activities of the Liberation Women's Union after the Complete Liberation of South Viet Nam," *Women of Vietnam*, no. 1 (1976): 22–23.

44. "Biographies of National Commissioners," in National Commission on the Observance of International Women's Year, *The Spirit of Houston*, 243–49, included in "How Did the National Women's Conference in Houston in 1977 Shape a Feminist Agenda for the Future?," in Sklar and Dublin, *Women and Social Movements in the United States*.

45. Judy Hansen, "Women in Vietnam: An Interview with Cora Weiss," *Pittsburgh Forum*, February 1, 1974.

46. Indochina Peace Campaign, "Women's Resources" (Santa Monica, Calif., ca. 1974), Folder "Miscellaneous Literature (over-sized)," Indochina Peace Campaign, SCPC.

47. Randall, interview with author.

48. Ibid.

49. Arlene Eisen Bergman, "Worldwide Family of Militant Women," *City Star*, March 1975, 10–11.

50. Randall, interview with author. See also Bergman, *Women of Viet Nam*; Randall, *Spirit of the People*.

51. Vu Can, "When the Intellectual Lives His People's Life," *Vietnam Courier*, April 1973, Box 88, 12–14, quotation on 12.

52. "International Women's Year in Viet Nam," *Vietnam Courier*, April 1975, 9. See also Nguyen Van Huong, "Women's Rights in the Democratic Republic of Viet Nam," *Vietnam Courier*, April 1975, 8–12.

53. "No Longer Slaves of Slaves," *Victoria University Student Newspaper*, April 29, 1975, 8–9, http://nzetc.victoria.ac.nz/tm/scholarly/tei-Salient38091975-t1-body-d20 .html#Salient38091975-fig-Salient38091975_009a (April 19, 2015).

54. Holmes, *A Joyous Revolt*, esp. chapter 5; U.S. Women's Campaign, "To Sisters" (January 20, 1975), Box 2, Folder "Women's Campaign (Donna Futterman, et al.)," Friendshipment, SCPC.

55. Holmes, *A Joyous Revolt*; Bambara, *The Seabirds Are Still Alive*.

56. Laura Whitehorn, "The Seabirds Don't Lie," *The Feminist Wire*, November 26, 2014, http://thefeministwire.com/2014/11/toni-cade-bambara-and-vietnam/ (May 18, 2015).

57. U.S. Women's Campaign, "To Aid the Institute for the Protection of Mothers and Children in Viet Nam" (Brochure, Minneapolis, n.d.), Box 2, Folder "Women's Campaign (Donna Futterman, et al.)," Friendshipment, SCPC. The alternative translation is the Institute for the Protection of Mothers and Children.

58. Dorothy Steffens, "To Viet Nam Women's Union," August 19, 1975, Part III, Series H, 4, Box 20, Folder "Correspondence with Vietnamese Women's Union, 1972–1975," WILPF, SCPC.

59. Ethel Taylor, "Keynote Address at WSP National Conference, Chicago, Illinois, October, 1973" (Chicago, October 1973), Series A, 1, Box 3, Folder "National Conference 1973, Chicago, IL," WSPR, SCPC, n.p.

60. Mary Ellen O'Donnell, "Minutes of National Consultative Meeting" (Chicago, October 1973), Series A, 1, Box 1, Folder "National Consultative Committee Minutes & Memos (Aug. 1970–1973)," WSPR, SCPC.

61. Richard Reston, "Private Group Starts Direct US-to-Hanoi Aid Next Week with Hospital Supplies," *Boston Globe*, December 19, 1974, 18; Bach Mai Hospital Relief Fund, "A Special Report to You from the Board of the Bach Mai Fund" (Cambridge, Mass., ca. 1975), Box 1, Folder "Financial Files, Tax Status," Friendshipment, SCPC; Bach Mai Hospital Relief Fund, "Special Bulletin!" (Cambridge, Mass., ca. 1975), Box 1, Folder "Financial Files, Tax Status," Friendshipment, SCPC;

Bella Abzug, "To Cora Weiss," June 16, 1975, Box 1, Folder "Financial Files, Legal Status," Friendshipment, SCPC; John Foristall, "To Bach Mai Hospital Emergency Relief Fund, Inc.," June 24, 1975, Box 1, Folder "Financial Files, Legal Status," Friendshipment, SCPC; Tom Davidson, "Loss of Tax-Deductibility for Our Work in Indochina and Implications for Your Organization" (Memo, Cambridge, Mass., June 25, 1975), Box 1, Folder "Financial Files, Legal Status," Friendshipment, SCPC; Eileen Shanahan, "IRS Disallows Tax Exemptions for Gifts to Hospital near Hanoi," *New York Times*, July 9, 1975, Box 1, Folder "Financial Files, Legal Status," Friendshipment, SCPC; Tom Davidson, "To Brewster Rhoads," July 11, 1975, Box 1, Folder "Financial Files, Legal Status," Friendshipment, SCPC; Bach Mai Hospital Relief Fund, "News" (Cambridge, Mass., July 23, 1975), Box 1, Folder "Financial Files, Tax Status," Friendshipment, SCPC; "August 14 Meeting," August 1975, Box 1, Folder "Financial Files, Tax Status," Friendshipment, SCPC.

62. Cora Weiss, "Aid from the US to Vietnam: A Brief and Incomplete Review," September 1975, Box 1, Folder "Aid Paper," Friendshipment, SCPC.

63. Larry McDonald, "Human Rights in Vietnam: U.S. Apologists for State Terrorism," *Congressional Record—House* 123, no. 7 (March 22, 1977): 8644–47.

64. Anita Fussell, "Vietnam Reconstruction Continues," *Nebraska Journal*, December 5, 1977, Box 8, Folder "Newsclippings Jan 1974–Jan 1978," Friendshipment, SCPC, 10; Janis Johnson, "US Urged to End Vietnam Ban," *Washington Post*, May 7, 1976; Heidi Kuglin, "To W. W. Wittkamper," November 18, 1976, Box 1, Folder "Correspondence Oct–Dec 1976," Friendshipment, SCPC; Heidi Kuglin, "To Murray Braverman," February 18, 1977, Box 1, Folder "Correspondence Jan–Mar 1977," Friendshipment, SCPC; Cora Weiss, "Cora Weiss' Vietnam Trip Report," ca. 1976, Box 2, Folder "Cora Weiss Trip, Articles," Friendshipment, SCPC; Midge Meinertz, "The Following Oral Testimony" (June 1977), Box 5, Folder "Misc. CWS Press," CWP, SCPC.

65. Moyn, "The Return of the Prodigal," 2. See also Kaufman, *Plans Unraveled*.

66. Ngo Ba Thanh, "Statement by Madame Ngo Ba Thanh," Ho Chi Minh City, February 15, 1977, Box 7, Folder "Ngo Ba Thanh," Friendshipment, SCPC, 1.

67. Martha Winnacker, "Recovering from Thirty Years of War," *Southeast Asia Chronicle*, June 1977, 1–10, 14–19, esp. 2–4.

68. Richard Goldensohn, "Interview with Cora Weiss" (1978), Box 6, Folder "Misc. Press Materials Re: Ship of Wheat," CWP, SCPC; Denis Grayo, "Hanoi Ready to Resume Talks with Washington," *Korea Times*, May 30, 1978, Box 6, Folder "Misc. Files Re: CWS Vietnam Trip," CWP, SCPC; "CWS Vietnam Wheat Shipment Press Conference" (New York, June 1, 1978), Box 6, Folder "Misc. Press Materials Re: Ship of Wheat," CWP, SCPC; "Minutes of Working Group on People-to-People Aid" (New York, September 24, 1977), Box 4, Folder "Conference Follow-up, September 24–25," Friendshipment, SCPC; Anita Fussell, "Vietnam Reconstruction Continues"; Church World Service, *CWS Sailed a Ship of Wheat to Vietnam*; Vietnam News Agency, "American People's Wheat for Viet Nam" (Hanoi, May 1978), Box 6, Folder "Misc. Press Materials Re: Ship of Wheat," CWP, SCPC; "CWS Press Conference San Francisco" (San Francisco, May 30, 1978), Box 6, Folder "Misc. Press Materials Re: Ship of Wheat," CWP, SCPC; "A Ship of Wheat—From Houston to Ho Chi Minh

City" (June 1978), Box 5, Folder "Misc. CWS Press," CWP, SCPC; *Join Us: People to People Aid*, Brochure, ca. 1978, Box 6, Folder "Church World Service, 1978," CWP, SCPC. See also the many newspaper clippings collected in Box 5, Folder "Newspaper Clippings: CWS Wheat Shipment 1978," CWP, SCPC.

69. "Churches Will Vote on Viet-Grain Deal," *Athens Daily Review*, January 31, 1978, Box 5, Folder "Newspaper Clippings: CWS Wheat Shipment 1978," CWP, SCPC.

70. Quoted in Peter Arnett, "Kansas Farmer Sees New World in Viet Visit," *Dallas Morning News*, May 11, 1978. See also "Farmers to Aid Vietnam," n.d., Box 7, Folder "Wheat Press May 1978 Church World Service," CWP, SCPC; "Memo on Religion in Vietnam" (June 1978), Box 5, Folder "Misc. CWS Press," CWP, SCPC; "American Visitor Refutes Persecution Allegations," *Vietnam News*, June 1, 1978, Box 6, Folder "Church World Service, 1978," CWP, SCPC; "Church Aid for Viet Nam," *Christianity Today*, June 13, 1978, Box 1, Folder "Financial Files, Legal Status," Friendshipment, SCPC; Peter Arnett, "Kansas Farmer Off to the City—Saigon," *Wichita Eagle*, May 11, 1978, Box 7, Folder "Wheat Press May 1978 Church World Service," CWP, SCPC; Peter Arnett, "He Left the Farm, Saw the World and Came Home," *Argus-Leader*, May 21, 1978, Box 7, Folder "Wheat Press May 1978 Church World Service," CWP, SCPC; Paul Stevens, "Farmer Returns from Vietnam," *Union Daily Times*, June 1, 1978, Box 7, Folder "Wheat Press May 1978 Church World Service," CWP, SCPC, and many other articles collected in Box 5, Folder "Newspaper Clippings: CWS Wheat Shipment 1978," CWP, SCPC.

71. Joining Lerner on the trip were associate director for the Interreligious Foundation for Community Organization Marilyn Clement, white; performer Vinie Burrows, African American; CWS coordinator Sally Benson, white; and tribal judge Marie Sanchez, Native American.

72. Viet Nam Women's Union, "Historic Session of National Assembly of Reunified Viet Nam" (Hanoi, July 1976), Part III, Series H, 4, Box 20, Folder "Correspondence, etc. re: Visit of Mme. Ngo ba Thanh, 1974–1976," WILPF, SCPC, 6.

73. James Feron, "Interview: A Hastings Woman Revisits Vietnam," *New York Times*, January 15, 1978, WC2.

74. Lerner, interview with author; Weiss, interview with author.

75. Lerner, interview with author; Pham Ngac, interview with author; Cu Dinh Ba, interview with author. Pham Ngac, Cu Dinh Ba, and other Vietnamese interviewed through this project remembered Cora Weiss by name and even sent their warm regards to her through me.

76. Feron, "Interview."

77. Marilyn Clement, "Ho Chi Minh Taught Us to Distinguish," n.d., Box 2, Folder "Vietnamese-American Friendship Day, 1978," Friendshipment, SCPC.

Conclusion

1. Scholarship on the memory and aftermath of the Viet Nam war includes Ngo, "Legacies Foretold"; Martini, *Invisible Enemies*; Laderman, *Tours of Vietnam*; Lewis, *Hardhats, Hippies, and Hawks*.

2. Christine Sylvester states that women have often looked abroad to evaluate their own rights but usually find a lack of rights in other nations. Sylvester, *Feminist International Relations*, 34.

3. "How Women the World over Feel about Their Vietnamese Sisters," *Women of Viet Nam*, no. 1 (1976): 28–31.

4. Viet Nam Women's Union, "Appeal to Women over the World" (Hanoi, February 19, 1979), Accession 07S-92, Box 4, Saralee Hamilton Collection, SSC.

5. "Riverside Church Hiring Organizer Carol [*sic*] Weiss," May 22, 1978, Box 7, Folder "Wheat Press May 1978 Church World Service," CWP, SCPC; "Riverside Church Disarmament Program" (New York City, 1983), Box 7, Folder "Riverside Disarmament History, 1978–1983," CWP, SCPC; Midge Meinertz, "To Cora Weiss," June 28, 1978, Box 6, Folder "Church World Service, 1978," CWP, SCPC.

6. Dutt, "Some Reflections on United States Women of Color and the United Nations Fourth World Conference on Women and NGO Forum in Beijing, China."

7. Hirschkind and Mahmood, "Feminism, the Taliban, and Politics of Counter-Insurgency"; Farrell and McDermott, "Claiming Afghan Women"; Fernandes, "The Boundaries of Terror."

8. Falcón, "Transnational Feminism and Contextualized Intersectionality at the 2001 World Conference against Racism." Falcón suggests that being able to note harmful U.S. foreign policies is key to building truly transnational feminist movements.

Bibliography

Primary Sources

Archival Sources

Albuquerque, N.M.
  University of New Mexico, Center for Southwest Research, University
     Libraries
    Radical Pamphlets Collection
    Margaret Randall Papers
    Underground Newspaper Collection
Berkeley, Calif.
  The Graduate Theological Union Archives
    Anne McGrew Bennett Collection, GTU 89-5-017
Cambridge, Mass.
  Harvard University, Radcliffe Institute, Schlesinger Library
    Charlotte Bunch Additional Papers
    Charlotte Bunch Papers
    Barbara Deming Papers
    Helen Boydon Lamb Papers
    Florence Luscomb Additional Papers
    Nancy Osterud Papers
Chicago, Ill.
  Chicago Historical Society
    Shirley Lens Papers
    Women for Peace Papers
Durham, N.C.
  Duke University, Rare Book, Manuscript, and Special Collections Library
    Documents from the Women's Liberation Movement: An On-line Archival
     Collection
    J. B. Matthews Papers
    Bobbye S. Ortiz Papers
    Victoria Ortiz Papers
    Irene Peslikis Papers
Los Angeles, Calif.
  UCLA, Charles E. Young Research Library, Department of Special
    Collections
    Steve Louie Asian American Movement Collection (Collection Number 1805)
    Collection of Underground, Alternative and Extremist Literature
    (Collection 50)

Madison, Wis.
  Wisconsin Historical Society
    Donna Allen Papers, M92-266
Northampton, Mass.
  Smith College, Sophia Smith Collection
    Joan Biren Collection
    Saralee Hamilton Collection
    Peace Collection
    Periodicals Collection
    Women's Liberation Collection
Palo Alto, Calif.
  Stanford University, Hoover Institution Archives
    Martin Florian Herz Collection
    New Left Collection
St. Paul, Minn.
  Minnesota Historical Society
    Marianne Hamilton Papers
Swarthmore, Pa.
  Swarthmore College Peace Collection
    Elise Boulding Papers
    Kay Camp Papers
    Committee of Liaison with Families of Servicemen Detained in North
      Vietnam Records
    Friendshipment/Bach Mai Hospital Relief Fund Records
    Indochina Peace Campaign
    Indochina Resource Center
    Vietnam Women's Union Records
    Cora Weiss Papers
    Women Strike for Peace Records
    Women's International League for Peace and Freedom Papers
Vancouver, British Columbia, Canada
  Simon Fraser University, Archives and Records Management Department
    Kathleen Hudson Women's Bookstore Collection
    Anne Roberts Women's Movement Fond
Washington, D.C.
  Library of Congress
    Muriel Rukeyser Papers
  Woodrow Wilson International Center for Scholars, Digital Archive
    Cold War International History Project

Oral History Interviews

Chen, May. Interview by Karen Harper, March 1, 1993. Women's History: Asian
  American Women's Movement Activists. The Virtual Oral/Aural History

Archive, California State University, Long Beach, Calif., http://www.csulb.edu
/voaha. November 21, 2011.

Iwataki, Miya. Interview by Karen Harper, November 26, 1991. Women's History:
Asian American Women's Movement Activists. The Virtual Oral/Aural History
Archive, California State University, Long Beach, Calif., http://www.csulb.edu
/voaha. November 21, 2011.

Martínez, Elizabeth (Betita). Interview by Anselmo F. Arellano, March 16, 1998.
Box 5, DVD 13, Oral History Projects and Video Recordings Collection. Center
for Southwest Research, University Libraries, University of New Mexico,
Albuquerque, N.M.

Martínez, Elizabeth (Betita). Interview by Loretta Ross, Transcript of Video
Recording, August 3, 2006. Voices of Feminism Oral History Project. Sophia
Smith Collection, Smith College, Northampton, Mass.

Interview with Vivian Rothstein, Student Activist, People's Century, Young Blood
Episode. Transcript, ca. 1999, http://www.pbs.org/wgbh/peoplescentury
/episodes/youngblood/rothsteintranscript.html. June 13, 2013.

Saika, Peggy. Interview by Loretta Ross, Transcript of Video Recording,
February 20, 2006. Voices of Feminism Oral History Project. Sophia Smith
Collection, Smith College, Northampton, Mass.

Yoshimura, Evelyn. Interview by Julie Bartolotto, May 5, 1995. Women's History:
Asian American Women's Movement Activists. The Virtual Oral/Aural History
Archive, California State University, Long Beach, Calif., http://www.csulb.edu
/voaha. November 21, 2011.

Author Interviews

Cu Dinh Ba. In-person interview, Da Nang, July 24, 2015.

Huynh Ngoc An. In-person interview, Ho Chi Minh City, July 27, 2015.

Le Mai. In-person interview, Hanoi, July 23, 2015.

Lerner, Judy. In-person interview, New York City, March 18, 2013.

Ngo Thi Phuong Thien. In-person interview, Ho Chi Minh City, July 27, 2015.

Ngo Thi Tuyet. In-person interview, Da Nang, July 24, 2015.

Nguyen Binh An. In-person interview, Da Nang, July 24, 2015.

Osterud, Nancy Grey. In-person interview, Newport, R.I., June 24, 2014.

Pham Khac Lam. In-person interview, Hanoi, July 22, 2015.

Pham Ngac. In-person interview, Hanoi, July 23, 2015.

Pham Van Chuong. In-person interview, Hanoi, July 22, 2015.

Phan Thi Minh. In-person interview, Da Nang, July 25, 2015.

Randall, Margaret. In-person interview, Albuquerque, N.M., January 10, 2012.

Rothstein, Vivian. Telephone interview, November 1, 2013.

Tran Minh Quoc. In-person interview, Hanoi, July 23, 2015.

Trinh Ngoc Thai. In-person interview, Hanoi, July 22, 2015.

Vo Anh Tuan. In-person interview, Ho Chi Minh City, July 28, 2015.

Weiss, Cora. Telephone interview, December 1, 2010.

Selected Newspapers and Periodicals

The Afro American
The Black Panther
 (Oakland, Calif.)
Chicano Student Move-
 ment (Los Angeles,
 Calif.)
Congressional Record
Documents and
 Information (WIDF)
El Grito del Norte
 (Española, N.M.)
Feminist Liberation
 Newsletter
Freedomways
Getting Together
 (New York, N.Y.)

Gidra (Los Angeles,
 Calif.)
Guardian
L.A. Free Press
Liberation
Medical Aid for Indochina
 News
Memo (WSP)
The Militant
Muhammad Speaks
New York Times
off our backs
Peace and Freedom
 (WILPF)
The Pedestal (Vancouver,
 Canada)

Philadelphia Inquirer
Rat
South Viet Nam in
 Struggle (Hanoi, DRV)
Vietnam (WIDF)
The Vietnam Courier
 (Hanoi, DRV)
Voice of Women
Washington Post
WIN
Women: A Journal of
 Liberation
Women of Vietnam
 (Hanoi, DRV)

FBI Files

Bennett, Anne McGrew
Camp, Katherine
Clarke, Mary
Committee of Liaison with Families of Servicemen Detained in North Vietnam
Deming, Barbara
Hasegawa, Marii
Lens, Shirley
McCarthy, Mary
Sontag, Susan
Sumi, Hideko "Patricia"
Third World Women's Alliance
Weiss, Cora
Wilson, Dagmar
Women Strike for Peace

Published Sources

Adams, Judith Porter. *Peacework: Oral Histories of Women Peace Activists*. Boston: Twayne, 1990.
Asian Women. Berkeley: University of California, 1971.
Bambara, Toni Cade. *The Seabirds Are Still Alive: Collected Stories*. New York: Random House, 1977.
Bergman, Arlene Eisen. *Women of Viet Nam*. 2nd ed. San Francisco: Peoples Press, 1975.
Brown, Elaine. *A Taste of Power: A Black Woman's Story*. New York: Anchor, 1992.

Burchett, Wilfred G. *Vietnam: Inside Story of the Guerrilla War*. New York: International Publishers, 1965.

Burris, Barbara. *Fourth World Manifesto: An Angry Response to an Imperialist Venture against the Women's Liberation Movement*. Detroit: The Advocate Press, 1971.

Church World Service. *CWS Sailed a Ship of Wheat to Vietnam*. New York: Church World Service, 1978.

Clinton, James W., ed. *The Loyal Opposition: Americans in North Vietnam, 1965–1972*. Niwot, Colo.: University Press of Colorado, 1995.

Committee on Armed Services. *Problems of Prisoners of War and Their Families*. Washington, D.C.: U.S. Government Printing Office, 1970.

Committee on Foreign Relations. *American Prisoners of War in Southeast Asia*. Washington, D.C.: U.S. Government Printing Office, 1971.

———. *Harrison E. Salisbury's Trip to North Vietnam*. Washington, D.C.: U.S. Government Printing Office, 1967.

Committee on Internal Security. *Investigation of Students for a Democratic Society Part 7-A*. Washington, D.C.: U.S. Government Printing Office, 1969.

———. *New Mobilization Committee to End the War in Vietnam Part II*. Washington, D.C.: U.S. Government Printing Office, 1970.

Committee on the Judiciary. *Extent of Subversion in "New Left."* Washington, D.C.: U.S. Government Printing Office, 1970.

Cotera, Marta. "Our Feminist Heritage." In *Chicana Feminist Thought: The Basic Historical Writings*, edited by Alma M. García, 41–44. New York: Routledge, 1997. Originally a speech given by Cotera in 1973.

Duckles, Madeline. Nguyen Thi Binh: Pacifica Radio Archive, October 1966, http://archive.org/details/MadelineDucklesInterviewsNguyenThiBinh. May 30, 2013.

Espinoza, Dionne, and Lorena Oropeza, eds. *Enriqueta Vasquez and the Chicano Movement: Writings from* El Grito Del Norte. Houston: Arte Público, 2006.

García, Alma, ed. *Chicana Feminist Thought: The Basic Historical Writings*. New York: Routledge, 1997.

Greene, Felix. *Vietnam! Vietnam!: In Photographs and Text*. Palo Alto, Calif.: Futon, 1966.

Gumbo Albert, Judy. "CounterPunch: Back to Viet Nam." *Yippie Girl*, January 13, 2014, http://yippiegirl.com/vietnam/back-to-viet-nam.html. July 31, 2014.

House Committee on Foreign Affairs. *The Treatment of Political Prisoners in South Vietnam by the Government of the Republic of South Vietnam*. Washington, D.C.: U.S. Government Printing Office, 1973.

"Interview with Mrs. Ngo Ba Thanh, 1981." *WGBH Media Library and Archives*, March 15, 1981, http://openvault.wgbh.org/catalog/vietnam-obb668-interview-with-mrs-ngo-ba-thanh-1981. April 14, 2015.

Kerry, John. "American Policy Makers Are Responsible for War Crimes in Vietnam." In *Vietnam War Crimes*, edited by Samuel Brenner, 32–40. Detroit: Thomson Gale, 2006.

Louie, Steve, ed. *Asian Americans: The Movement and the Moment*. Los Angeles, Calif.: UCLA Asian American Studies Center Press, 2001.

Mariscal, George, ed. *Aztlán and Viet Nam: Chicano and Chicana Experiences of the War*. Berkeley: University of California Press, 1999.

Martínez, Elizabeth Sutherland. *500 Years of Chicana Women's History*. Bilingual ed. New Brunswick, N.J.: Rutgers University Press, 2008.

McCarthy, Mary. *Hanoi*. New York: Harcourt, Brace and World, 1968.

McEldowney, Carol Cohen. *Hanoi Journal, 1967*. Edited by Suzanne Kelley McCormack and Elizabeth Mock. Amherst: University of Massachusetts Press, 2007.

Moynihan, Daniel Patrick. *The Negro Family: The Case for National Action*. Washington, D.C.: United States Department of Labor, 1965.

Nakamura, Norman. "The Nature of G.I. Racism." In *Roots: An Asian American Reader*, edited by Amy Tachiki, Eddie Wong, and Franklin Odo, 24–26. Los Angeles: Continental Graphics, 1971. Originally published in *Gidra* (June/July 1970).

National Commission on the Observance of International Women's Year. *The Spirit of Houston: The First National Women's Conference*. Washington, D.C.: U.S. Government Printing Office, 1978.

Ngo Ba Thanh, ed. *Thuc the Chinh Tri Thu Ba Tai Mien Nam Viet-Nam Dong Gop Vao Cham Dut Chien Tranh va Lap Lai Hoa Binh O Viet Nam (The Third Political Force in Viet Nam Contributing to the End of the War and the Restoration of Peace in Viet Nam)*. Vol. 1. Saigon: Vietnamese Women's Movement for the Right to Live, Vietnamese People's Front Struggling for Peace, 1974.

———. *Thuc the Chinh Tri Thu Ba Tai Mien Nam Viet-Nam (The Third Political Force of Southern Viet Nam)*. Saigon: Vietnamese Women's Movement for the Right to Live, Vietnamese People's Front Struggling for Peace, 1975.

Nguyen Quy, ed. History and Public Policy Program Digital Archive, Van Kien Dang Qoan Tap, 30, 1969 [Collected Party Documents, Volume 30, 1969]. Hanoi: National Political Publishing House, 2004.

Nguyen Thi Binh. *Family, Friends and Country: A Memoir*. Translated by Lady Borton. Hanoi: Tri Thuc, 2015.

Patitucci, Jean. *Chronology of Developments in Vietnam: December 1969*. Washington, D.C.: Congressional Research Service, 1970.

Rafalko, Frank J. *MH/Chaos: The CIA's Campaign against the Radical New Left and the Black Panthers*. Annapolis, Md.: Naval Institute Press, 2011.

Randall, Margaret. *Spirit of the People*. Vancouver: New Star, 1975.

Rincón, Bernice. "La Chicana: Her Role in the Past and Her Search for a New Role in the Future." In *Chicana Feminist Thought: The Basic Historical Writings*, edited by Alma M. García, 24–28. New York: Routledge, 1997. Originally published in *Regeneración* 1, no. 10 (1971): 15–18.

Rowbotham, Sheila. *Women, Resistance and Revolution: A History of Women and Revolution in the Modern World*. London: Allen Lane the Penguin Press, 1972.

Sklar, Kathryn Kish, and Thomas Dublin, eds. *Women and Social Movements in the United States, 1600–2000*. Binghamton: State University of New York at Binghamton, 2004.

Tachiki, Amy, Eddie Wong, and Franklin Odo, eds. *Roots: An Asian American Reader*. Los Angeles: Continental Graphics, 1971.

Takemoto, Cindy. "Pat Sumi: Off the Pedestal." In *Asian Women*, 107–11. Berkeley: University of California, 1971.

Taylor, Ethel Barol. *We Made a Difference: My Personal Journey with Women Strike for Peace*. Philadelphia: Camino, 1998.

Vietnamese Women. Vietnamese Studies 10. Hanoi: Xunhasaba, 1966.

Women's International Democratic Federation. *The Situation in the Countries of Indochina and Solidarity with Their Peoples*. Berlin: International Viet Nam Solidarity Committee, Women's International Democratic Federation, 1970.

———. *Vietnam*. Berlin: International Viet Nam Solidarity Committee, 1973.

Women's Work on Peace and War. Boston: Pandora, 1984.

Ybara, Lea, and Nina Genera. *La Batalla Está Aquí: Chicanos and the War*. El Cerrito, Calif.: Chicano Draft Help, 1972.

Yokota, Ryan Masaaki. "Interview with Pat Sumi: In Memoriam May 15, 1944–August 15, 1997." In *Asian Americans: The Movement and the Moment*, edited by Steve Louie, 16–31. Los Angeles, Calif.: UCLA Asian American Studies Center Press, 2001.

Secondary Sources

Adams, Nina. "The Women Who Left Them Behind." In *Give Peace a Chance: Exploring the Vietnam Antiwar Movement: Essays from the Charles DeBenedetti Memorial Conference*, edited by Melvin Small and William D. Hoover, 182–95. Syracuse, N.Y.: Syracuse University Press, 1992.

Allen, Michael J. *Until the Last Man Comes Home: POWs, MIAs, and the Unending Vietnam War*. Chapel Hill: University of North Carolina Press, 2009.

Alonso, Harriet Hyman. *Peace as a Women's Issue: A History of the U.S. Movement for World Peace and Women's Rights*. Syracuse, N.Y.: Syracuse University Press, 1993.

Anderson, Benedict R. *Imagined Communities: Reflections on the Origin and Spread of Nationalism*. New York: Verso, 1991.

Anderson, Carol. *Eyes off the Prize: The United Nations and the African American Struggle for Human Rights, 1944–1955*. New York: Cambridge University Press, 2003.

Anderson, Helen. "Fighting for Family: Vietnamese Women and the American War." In *The Columbia History of the Vietnam War*, edited by David L. Anderson, 297–316. New York: Columbia University Press, 2013.

Anderson-Bricker, Kristin. "'Triple Jeopardy': Black Women and the Growth of Feminist Consciousness in SNCC, 1964–1975." In *Still Lifting, Still Climbing: Contemporary African American Women's Activism*, edited by Kimberly Springer, 49–69. New York: New York University Press, 1999.

Berkeley, Kathleen C. *The Women's Liberation Movement in America*. Westport, Conn.: Greenwood, 1999.

Blackwell, Joyce. *No Peace without Freedom: Race and the Women's International League for Peace and Freedom, 1915–1975*. Carbondale: Southern Illinois University Press, 2004.

Blackwell, Maylei. *¡Chicana Power!: Contested Histories of Feminism in the Chicano Movement*. Austin: University of Texas Press, 2011.

Bolt, Christine. *Sisterhood Questioned?: Race, Class and Internationalism in the American and British Women's Movements, c.1880s–1970s*. New York: Routledge, 2004.

Borstelmann, Thomas. *The Cold War and the Color Line: American Race Relations in the Global Arena.* Cambridge, Mass.: Harvard University Press, 2001.

Brigham, Robert K. *Guerrilla Diplomacy: The NLF's Foreign Relations and the Viet Nam War.* Ithaca, N.Y.: Cornell University Press, 1998.

Brocheux, Pierre. *Ho Chi Minh: A Biography.* New York: Cambridge University Press, 2007.

Brookfield, Tarah. *Cold War Comforts: Canadian Women, Child Safety, and Global Insecurity.* Waterloo: Wilfrid Laurier University Press, 2012.

Burke, Roland. "From Individual Rights to National Development: The First UN International Conference on Human Rights, Tehran, 1968." *Journal of World History* 19, no. 3 (September 2008): 275–96.

Burton, Antoinette M. *Burdens of History: British Feminists, Indian Women, and Imperial Culture, 1865–1915.* Chapel Hill: University of North Carolina, 1994.

———. "The White Woman's Burden: British Feminists and 'The Indian Woman,' 1865–1915." In *Western Women and Imperialism: Complicity and Resistance*, edited by Nupur Chaudhuri and Margaret Strobel, 137–57. Bloomington: Indiana University Press, 1992.

Bussey, Gertrude Carman, and Margaret Tims. *Pioneers for Peace: Women's International League for Peace and Freedom, 1915–1965.* London: WILPF, British Section, 1980.

Busto, Rudy V. *King Tiger: The Religious Vision of Reies López Tijerina.* Albuquerque, N.M.: University of New Mexico Press, 2005.

Casey, Caitlin. "Vanguards of Globalization: Transnationalism in American Activism, 1960–1975." Ph.D. diss., Yale University, 2011.

Castledine, Jacqueline. *Cold War Progressives: Women's Interracial Organizing for Peace and Freedom.* Urbana: University of Illinois Press, 2012.

Chan, Sucheng. "The Exclusion of Chinese Women, 1870–1943." In *Entry Denied: Exclusion and the Chinese Community in America, 1882–1943*, edited by Sucheng Chan, 94–146. Philadelphia: Temple University Press, 1991.

Chavez, Marisela. "'We Have a Long, Beautiful History': Chicana Feminist Trajectories and Legacies." In *No Permanent Waves: Recasting Histories of U.S. Feminism*, edited by Nancy A. Hewitt, 77–97. New Brunswick, N.J.: Rutgers University Press, 2010.

Chong, Denise. *The Girl in the Picture: The Story of Kim Phuc, the Photograph, and the Vietnam War.* New York: Viking, 2000.

Chow, Esther Ngan-Ling. "The Development of Feminist Consciousness among Asian American Women." *Gender and Society* 1, no. 3 (September 1987): 284–99.

———. "The Feminist Movement: Where Are All the Asian American Women?" *U.S.-Japan Women's Journal*, no. 2 (1992): 96–111.

Cleaver, Kathleen. "Women, Power, and Revolution." In *Liberation, Imagination, and the Black Panther Party: A New Look at the Panthers and Their Legacy*, edited by Kathleen Cleaver and George N. Katsiaficas, 123–27. New York: Routledge, 2001.

Cobble, Dorothy Sue. *The Other Women's Movement: Workplace Justice and Social Rights in Modern America.* Princeton, N.J.: Princeton University Press, 2004.

Davies, Carole Boyce. *Left of Karl Marx: The Political Life of Black Communist Claudia Jones*. Durham, N.C.: Duke University Press, 2008.

Davin, Anna. "Imperialism and Motherhood." In *Tensions of Empire: Colonial Cultures in a Bourgeois World*, edited by Frederick Cooper and Ann Laura Stoler, 87–151. Berkeley, Calif.: University of California Press, 1997.

De Haan, Francisca. "Eugenie Cotton, Pak Chong-ae, and Claudia Jones: Rethinking Transnational Feminism and International Politics." *Journal of Women's History* 25, no. 4 (Winter 2013): 174–89.

DeBenedetti, Charles. *An American Ordeal: The Antiwar Movement of the Vietnam Era*. Syracuse, N.Y.: Syracuse University Press, 1990.

Duberman, Martin B. *A Saving Remnant: The Radical Lives of Barbara Deming and David McReynolds*. New York: New Press, 2011.

Dudziak, Mary L. *Cold War Civil Rights: Race and the Image of American Democracy*. Princeton, N.J.: Princeton University Press, 2000.

Dutt, Mallika. "Some Reflections on United States Women of Color and the United Nations Fourth World Conference on Women and NGO Forum in Beijing, China." In *Global Feminisms since 1945*, edited by Bonnie G. Smith, 305–13. New York: Routledge, 2000.

Early, Frances. *A World without War: How U.S. Feminists and Pacifists Resisted World War I*. Syracuse, N.Y.: Syracuse University Press, 1997.

Echols, Alice. *Daring to Be Bad: Radical Feminism in America, 1967–1975*. Minneapolis: University of Minnesota Press, 1989.

———. "'Women Power' and Women's Liberation: Exploring the Relationship between the Antiwar Movement and the Women's Liberation Movement." In *Give Peace a Chance: Exploring the Vietnam Antiwar Movement: Essays from the Charles DeBenedetti Memorial Conference*, edited by Melvin Small and William D. Hoover, 171–81. Syracuse, N.Y.: Syracuse University Press, 1992.

Elbaum, Max. *Revolution in the Air: Sixties Radicals Turn to Lenin, Mao and Che*. New York: Verso, 2002.

Encarguez Perez, Beverly. "Woman Warrior Meets Mail-Order Bride: Finding an Asian American Voice in the Women's Movement." *Berkeley Women's Law Journal* 18 (2003): 211–36.

Enke, Anne. *Finding the Movement: Sexuality, Contested Space, and Feminist Activism*. Durham, N.C.: Duke University Press, 2007.

Enloe, Cynthia H. *Bananas, Beaches & Bases: Making Feminist Sense of International Politics*. Berkeley: University of California Press, 1990.

Espiritu, Yen Le. "Panethnicity and Asian American Activism." In *Major Problems in Asian American History*, edited by Lon Kurashige and Alice Yang Murray, 442–49. Boston: Houghton Mifflin, 2003.

Estepa, Andrea. "Taking the White Gloves Off: Women Strike for Peace and 'the Movement,' 1967–73." In *Feminist Coalitions: Historical Perspectives on Second-Wave Feminism in the United States*, edited by Stephanie Gilmore, 84–112. Urbana: University of Illinois Press, 2008.

Evans, Sara M. *Personal Politics: The Roots of Women's Liberation in the Civil Rights Movement and the New Left*. New York: Knopf, 1979.

————. "Women's Liberation: Seeing the Revolution Clearly." *Feminist Studies* 41, no. 1 (2015): 138–49.

Ezekiel, Judith. *Feminism in the Heartland*. Columbus: Ohio State University Press, 2002.

Falcón, Sylvanna. "Transnational Feminism and Contextualized Intersectionality at the 2001 World Conference against Racism." *Journal of Women's History* 24, no. 4 (Winter 2012): 99–120.

Farrell, Amy, and Patrice McDermott. "Claiming Afghan Women: The Challenge of Human Rights Discourse for Transnational Feminism." In *Just Advocacy?: Women's Human Rights, Transnational Feminisms, and the Politics of Representation*, edited by Wendy S. Hesford and Wendy Kozol, 33–55. New Brunswick, N.J.: Rutgers University Press, 2005.

Fernandes, Leela. "The Boundaries of Terror: Feminism, Human Rights, and the Politics of Global Crisis." In *Just Advocacy?: Women's Human Rights, Transnational Feminisms, and the Politics of Representation*, edited by Wendy S. Hesford and Wendy Kozol, 56–74. New Brunswick, N.J.: Rutgers University Press, 2005.

Fischer, Marilyn. "Addams's Internationalist Pacifism and the Rhetoric of Maternalism." *NWSA Journal* 18, no. 3 (Fall 2006): 1–19.

Foster, Catherine. *Women for All Seasons: The Story of the Women's International League for Peace and Freedom*. Athens: University of Georgia Press, 1989.

Frazier, Robeson Taj. *The East Is Black: Cold War China in the Black Radical Imagination*. Durham, N.C.: Duke University Press, 2014.

Giddings, Paula. *When and Where I Enter: The Impact of Black Women on Race and Sex in America*. New York: Morrow, 1984.

Gill, Gerald. "From Maternal Pacifism to Revolutionary Solidarity: African-American Women's Opposition to the Vietnam War." In *Sights on the Sixties*, edited by Barbara L. Tischler, 177–95. New Brunswick, N.J.: Rutgers University Press, 1992.

Gitlin, Todd. *The Sixties: Years of Hope, Days of Rage*. New York: Bantam, 1987.

Gluck, Sherna. "Whose Feminism, Whose History? Reflections on Excavating the History of (the) U.S. Women's Movement(s)." In *Community Activism and Feminist Politics: Organizing Across Race, Class, and Gender*, edited by Nancy Naples, 31–56. New York: Routledge, 1998.

Goldstein, Joshua S. *War and Gender: How Gender Shapes the War System and Vice Versa*. Cambridge: Cambridge University Press, 2001.

Goossen, Rachel Waltner. *Women against the Good War: Conscientious Objection and Gender on the American Home Front, 1941–1947*. Chapel Hill: University of North Carolina Press, 1997.

Gore, Dayo F. *Radicalism at the Crossroads: African American Women Activists in the Cold War*. New York: New York University Press, 2012.

Hammond, William M. *Reporting Vietnam: Media and Military at War*. Lawrence: University Press of Kansas, 1998.

Harris, Duchess. "From the Kennedy Commission to the Combahee Collective: Black Feminist Organizing 1960–80." In *Sisters in the Struggle: African American*

Women in the Civil Rights–Black Power Movement, edited by Bettye Collier-Thomas and V. P. Franklin, 280–305. New York: New York University Press, 2001.

Hart, Justin. *Empire of Ideas: The Origins of Public Diplomacy and the Transformation of U. S. Foreign Policy.* New York: Oxford University Press, 2013.

Hershberger, Mary. *Jane Fonda's War: A Political Biography of an Antiwar Icon.* New York: New Press, 2005.

———. *Traveling to Vietnam: American Peace Activists and the War.* Syracuse, N.Y.: Syracuse University Press, 1998.

Hesford, Victoria. *Feeling Women's Liberation.* Durham, N.C.: Duke University Press, 2013.

Hewitt, Nancy A., ed. *No Permanent Waves: Recasting Histories of U.S. Feminism.* New Brunswick, N.J.: Rutgers University Press, 2010.

Hirschkind, Charles, and Saba Mahmood. "Feminism, the Taliban, and Politics of Counter-insurgency." *Anthropological Quarterly* 75, no. 2 (Spring 2002): 339–54.

Hoganson, Kristin L. *Fighting for American Manhood: How Gender Politics Provoked the Spanish-American and Philippine-American Wars.* New Haven, Conn.: Yale University Press, 1998.

Holmes, Linda Janet. *A Joyous Revolt: Toni Cade Bambara, Writer and Activist.* Santa Barbara, Calif.: Praeger, 2014.

Hsiao, Andrew. "The Hidden History of Asian-American Activism in New York City." *Social Policy* 28, no. 4 (Summer 1998): 23–31.

Iwataki, Miya. "The Asian Women's Movement—A Retrospective." *East Wind* 2, no. 1 (Spring/Summer 1983): 35–41.

Jacobs, Margaret D. *White Mother to a Dark Race: Settler Colonialism, Maternalism, and the Removal of Indigenous Children in the American West and Australia, 1880–1940.* Lincoln: University of Nebraska Press, 2009.

Jeffreys-Jones, Rhodri. *Peace Now!: American Society and the Ending of the Vietnam War.* New Haven, Conn.: Yale University Press, 1999.

Jensen, Kimberly, and Erika A. Kuhlman, eds. *Women and Transnational Activism in Historical Perspective.* Dordrecht: Republic of Letters, 2010.

Joseph, Peniel E. *Waiting 'Til the Midnight Hour: A Narrative History of Black Power in America.* New York: Henry Holt, 2006.

———. ed. *The Black Power Movement: Rethinking the Civil Rights–Black Power Era.* New York: Routledge, 2006.

Jung, Moon-Ho. *The Rising Tide of Color: Race, State Violence, and Radical Movements across the Pacific.* Seattle: University of Washington Press, 2014.

Kaplan, Amy. "Left Alone with America: The Absence of Empire in the Study of American Culture." In *Cultures of United States Imperialism*, edited by Donald Pease and Amy Kaplan, 3–21. Durham, N.C.: Duke University Press, 1993.

———. ed. *The Anarchy of Empire in the Making of U.S. Culture.* Cambridge, Mass.: Harvard University Press, 2002.

Kaufman, Scott. *Plans Unraveled: The Foreign Policy of the Carter Administration.* DeKalb: Northern Illinois University Press, 2008.

Kelley, Robin D. G., and Betsy Esch. "Black Like Mao: Red China and Black Revolution." *Souls: A Critical Journal of Black Politics, Culture, and Society* 1, no. 4 (Fall 1999): 6–41.

Kimball, Jeffrey. "Richard M. Nixon and the Vietnam War: The Paradox of Disengagement with Escalation." In *The Columbia History of the Vietnam War*, edited by David L. Anderson, 217–43. New York: Columbia University Press, 2013.

Ko, Dorothy. *Cinderella's Sisters: A Revisionist History of Footbinding.* Berkeley, Calif.: University of California Press, 2005.

Koven, Seth, and Sonya Michel. *Mothers of a New World: Maternalist Politics and the Origins of Welfare States.* New York: Routledge, 1993.

Kwan, Peter. "Invention, Inversion and Intervention: The Oriental Woman in the World of Suzie Wong, M. Butterfly, and the Adventures of Priscilla, Queen of the Desert." *Asian Law Journal* 5 (May 1998): 99–137.

Laderman, Scott. *Tours of Vietnam: War, Travel Guides, and Memory.* Durham, N.C.: Duke University Press, 2009.

Laville, Helen. *Cold War Women: The International Activities of American Women's Organisations.* Manchester: Manchester University Press, 2002.

Lawson, Steven F. "Freedom Then, Freedom Now: The Historiography of the Civil Rights Movement." *American Historical Review* 96, no. 2 (April 1991): 456–71.

Lazerow, Jama, and Yohuru R. Williams, eds. *In Search of the Black Panther Party: New Perspectives on a Revolutionary Movement.* Durham, N.C.: Duke University Press, 2006.

Lembcke, Jerry. *Hanoi Jane: War, Sex, and Fantasies of Betrayal.* Amherst: University of Massachusetts Press, 2010.

Lewis, Penny W. *Hardhats, Hippies, and Hawks: The Vietnam Antiwar Movement as Myth and Memory.* Ithaca, N.Y.: Cornell University Press, 2013.

Ling, Susie. "The Mountain Movers: Asian American Women's Movement in Los Angeles." *Amerasia* 15, no. 1 (1989): 51–67.

Liu, Michael, Kim Géron, and Tracy A. M. Lai. *The Snake Dance of Asian American Activism: Community, Vision, and Power in the Struggle for Social Justice, 1945–2000.* Lanham, Md.: Lexington Books, 2008.

Loyd, Jenna. "'War Is Not Healthy for Children and Other Living Things.'" *Environment and Planning D: Society and Space* 27 (April 2009): 403–24.

Maeda, Daryl J. *Chains of Babylon: The Rise of Asian America.* Minneapolis: University of Minnesota Press, 2009.

Mariscal, George. "Mexican Americans and the Viet Nam War." In *A Companion to the Vietnam War*, edited by Marilyn Blatt Young and Robert Buzzanco, 348–66. Malden, Mass.: Blackwell, 2002.

Martini, Edwin A. *Invisible Enemies: The American War on Vietnam, 1975–2000.* Amherst: University of Massachusetts Press, 2007.

McCormack, Suzanne Kelley. "'Good Politics Is Doing Something': Independent Diplomats and Anti-war Activists in the Vietnam-era Peace Movement, a Collective Biography." Ph.D. diss., Boston College, 2002.

Michel, Sonya, and Robyn Rosen. "The Paradox of Maternalism: Elizabeth Lowell Putnam and the American Welfare State." *Gender & History* 4, no. 3 (Autumn 1992): 364–86.

Midgley, Clare. "Anti-slavery and the Roots of Imperial Feminism." In *Gender and Imperialism*, edited by Clare Midgley, 161–79. Manchester: Manchester University Press, 1998.

———. *Feminism and Empire: Women Activists in Imperial Britain, 1790–1865*. London: Routledge, 2007.

The Military History Institute of Vietnam. *Victory in Vietnam: The Official History of the People's Army of Vietnam, 1954–1975*. Translated by Merle Pribbenow. Lawrence: University Press of Kansas, 2002.

Miller, Jim. *Democracy Is in the Streets: From Port Huron to the Siege of Chicago*. New York: Simon and Schuster, 1987.

Mohanty, Chandra Talpade. "Under Western Eyes: Feminist Scholarship and Colonial Discourses." In *Third World Women and the Politics of Feminism*, edited by Chandra Talpade Mohanty and Ann Russo, 51–80. Bloomington: Indiana University Press, 1991.

Mollin, Marian. *Radical Pacifism in Modern America: Egalitarianism and Protest*. Philadelphia: University of Pennsylvania Press, 2006.

Moyn, Samuel. "The Return of the Prodigal: The 1970s as a Turning Point in Human Rights History." In *The Breakthrough: Human Rights in the 1970s*, edited by Jan Eckel and Samuel Moyn, 1–14. Philadelphia: University of Pennsylvania Press, 2014.

Newman, Louise Michele. *White Women's Rights: The Racial Origins of Feminism in the United States*. New York: Oxford University Press, 1999.

Ngo Vinh Long. "Legacies Foretold: Excavating the Roots of Postwar Viet Nam." In *Four Decades On: Vietnam, the United States, and the Legacies of the Second Indochina War*, edited by Scott Laderman and Edwin A. Martini, 16–43. Durham, N.C.: Duke University Press, 2013.

Nguyen, Lien-Hang T. *Hanoi's War: An International History of the War for Peace in Vietnam*. Chapel Hill: University of North Carolina Press, 2012.

———. "Revolutionary Circuits: Toward Internationalizing America in the World." *Diplomatic History* 39, no. 3 (June 1, 2015): 411–22.

Ogbar, Jeffrey O. G. *Black Power: Radical Politics and African American Identity*. Baltimore: Johns Hopkins University Press, 2004.

Olcott, Jocelyn. "Empires of Information: Media Strategies for the 1975 International Women's Year." *Journal of Women's History* 24, no. 4 (2012): 24–48.

Oropeza, Lorena. *¡Raza Sí!, ¡Guerra No!: Chicano Protest and Patriotism during the Viet Nam War Era*. Berkeley: University of California Press, 2005.

———. "*Viviendo y Luchando*: The Life and Times of Enriqueta Vasquez." In *Enriqueta Vasquez and the Chicano Movement: Writings from* El Grito Del Norte, edited by Dionne Espinoza and Lorena Oropeza, xix–liii. Houston: Arte Público, 2006.

Pascoe, Peggy. *Relations of Rescue: The Search for Female Moral Authority in the American West, 1874–1939*. New York: Oxford University Press, 1990.

Plastas, Melinda. *A Band of Noble Women: Racial Politics in the Women's Peace Movement*. Syracuse, N.Y.: Syracuse University Press, 2011.

Prevost, Elizabeth. "Assessing Women, Gender, and Empire in Britain's Nineteenth-Century Protestant Missionary Movement." *History Compass* 7, no. 3 (May 1, 2009): 765–99.

Pripas-Kapit, Sarah. "Piety, Professionalism and Power: Chinese Protestant Missionary Physicians and Imperial Affiliations between Women in the Early Twentieth Century." *Gender & History* 27, no. 2 (August 1, 2015): 349–73.

Pulido, Laura. *Black, Brown, Yellow, and Left: Radical Activism in Los Angeles.* Berkeley: University of California Press, 2006.

Rincón, Bernice. "La Chicana: Her Role in the Past and Her Search for a New Role in the Future." In *Chicana Feminist Thought: The Basic Historical Writings*, edited by Alma M. García, 24–28. New York: Routledge, 1997. Originally published in *Regeneración* 1, no. 10 (1971): 15–18.

Rosen, Ruth. *The World Split Open: How the Modern Women's Movement Changed America.* New York: Viking, 2000.

Roth, Benita. *Separate Roads to Feminism: Black, Chicana, and White Feminist Movements in America's Second Wave.* Cambridge: Cambridge University Press, 2004.

Rupp, Leila J. *Worlds of Women: The Making of an International Women's Movement.* Princeton, N.J.: Princeton University Press, 1997.

Schneidhorst, Amy C. *Building a Just and Secure World: Popular Front Women's Struggle for Peace and Justice in Chicago during the 1960s.* New York: Continuum International Publishing Group, 2011.

Schott, Linda K. *Reconstructing Women's Thoughts: The Women's International League for Peace and Freedom before World War II.* Stanford, Calif.: Stanford University Press, 1997.

Schulzinger, Robert. "The Legacy of the Vietnam War." In *The Columbia History of the Vietnam War*, edited by David L. Anderson, 385–408. New York: Columbia University Press, 2013.

Shah, Sonia, ed. *Dragon Ladies: Asian American Feminists Breathe Fire.* Boston: South End, 1997.

Sharer, Wendy B. *Vote and Voice: Women's Organizations and Political Literacy, 1915–1930.* Carbondale: Southern Illinois University Press, 2004.

Singh, Nikhil Pal. *Black Is a Country: Race and the Unfinished Struggle for Democracy.* Cambridge, Mass.: Harvard University Press, 2004.

Sklar, Kathryn Kish. "'Some of Us Who Deal with the Social Fabric': Jane Addams Blends Peace and Social Justice, 1907–1919." *Journal of the Gilded Age and Progressive Era* 2, no. 1 (January 2003): 80–96.

Small, Melvin. *Antiwarriors: The Vietnam War and the Battle for America's Hearts and Minds.* Wilmington, Del.: Scholarly Resources, 2002.

———, and William D. Hoover, eds. *Give Peace a Chance: Exploring the Vietnam Antiwar Movement: Essays from the Charles DeBenedetti Memorial Conference.* Syracuse, N.Y.: Syracuse University Press, 1992.

Sneider, Allison L. *Suffragists in an Imperial Age: U.S. Expansion and the Woman Question, 1870–1929.* New York: Oxford University Press, 2008.

Springer, Kimberly. "Black Feminists Respond to Black Power Masculinism." In *The Black Power Movement: Rethinking the Civil Rights–Black Power Era*, edited by Peniel E. Joseph, 105–18. New York: Routledge, 2006.

———. *Living for the Revolution: Black Feminist Organizations, 1968–1980*. Durham, N.C.: Duke University Press, 2005.

Storrs, Landon, R. Y. *The Second Red Scare and the Unmaking of the New Deal Left*. Princeton, N.J.: Princeton University Press, 2013.

Strobel, Margaret. "Gender, Sex, and Empire." In *Islamic & European Expansion: The Forging of a Global Order*, edited by Michael Adas, 345–75. Philadelphia: Temple University Press, 1993.

Stur, Heather Marie. *Beyond Combat: Women and Gender in the Vietnam War Era*. Cambridge: Cambridge University Press, 2011.

Swerdlow, Amy. "Ladies' Day at the Capitol: Women Strike for Peace versus HUAC." *Feminist Studies* 8, no. 3 (Autumn 1982): 493–520.

———. "'Not My Son, Not Your Son, Not Their Sons': Mothers against the Vietnam Draft." In *Give Peace a Chance: Exploring the Vietnam Antiwar Movement: Essays from the Charles DeBenedetti Memorial Conference*, edited by Melvin Small and William D. Hoover, 159–70. Syracuse, N.Y.: Syracuse University Press, 1992.

———. *Women Strike for Peace: Traditional Motherhood and Radical Politics in the 1960s*. Chicago: University of Chicago Press, 1993.

Sylvester, Christine. *Feminist International Relations: An Unfinished Journey*. New York: Cambridge University Press, 2002.

Taylor, Sandra C. *Vietnamese Women at War: Fighting for Ho Chi Minh and the Revolution*. Lawrence: University Press of Kansas, 1999.

Thomas, Lynn M. *Politics of the Womb: Women, Reproduction, and the State in Kenya*. Berkeley: University of California Press, 2003.

Trujillo, Armando L. *Chicano Empowerment and Bilingual Education: Movimiento Politics in Crystal City, Texas*. New York: Garland, 1998.

Turner, Karen Gottschang. *Even the Women Must Fight: Memories of War from North Vietnam*. New York: Wiley, 1998.

Turse, Nick. *Kill Anything That Moves: The Real American War in Vietnam*. New York: Metropolitan Books, 2013.

Tyson, Timothy B. *Radio Free Dixie: Robert F. Williams and the Roots of Black Power*. Chapel Hill: University of North Carolina Press, 1999.

Von Eschen, Penny M. *Race against Empire: Black Americans and Anticolonialism, 1937–1957*. Ithaca, N.Y.: Cornell University Press, 1997.

Vuic, Kara Dixon. *Officer, Nurse, Woman: The Army Nurse Corps in the Vietnam War*. Baltimore: The Johns Hopkins University Press, 2011.

Ward, Stephen. "The Third World Women's Alliance: Black Feminist Radicalism and Black Power Politics." In *The Black Power Movement: Rethinking the Civil Rights–Black Power Era*, edited by Peniel E. Joseph, 119–44. New York: Routledge, 2006.

Wei, William. *The Asian American Movement*. Philadelphia: Temple University Press, 1993.

White, Deborah G. *Too Heavy a Load: Black Women in Defense of Themselves, 1894–1994*. New York: Norton, 1999.

Williams, Rhonda. "Black Women, Urban Politics, and Engendering Black Power." In *The Black Power Movement: Rethinking the Civil Rights–Black Power Era*, edited by Peniel E. Joseph, 79–103. New York: Routledge, 2006.

Wong, K. Scott. "War Comes to Chinatown: Social Transformation and the Chinese of California." In *The Way We Really Were: The Golden State in the Second Great War*, edited by Roger W. Lotchin, 164–86. Urbana: University of Illinois Press, 2000.

Wu, Judy Tzu-Chun. *Radicals on the Road: Internationalism, Orientalism, and Feminism during the Viet Nam Era*. Ithaca, N.Y.: Cornell University Press, 2013.

———. "Rethinking Global Sisterhood: Peace Activism and Women's Orientalism." In *No Permanent Waves: Recasting Histories of U.S. Feminism*, edited by Nancy A. Hewitt, 193–220. New Brunswick, N.J.: Rutgers University Press, 2010.

Young, Cynthia Ann. *Soul Power: Culture, Radicalism, and the Making of a U.S. Third World Left*. Durham, N.C.: Duke University Press, 2006.

Young, Marilyn Blatt. *The Vietnam Wars, 1945–1990*. New York: HarperCollins, 1991.

Index

Abzug, Bella, 132
Activists of color, 54–78; and Angela
  Davis case, 114; and anti-imperialism,
  54, 55, 66, 67–68, 69, 73, 76, 77, 93;
  Anti-Imperialist Delegation (1970),
  64–65, 66, 70, 76–77, 164–65n52; and
  anti-imperialist feminist delegation
  (1975), 135–36; and colonialism, 56–57,
  59; and critiques of U.S. society, 66,
  71–72, 76, 77, 142; and Dec. 1966
  delegation, 18, 19, 21, 153n42; and
  Djakarta conference, 151n15; and ethnic separations, 71, 166–67n95; and
  feminism, 55, 57, 64–65, 66–69, 73–74,
  82, 93; and idealization of North
  Viet Nam, 54, 60–61, 69, 76–77,
  168n128; and Indochinese Women's
  Conference, 89–90, 91; and land, 57,
  58–60, 61, 163n10, 163n23; Martínez
  background, 55–58; and maternalism,
  26, 62–63, 75; and North Vietnamese
  women's equality, 55, 74, 75–76; and
  POWs/MIAs, 65; and sexism, 67–68,
  72–73, 78; and terminology, 162n3;
  and women's resistance roles, 4, 22,
  61–62, 69–70, 74–75
African-American activists, 64, 65–70;
  and Angela Davis case, 114; and anti-
  imperialist feminist delegation (1975),
  135–36; and Dec. 1966 delegation,
  18, 19, 21, 26, 153n42; and feminism,
  67–69, 82; and POWs/MIAs, 65; and
  sexism, 67–68, 78; and women's resistance roles, 70. *See also specific people*
Agnew, Spiro, 109
Alonso, Harriet, 86
American Friends Service Committee
  (AFSC), 131

Anderson, Benedict, 35
Anderson, William, 174n14
Anticommunism: and activists of color,
  58; and Canada conference (1969),
  44; and détente, 123, 131; and Djakarta
  conference, 15–16; and humanitarian aid, 137; and idealization of
  North Viet Nam, 76, 113–14; and
  maternalism, 9; and origins of Viet
  Nam war, 8; and pushback against
  WSP, 156n89; and South Vietnamese
  women, 126
Anti-imperialism: and activists of color,
  54, 55, 66, 67–68, 69, 73, 76, 77, 93;
  and feminism, 85–86, 88, 90–91,
  93–95, 97
Anti-Imperialist Delegation (1970),
  64–65, 66, 70, 76–77, 164–65n52
Asian-American activists, 70–76;
  backgrounds of, 70–71; and ethnic
  separations, 71, 166–67n95; and feminism, 73–74; and military racism,
  71–72, 167n104; and sexism, 72–73;
  and women's resistance roles, 74–75.
  See also specific people
Association of International Women,
  108, 176n40
Atrocities. *See* Civilian casualty accusations; South Vietnamese conditions
Austin, Jan, 164n52
Axelrod, Beverly, 150n15

Bach Mai Hospital Relief Fund, 128,
  136–37
Baez, Joan, 35, 119–20, 127
Bambara, Toni Cade, 135–36
Barrow, Willie, 114
Beal, Frances, 69

Collaboration vs. cultural imperialism, 3–4, 101, 145–46
the Collective (Women's Liberation Anti-Imperialist Collective), 83, 85, 170n20
Collingwood, Charles, 36
Colonialism, 56–57, 59, 76
Committee for Solidarity with the American People (Viet-My), 102, 116, 118, 127
Committee of Reconciliation, 183n20
Conscription, 35, 38
Costain, Pam, 135
Cu Dinh Ba, 188n75
Cultural imperialism vs. collaboration, 3–4, 101, 145–46
CWS (Church World Service), 138–39

Davis, Angela, 114
Davis, Rennie, 47
Delegations to Viet Nam: Anti-Imperialist Delegation (1970), 64–65, 66, 70, 76–77, 164–65n52; anti-imperialist feminist delegation (1975), 135–36; and Bratislava conference, 81–82; and civilian casualty accusations, 19–20, 23–24, 25–26, 28, 47–48, 50–51; Dec. 1966, 18–27, 153n42; and maternalism, 18, 20–21, 26, 28, 29, 30–31, 33; post-reunification period, 135–36, 139, 140; post-U.S. withdrawal period, 122–25, 126–27, 128–31; and POWs/MIAs, 29–30, 44–46, 47–48, 49–50, 51–52, 116, 117–18, 180n94; and U.S. government policies, 1, 27, 32; WILPF 1971 delegation, 109–11, *111*, 177n52; and women's resistance roles, 21–23, 31–32, 34; WSP Clarke-Gordon delegation (1965), 1, *2*, 9; WSP Dec. 1969 delegation, 44–45, 49–52; WSP Sept. 1967 delegation, 28–33, *29*
Dellinger, Dave, 18–19, 30, 117
Deming, Barbara: and Dec. 1966 delegation, 18, 19, 21, 22, 23, 24–25, 27;

and maternalism, 21, 34; and Operation Babylift, 133; pushback against, 26–27; and women's resistance roles, 22, 32
Desertion, encouragement of, 41, 66
Détente, 123, 131
Dinh Thi Huong, 92, 94–95, 169n5, 172n59
Djakarta conference (1965), 11–17, *12*; attendance, 11–12, 150–51n15; and Canada conference (1969), 43; joint communiqué, 14, 151–52n21; and maternalism, 11, 13–14, 15, 16, 17; planning for, 9, 149n2; reports on, 15–17; and South Vietnamese women, 12, 151n18
Domestic violence, 86
Draft, 35, 38
Draft resistance, 35–36, 38
DRV government: and African-American activists, 66; and conscription, 38; and idealization of North Viet Nam, 76; and maternalism, 6; people's diplomacy, 2–3, 6, 17–18, 99–100; and POWs/MIAs, 45, 46, 47, 48–49, 115–17, 118, 119; and women's resistance roles, 10–11
Duckles, Madeline, 49–52, 117
Dumont, Yvonne, 37
Duong Van Minh, 112, 114–15

Eaton, Anne, 51
Eaton, Cyrus, 51
Ecofeminism, 48
Eisen, Arlene (Bergman), 134–35
Empire of Ideas (Hart), 183n17
Evans, Linda, 47
Evans, Sara, 169n7

Falcón, Sylvanna, 189n8
Fanon, Frantz, 65
Feminism, 4–5, 79–98, 143; and activists of color, 55, 57, 64–65, 67–69, 73–74, 82, 93; and anti-imperialism, 85–86, 88, 90–91, 93–95, 97; and Bratislava

Middleton, Donna, 69
Mirikitani, Janice, 73, 74
Missing in action. *See* POWs/MIAs
Mollin, Marian, 149n17
Morton, Peggy, 84
Moynihan, Daniel Patrick, 68, 166n72
"MS." (Mirikitani), 73, 74
My Lai massacre, 50–51, *129*

Nash, Diane: and activists of color, 18, 19, 153n42; and civilian casualty accusations, 20–21, 23, 26; government penalization of, 27; and maternalism, 18, 20–21, 26, 34; and women's resistance roles, 32
National Liberation Front (NLF): and African-American activists, 66; and Bratislava conference, 80–81; and maternalism, 6; and 1971 elections, 114–15; origins of, 7–8, 16; political prisoners from, 102–3; and women's resistance roles, 14. *See also* Provisional Revolutionary Government; South Vietnamese women
National Organization for Women (NOW), 169n7
National Student Association, 115
National Women's Conference (Houston, 1977), 134, 139
The Negro Family: The Case for National Action (Moynihan), 68
Newman, Grace Mora, 18, 23, 27
New Mobe (New Mobilization Committee to End the War in Vietnam), 82–83
News coverage. *See* Media
Newton, Huey, 65, 68, 77, 78
Ngo Ba Thanh: background of, 107–9; incarceration of, 112–13, 125–26; and International Women's Year, 134; and post-reunification activism, 138; and post-U.S. withdrawal activism, 131–32; and Right to Live, 109, 110, *111*
Ngo Dinh Diem, 7, 16

Ngo Thi Tuyet, 38, 39
Nguyen Binh Thanh, 99–100
Nguyen Khoa Dieu Hong, 151n16
Nguyen My Dung, 19
Nguyen Ngoc Dung, *37*, 42–43, 44, 99–100, 151n17
Nguyen Thi Binh: on Christmas bombings, 120; and Djakarta conference, 12, *12*, 14–15; and feminism, 80–81; historical literature on, 7; and Paris Conference of Concerned Women, *37*, 39; and Paris Peace Talks, 40, 99–100; and post-reunification activism, 139–40; and post-U.S. withdrawal activism, 130; as source, 5; and women's resistance roles, 14–15, 39
Nguyen Thi Dinh, 7
Nguyen Thi Truc, 151n16
Nguyen Thi Xiem, 91–92, 96, 169n5
Nguyen Van Thieu administration: and 1971 elections, 112, 115; and Paris Peace Talks, 119; and post-U.S. withdrawal activism, 125–26, 130, 132; and Right to Live, 111, 112; and Third Force, 107, 108
Nixon administration: and bombing of North Vietnam, 115, 119; Cambodia invasion, 63–64; and Paris Peace Talks, 119; and POWs/MIAs, 46, 49, 115–16, 118–19; Vietnamization policy, 64, 92; and Watergate scandal, 132
Nonviolence, 22, 32–33, 124. *See also* Women's resistance roles
North Vietnamese foreign relations fronts, 2, 148n3. *See also* People's diplomacy
North Vietnamese women's equality: and activists of color, 55, 74, 75–76; and delegations to Viet Nam, 1, 21; and feminism, 4, 81–82, 84, 96–97, 134–35, 143, 189n2; limits of, 83, 84, 96–97, 100, 135; and post-reunification activism, 5, 135, 139–40; and resistance roles, 21, 22, 32; and

ese women's equality, 113–14; and women's resistance roles, 15. *See also* Djakarta conference; Maternalism

Women's Union of Liberation (WUL): and Bratislava conference, 80–81; and Canada conference (1969), 42–44; and Djakarta conference, 12, 13, 14–16, 151n17; importance of, 143–44; and Indochinese Women's Conference, 169n5; and International Women's Year, 134; and maternalism, 6, 10; and Paris Conference of Concerned Women, 36–40

Wu, Judy, 4, 5, 54

Wyman, Louis, 27

Yoshimura, Evelyn, 70

Young, Ron, 102, 103, 105

Young, Trudi (Schutz), 102, 103, *104*, 105, 170n21

CPSIA information can be obtained
at www.ICGtesting.com
Printed in the USA
LVOW11*2117280917
550420LV00007B/110/P